I$ ⸀⸀ ⁀⸀ POLITICAL THEORY

Political Theory has undergone a remarkable development in recent years. From a state in which it was once declared dead, it has come to occupy a central place in the study of Politics. Both political ideas and the wide-ranging arguments to which they give rise are now treated in a rigorous, analytical, fashion, and political theorists have contributed to disciplines as diverse as economics, sociology and law. These developments have made the subject more challenging and exciting, but they have also added to the difficulties of students and others coming to the subject for the first time. Much of the burgeoning literature in specialist books and journals is readily intelligible only to those who are already well-versed in the subject.

Issues in Political Theory is a series conceived in response to this situation. It consists of a number of detailed and comprehensive studies of issues central to Political Theory which take account of the latest developments in scholarly debate. While making original contributions to the subject, books in the series are written especially for those who are new to Political Theory. Each volume aims to introduce its readers to the intricacies of a fundamental political issue and to help them find their way through the detailed, and often complicated, argument that that issue has attracted.

PETER JONES
ALBERT WEALE

ISSUES IN POLITICAL THEORY

Series editors: PETER JONES and ALBERT WEALE

Published

David Beetham: **The Legitimation of Power**
Tom Campbell: **Justice** (3rd edition)
John Horton: **Political Obligation** (2nd edition)
Peter Jones: **Rights**
Albert Weale: **Democracy** (2nd edition)

Forthcoming
Raymond Plant: **Equality**

Issues in Political Theory series
Series Standing Order

ISBN 978–0–230–54394–2 paperback
ISBN 978–0–230–54393–5 hardback
(outside North America only)

You can receive future titles in this series as they are published by a placing a stand-ing order. Please contact your bookseller or, in the case of difficulty, write to us at the address below with your name and address, the title of the series and an ISBN quoted above.

Customer Services Department, Palgrave Macmillan Ltd,
Houndmills, Basingstoke, Hampshire RG21 6XS, England, UK

Political Obligation

Second Edition

John Horton

First edition 1992
Second edition 2010

Published by
PALGRAVE MACMILLAN

Palgrave Macmillan in the UK is an imprint of Macmillan Publishers Limited,
registered in England, company number 785998, of Houndmills, Basingstoke,
Hampshire RG21 6XS.

Palgrave Macmillan in the US is a division of St Martin's Press LLC,
175 Fifth Avenue, New York, NY 10010.

Palgrave Macmillan is the global academic imprint of the above companies
and has companies and representatives throughout the world.

Palgrave® and Macmillan® are registered trademarks in the United States,
the United Kingdom, Europe and other countries.

ISBN 978–0–230–57650–6   hardback
ISBN 978–0–230–57651–3   paperback

This book is printed on paper suitable for recycling and made from fully
managed and sustained forest sources. Logging, pulping and manufacturing
processes are expected to conform to the environmental regulations of the
country of origin.

A catalogue record for this book is available from the British Library.

A catalog record for this book is available from the Library of Congress.

10 9 8 7 6 5 4 3 2 1
19 18 17 16 15 14 13 12 11 10

Printed in China

To Chris

Contents

Preface to the Second Edition

The aim of this revised edition is, as with the original, to introduce a range of philosophical questions and arguments concerning political obligation that will be useful for students and, I hope, also of some interest to fellow political theorists. Much of the book is taken up with the attempt to sketch the more prominent arguments that seek to justify political obligation; to explore some of their assumptions and implications; and to suggest what seem to me to be both their virtues and weaknesses. However, an increased proportion of the book is concerned with my attempt to offer a distinctive alternative to the traditional theories, in terms of an associative account of political obligation. The approach adopted in the book is analytical rather than historical, and my concern to address arguments of particular relevance in the modern world is reflected in the focus primarily being on contemporary writings rather than the history of political thought.

Returning to revise a book that one wrote around twenty years ago is a slightly odd and unnerving experience, and inevitably raises the question of whether indeed it is worth revising. Somewhat to my surprise, I felt that I could still stand by the substance of much, although by no means all, of what I had written. Moreover, having continued to think off and on about many of the issues in the intervening period, I also thought that I could significantly improve it. And it remains one of only a few books that seek to combine an accessible overview of the terrain with the attempt to defend a distinctive view. Further, encouraged by a number of friends and colleagues who were kind enough to tell me that they still found the book useful both for teaching purposes and in thinking about the issues, even if as is often the case they do not agree with me, and assisted by Steven Kennedy, my indefatigable, enthusiastic and long-suffering editor at Palgrave Macmillan, a new edition, therefore, seemed worthwhile. I can only hope that readers will agree.

I would not, though, want anyone to think that I have been unable to see quite a lot of flaws in the original book. Some of the most embarrassing are stylistic, and I have to confess that I have not found reading my earlier prose an especially enjoyable experience. For the most part, at least, I do think that it had the merit of clarity, but I hope that this new edition, while retaining that clarity, will read a touch more fluently. Seeking to make the writing rather less stilted has meant that there is scarcely a paragraph that remains entirely unchanged, although many of these changes are merely verbal or trivial. (At least those readers sensitive to the distinction between 'which' and 'that' should find reading the book a less painful experience!)

Substantive changes to Chapters 2–4 have been, for the most part, relatively modest: the arguments for and against many of the standard views have not altered dramatically. Therefore, I have not necessarily discussed more recent work simply because it is more recent, although there is for example an entirely new section on Samaritanism in Chapter 4. I have, though, made major revisions to some parts of the text, including, along with comprehensive revisions of Chapters 1 and 8, a complete rewriting and restructuring of what was formerly Chapter 6, now spread over and enlarged into two chapters (6 and 7). This reflects the fact that there was general agreement among critics, with which I concur, that the view set out in Chapter 6 was too underdeveloped. I have also tried, to a degree, to remedy a related weakness. This is that in my desire to resist, as I see it, a particular kind of justificatory excess common among philosophers, I underestimated the extent to which I still needed to say something more substantial by way of explanation of political obligation. I have come to the view that George Klosko is basically correct when he remarked that 'saying that no explanation is necessary does not constitute an explanation' (Klosko, 2005, p. 114). I have also tended to find a little more merit in many of the views that I criticize. I have not been won over by any of them as convincing general theories of political obligation, but I had previously understated the extent to which some of them could be seen to offer good reasons why at least some people should acknowledge obligations to their polity. There are other changes of emphasis that readers inclined to make detailed comparisons with the earlier edition will easily identify, but which it would be tiresome to document in detail. Much of the new material in Chapters 6 and 7 draws on my two-part article in *Political Studies* (vol. 54, 2006, pp. 427–43, and vol. 55, 2007, pp. 1–19), and I am most grateful to the editors and publishers for permission to use that material here.

I have come to identify my own account as an 'associative theory' of political obligation. I sometimes have doubts about whether that is, perhaps, the best label - commentators on the first edition also called it, *inter alia*, a 'communitarian theory' or an 'identity theory', to neither of which designations do I have any particular antipathy – but, on balance, I am content to stick with 'associative', especially as it now has a certain currency in the literature. And, for all the dangers of labelling and its intrinsic unimportance, a label has its uses, too.

I should reiterate my thanks to those who helped with comments, suggestions, personal support and in other ways with the original edition. These include: Keith Alderman, Alex Callinicos, the late John Crump, Pamela Dowswell, David Edwards, Margaret Gilbert, Terry Hopton, Peter Jones, Paul Kelly, Preston King, Adrian Leftwich, John Liddington, Barbara McGuinness, Chris Megone, Jackie Morgan, David Morland, Glen Newey, Dorothy Nott, Igor Primoratz, Keith Povey, Steve Reilly, Claire Roberts, Rian Voet, Albert Weale and especially Jenny Bradford, Susan Mendus and Peter Nicholson. I should also reiterate my gratitude to the C. & J. B. Morrell Trust for their generous support of my writing the first edition. Similarly, I would like to repeat my acknowledgement to my original teacher and inspiration, the late John Rees.

Versions of papers that formed the basis of some of the more important revisions were helpfully discussed at workshops/seminars/panels at the Universities of Essex, Keele, Newcastle, Pennsylvania, Sheffield and Stirling; at the 2001 American Political Science Association Conference in San Francisco; and at the 'Hobbes, Theories of Justice and the Social Contract in the Twentieth Century' seminars in London, Paris and Berlin, supported by the British Academy and the Centre National de la Recherche Scientifique. I am especially grateful to the following who made particularly helpful contributions on one or more of those occasions or commented in writing: Andrea Baumeister, Chris Brewin, Thom Brooks, Richard Dagger, Andy Dobson, Cecile Fabre, Matthew Festenstein, Luc Foisneau, Eve Garrard, Iain Hampsher-Monk, Ian Harris, Nancy Hirschmann, Iseult Honohon, Peter Jones, Duncan Kelly, Ellen Kennedy, George Klosko, Yoke-Lian Lee, Graham Long, Jeff Lustig, Andrew Mason, Dan McDermott, Veronique Munoz-Darde, Anne Norton, Peter Nicholson, Rosemary O'Kane, Emmanuel Picavet, Massimo Renzo, John Rogers, Jonathan Seglow, Kara Shaw, Rogers Smith, Tom Sorell, Hidemi Suganami, Andrew Vincent, Rob Walker, Steven Wall, Albert Weale and Jo Wolff. I am also grateful to Paul Kelly and several anonymous referees for *Political Studies*. For their contributions, often in a gently sceptical vein, to my thinking about political obligation more generally I am especially indebted to Margaret Canovan, Margaret Gilbert, Massimo Renzo, Richard Vernon and, especially, Ryan Windeknecht and Glen Newey. I am also pleased to acknowledge the generosity of Keele University in granting me research leave that enabled me to work on the revision. Finally, I am particularly grateful for comments on all or most of a final draft of the text to Glen Newey,

Massimo Renzo, Richard Vernon, Bas van der Vossen, Ryan Windeknecht and the two editors of the series, Peter Jones and Albert Weale. They all had better things to do with their time, but each made valuable corrections and suggestions to help improve the final version. Of course, none of them can properly be blamed for what remains.

I have also incurred numerous additional debts to colleagues at York, Keele and elsewhere who have helped me in significant ways intellectually and/or practically over the last twenty years. These include, in addition to those people mentioned earlier, Sorin Baiasu, Paul Bou-Habib, Paula Casal, Alex Danchev, Maria Dimova-Cookson, Josie D'Oro, John Gray, Bruce Haddock, Susanne Karstedt, Cecile Laborde, Peter Lassman, Rex Martin, Caroline Merritt, Monica Mookherjee, Enzo Rossi, Gabriella Slomp, Pauline Weston and Anne Worrall. In addition to Steven Kennedy, I am also grateful to Stephen Wenham at Palgrave Macmillan, and to Keith Povey and Nick Fox for their editorial work on the text. As I have grown older I have become increasingly forgetful, so I hope that anyone I have inadvertently omitted to acknowledge will accept my sincere apologies. And, if I do not thank successive classes of students over the years, this is not because I think that I have never learnt anything from students – several of my former graduate students are acknowledged individually above – but because, curiously enough, in over thirty-five years of university teaching I have still to teach a class specifically on political obligation!

Keele, 2010   JOHN HORTON

1 Problems of Political Obligation

The term 'political obligation' is not one that has much currency in contemporary political discourse, and will likely be unfamiliar even to those who are generally well-educated and politically informed. It is not a term like 'rights', 'freedom' or 'justice', which although also the subjects of extensive academic debate and inquiry, some of it quite technical and difficult, are omnipresent in popular political discussion. Most people have views about rights, freedom and justice, however naive and unreflective, whereas if challenged to say what they think about 'political obligation', without further explanation, the same people would be unlikely to have much idea what they are being asked. In fact, political obligation is something that appears scarcely to be mentioned outside books and articles on political philosophy; and even in that context the best evidence suggests that it dates from as recently as the late nineteenth century (Green, 1986). It is not, therefore, possible to begin by assuming even a rudimentary understanding of the term.

It would be a mistake, however, to infer from this fact that the complex of issues that the term denotes are only of recent origin, or that it is solely the concern of professional philosophers and academic political theorists. In truth, it is only the term that is arcane or unknown, as the idea that political obligation marks is a familiar one of considerable importance. The cluster of questions and issues with which it is concerned lie at the heart of political life and have done so, with greater or lesser urgency and self-consciousness, for as long as people have reflected on their relationship to the political community that claims them as members. It is this relationship – that between people and their political community – with which political obligation is fundamentally concerned. The problem of political obligation is about how this relationship is to be understood and what, if anything, it implies about the responsibilities we have to our political community. In particular, it is

1

about whether we can properly be understood to have some ethical bond with our polity, and if so how this manifests itself. The purpose of this chapter is, thus, to introduce the problem, to sketch some important preliminary distinctions, and to indicate in general terms the concerns of this book. I shall begin, however, by trying to show in a very simple way both the kind of issues involved in political obligation and why they matter. The task of characterizing a more refined and precise understanding of political obligation will be taken up later in the chapter.

Political obligation in context

The vast majority of people reading these words will be members of some political entity (today, most commonly, a state), and the lives of all of us who are members of a polity are crucially shaped and structured in a multiplicity of ways by this apparently simple fact. Even the most resolutely unpolitical people have to recognize that the nature of the political community in which they live, what it demands of them and what it permits them, is crucial to their being able to live the lives they do. Where citizens are generally tolerably content with the political arrangements of their society, they may not choose and will not be compelled to think much about their relationship to the political community of which they are members. Many features of this relationship may be taken for granted, and meeting the requirements that are imposed upon us by it may often be unreflective and habitual: we pay our taxes, apply for a passport if we wish to travel abroad, obey the law, complete our census returns, and much else. In this respect our relationship to our polity is like many of our other relationships and commitments – familial, professional, religious, and so on – in being experienced as an important but often practically unproblematic, even routine, feature of our daily lives to which we give little serious thought much of the time. However, we are all equally aware that these relationships and commitments can at any time become deeply problematic and troubling, threatening to destabilize us. Indeed, at times, they can give rise to questions so challenging that they require us to rethink our sense of who we are and how we should live, and in this way they have the potential to transform our lives.

It is only to be expected, therefore, that people are likely to be most acutely aware of their relationship to their political community when, for whatever reason, this relationship becomes problematic: the ways in which people's lives are intimately bound up with the wider polity will probably become a cause for serious reflection when, for example, demands are made of them or prohibitions imposed upon them that they find excessively burdensome or simply unacceptable. It is for this reason, primarily, that it is in times of political crisis, of serious dissent or discontent, of social breakdown or dislocation, that political obligation is most likely to become a major topic of political debate. It is in circumstances such as these that people are most likely to question the authority of their government and to think seriously about the terms and basis of their relationship to their political community. In particular, they may come to ask what legitimate claims the political community has on them and what they owe it; and how both of these matters are to be decided. It is in this way that people are most likely to be led to reflect *generally* on their relationship to their political community, and that the need for some general, theoretical or philosophical understanding of political obligation is likely to be felt most pressing. Yet, although it is in circumstances such as these that political obligation will most probably be experienced as a *problem*, it is to less troubled times that we should look for an 'answer'. It is something of an irony that it is precisely in those circumstances in which our need for an answer to our questions is most urgent, that it is also most difficult to give one.

It is, therefore, unsurprising to find that political theorists' and philosophers' sense of the importance of the problem of political obligation has varied with changing circumstances, and that philosophical reflection about it has often been most intense when some people have found themselves to be in radical conflict with their political community or when the political community itself has been perceived to be under serious threat or close to dissolution. Thus, one of the earliest sustained philosophical discussions of what we can now plausibly understand as an instance of the problem of political obligation occurs in the fourth century BC in the context of Plato's report of Socrates's meditations on his relationship to the Athenian *polis*, which had condemned him to death. Encouraged by his friends to escape and seek exile outside his *polis*, but rejecting the possibility of giving up his vocation as a teacher to appease his critics, Socrates reflects on what his obligations to Athens require of him. In brief compass, he considers a number of arguments, many of which continue to reverberate to the present time, and concludes that he must do whatever his city and country command, or else persuade it 'in accordance with universal justice' to change its view. Unlawful resistance, he concludes, would be wrong (Plato, 1969, p. 91). In Socrates's case, his own arguments led him to believe that he should make the ultimate sacrifice and accept the sentence of execution handed down to him. Whatever the merits of his particular arguments – and in some respects they are astonishingly percipient – Socrates shows us the seriousness of the issues: ultimately political obligation can be a matter of life or death.

A very different time and place in which the problem of political obligation became especially pressing was seventeenth-century England. In a country riven by religious conflict and civil war, involving armed insurrection and the execution of the king, the work of Thomas Hobbes and John Locke emerged as an attempt to formulate an account of political obligation that would help to hold together a country apparently on the verge of chaos and disintegration. In this context, one of the most formidable and enduring traditions of thought about political obligation, the social contract tradition, developed as a way of thinking about the relations between the individual and the polity. To simplify greatly, while the idea of a contract between a polity and its citizens is clearly present as far back as Socrates's arguments in the *Crito*, it is in response to the consequences of the wars of religion and the increasingly rapid growth of a bourgeois, commercial society and associated forms of individualism in seventeenth-century Europe that this approach begins to be fully explored. As a very broad generalization, it is probably true to say that modern thinking about political obligation has its roots in this period.

In so far as the potential for antagonism between personal autonomy and individual conscience, on the one hand, and the claims to authority and the right to command of the state, on the other, has not merely persisted but become sharper as a result of subsequent historical developments, such as increased individualism and the massive extension of the role of the state, then the problem of political obligation can be seen to have become more rather than less of a challenge. It is not, therefore, a problem that is of concern only to earlier generations. We need only consider the tumultuous events in Eastern Europe in the late 1980s, a variety of modern nationalisms and recurrent civil wars, to survey a panorama of recent contexts within which political obligation has been experienced as deeply problematic. Furthermore, while situations of radical conflict or political dislocation provide the most dramatic instances, there are less extreme but none the less serious examples of circumstances where thinking about political obligation can become urgent. A good case would be that of many patriotic young United States citizens in the 1960s and early 1970s drafted into the army to fight on behalf of their country in what they believed to be a fundamentally unjust war in Vietnam.

All these historical events and situations are extraordinarily complex and it would be simplistic to attempt to incorporate all these complexi-

ties within one simple notion of political obligation. Yet, at their heart
lies a cluster of recurring questions that are central to an understanding
of political obligation: what political community does a person belong
to? How is membership of a polity determined? What duties or obligations does a person have by virtue of his or her membership? How are
those duties or obligations to be judged relative to other commitments
and obligations? The answers to these, and other related questions, are
central to any understanding of political obligation. However, political
theorists or philosophers have tended to see one question as more fundamental than any other. This is: what is the basis, or in virtue of what
reasons, should we ever rightly ascribe political obligations to people? It
is this question of justification or explanation – and it is not always
possible to separate them – that is the focus of most philosophical
discussions of political obligation; and it is the principal concern of this
book.

One problem or many?

The idea that there is one, single, clearly defined problem of political
obligation, which different political philosophers at different times have
sought to answer, is, however, open to a powerful objection. This objection is encapsulated in the claim that there is nothing that can be identified as *the* problem of political obligation, but only a succession of
historically different and distinct problems. Thus, it is argued that it is
grossly anachronistic and seriously misleading to think that the issue
confronting Socrates in Athens, or Hobbes's or Locke's circumstances in
seventeenth-century England, or 'the problem of political obligation' as
seen by a political philosopher today, are all the *same* problem. There is
certainly a good deal of truth in this view: we cannot simply pretend that
Socrates, Hobbes and the political philosopher today are all contempo-
raries joined in a single debate about something called 'political obligation'. Their social and political circumstances, background beliefs and
assumptions, and even perhaps their conceptions of argument, vary, and
these differences are surely relevant to how they think about the question
and go about answering it. Yet, it is not self-evident that we cannot, to
some extent at least, not merely come to understand the concerns that
exercised Socrates, but also relate them to our own circumstances and
problems. After all, Socrates's arguments, or at least some of them,
continue to have considerable resonance in the very different conditions
of the modern world.

Thus, while it would be manifestly absurd, for example, to treat a young American in the 1960s facing the draft to fight in Vietnam as being in a situation identical to that of Socrates in Athens in the fourth century BC, at a certain level of generality (and some level of generality is unavoidable), it is not obviously absurd to see some similarities in their predicaments; to see how what Socrates says about his situation might relate, with suitable modifications, to that of the potential conscript. This is possible because, while they are separated by very different historical circumstances, they also share a common human condition in which reconciling the claims of individuals with those of the larger political community to which they belong is a problem that has the potential to arise wherever people are members of political communities and are also capable of distinguishing themselves from it. So, while there are many significant differences – for example between the way in which the problem of political obligation is formulated and interpreted in ancient and modern political philosophy – we can still trace a kinship of concerns (O'Sullivan, 1987, ch. 1). The arguments of earlier philosophers are variously developed and rejected by later philosophers, and most philosophers have certainly believed themselves to be presenting accounts of political obligation of very much wider relevance than to their own specific historical circumstances.

There is, therefore, no convincing reason to think that we are forced to choose between these two extreme positions. It is not the case either that there is one simple, perennial, unchanging, uniform problem that constitutes *the* problem of political obligation, or that because every historical situation is in some sense unique there can be *no* common, or at least closely related, concerns that transcend such variable circumstances. There can be identity in difference: the precise form in which questions pertaining to political obligation present themselves will inevitably vary according to the circumstances in which they arise; as will the answers. Yet, they can also be recognized as related to similar or overlapping concerns rooted in a broadly common human predicament. Such considerations also apply to social and cultural differences that exist at the same historical time. Although, for instance, the rhetoric of democracy is very widespread in the contemporary world, polities continue to take a great many different forms: Iran, China, Saudi Arabia, Denmark and the US are clearly very different kinds of political community. Philosophers certainly need to be alert and sensitive to historical and cultural differences, but there is no good reason to begin such an inquiry by assuming that it is impossible to say *anything* about political obligation that transcends highly specific contexts. The question of precisely how much it is possible to say about political obligation in general, and to what extent understanding needs to be contextualized and related concretely to particular historical circumstances, is an issue about which it is at least initially appropriate to have an open mind.

Political obligation, therefore, is fundamentally concerned with the relationship between people and the political community of which they are members. It gives rise to questions of considerable practical and philosophical importance concerning the obligations or duties one has in virtue of one's membership of a particular polity. How does this affect one's relations with other members and how do they differ from those of non-members? What is one's relationship to the political authority, to law and to the institutions and personnel of government? These are all questions that can be raised at a more or less general, or more or less specific, level. In fact, I shall conclude that there are significant limits to what can be said about political obligation in general, especially so far as its content is concerned, but this should be understood as the outcome of the argument rather than as a presupposition of it. In part, however, what is being contested in this debate is the nature of political theory or philosophy itself. It is to a preliminary consideration of this issue that we must now turn, leaving until the final section further clarification and refinement of the problem of political obligation.

Political philosophy, theory, justification and explanation

This book is a work of 'political theory' or 'political philosophy'. Some writers make a distinction between the two terms, often along the lines that the former is more abstract and largely independent of empirical concerns, whereas the latter is more applied and 'practical'. I shall not observe any such distinction, and the two terms will be used interchangeably. My own view, which I will not seek to defend here, is that even political philosophy should be sensitive to the broader 'realities' of politics if it is to be able to say much of interest about it. There is no point, for instance, in premising a political philosophy on assumptions about human beings that we are convinced are impossibly utopian, which is not of course to deny that what we regard as 'impossibly utopian' is itself something that is open to argument.

However, because the approach adopted here does try to be sensitive to the world in which politics has its place, it is even more important to be clear that it is not political sociology or history. Although it contains both historical and sociological considerations, it does not aim to offer either an historical narrative of changing relations between individuals and their particular polity or a sociological explanation of the way such relations actually operate. It is not concerned with explaining why in fact people obey the law, interesting and worthwhile though such an inquiry is in its own right (Tyler, 1990). Nor does this book attempt a complete or systematic history of ideas about political obligation, although the ideas of some of the principal figures in the history of political philosophy figure prominently in the ensuing discussion. Disciplinary boundaries, such as those between history, sociology and philosophy, are sometimes regarded as obstacles to a proper or clear understanding of issues, because they lead to a fragmentation of knowledge. However, while it cannot be denied that an over-insistence on narrow disciplinary perspectives can have such an effect, different disciplines characteristically address different sorts of question. This is not to suggest that history and sociology are always irrelevant to political philosophy: for example, historical misunderstanding and insensitivity to sociological explanations of how things are in fact likely to work can sometimes make for poor political philosophy. The point is, though, that each form of inquiry should be assessed on its own terms and in relation to its own goals or purposes. It is simply misguided to judge philosophy as if, for example, it were history; and vice versa.

In describing this as a work of political theory or philosophy I intend to indicate that it attempts to explore the problem of political obligation through the interpretation of concepts and an assessment of the persuasiveness of various moral arguments and not through empirical research. Rather, it aims to give an account of the meaning of political obligation; to assess the merits of various arguments for and against it; and generally to contribute to an understanding of its ethical significance and place in political life. However, beyond this level of rather anodyne generality about political theory or philosophy, the nature of the activity is itself somewhat controversial and disputed. I shall to some extent take sides on some of these disputes, leaning towards one conception of political philosophy and evincing a degree of scepticism about the more ambitious claims for philosophy of some other philosophers. However, this is not something that can be directly argued for here. Moreover, it would be wrong to exaggerate the significance of these differences, which are perhaps mostly matters of emphasis, but it does sometimes mean that there can be something of a mismatch between my own approach and some of the other theorists I discuss. For this reason it seems useful to make a few remarks about these differences, and also explain the conditions that I believe a general theoretical account of political obligation needs to meet.

Much of contemporary political philosophy is strongly normative. That is, it sees itself as primarily in the business of seeking moral justifications for political institutions, practices or principles. It also tends to operate with a particular model of what a moral justification should look like. Typically, it is thought that moral justifications need to be grounded in first principles that are intuitively convincing or that are part of a broader picture that convincingly hangs together. This is an enormous generalization that does scant justice to the diversity of political philosophy; and what exactly this means is variously interpreted by different political philosophers, some employing more rigorously demanding standards of justification than others. In what follows I do not entirely depart from a weaker reading of what this involves, but I also see the theoretical or philosophical task as more one of interpretation, more 'hermeneutical', than a matter of justification from first principles. Interpretation can itself be understood as a kind of justification, and to some extent that tends to be how it plays out in the subsequent argument. However, it is a rather more informal and relaxed conception of justification than many philosophers would find acceptable. My preferred designation is that what is sought is a philosophical or theoretical explanation. For my guiding thought is that if we can make sense of the idea of political obligation in a way that is intellectually coherent and morally unobjectionable then this constitutes a convincing theoretical or philosophical explanation of it. But it may be helpful at this point, rather than focusing on generalities about the nature of political philosophy, to set out how I shall approach the search for a convincing philosophical account of political obligation.

Thus, any satisfying theoretical explanation of political obligation should, in my view, at least go some way to meeting the following desiderata, which are listed in no particular order of importance:

1. The account must make sense of the idea of political obligation in a way that coheres with other ideas that we would not want to give up. It should explain how political obligation is to be understood and why it is valuable. It should also be able to explain why and when political obligation may be absent or problematic in various ways. So far as possible, although how far it is possible is necessarily an open question, it should seek to accommodate the central features of ordinary thought about these matters (although 'ordinary thought' will always be complex and messy in various ways), where ordinary thought is not obviously morally objectionable or contradictory, and especially if its central features are widespread across many different societies and deeply embedded in social life.

2.   The account needs to explain what can plausibly be thought of as the standard case of political obligation: this is the situation in which members acquire their political obligations to the polity in which they are born. Of course, not everyone acquires their political obligations in this way, but cases such as voluntary immigration are not the norm and are potentially easier to explain. The standard case, as I call it, is both the norm and the most difficult to explain. If we can give a satisfying account of that then the hardest task has been accomplished. Thus, a general account of political obligation, although needing to cover at least the standard case, does not have to explain why *everyone* has political obligations. That would be to set the bar for such an account impossibly and inappropriately high. There are always likely to be exceptions, special circumstances and difficult cases.

3.   Similarly, the account also needs only to explain cases where political obligation is thought to be significant. It does not need to explain why someone is supposedly under a political obligation to stop at a red light on a freeway in the middle of a desert when nobody is around. Thus, I reject William Edmundson's claim that although 'this type of case is, *in a sense*, "trivial and unimportant", a counterexample is a counterexample' (Edmundson, 1998, p. 28). If this example captured what political obligation were centrally about then Edmundson might be right. However, it does trivialize political obligation, and because we might be uncertain about whether there really is an obligation in this case nothing follows about the important cases. (Analogously, just because we can come up with a suitably trivial example of a promise, where we might think it neither here nor there that the promise is kept, this does not undermine the idea that we are generally under an obligation to keep our promises.) Our ideas are 'designed' to deal with a certain range of problems and circumstances, and when extended to trivial (or far-fetched) examples, they may be inappropriate in a variety of ways. That, though, is not a criticism of those ideas, but of their misapplication.

4.   The account must also meet what has become known as the 'particularity requirement' (Simmons, 1979, pp. 31–5). This is the claim that any adequate theory of political obligation must explain why members owe an obligation specifically to the particular polity of which they are members, rather than to any other polity. Political obligation is understood to concern the special moral relationship that obtains between members and *their* political community.

Failure to appreciate this point effectively debars a theory from being an account of *political* obligation, whatever merits it may otherwise possess.

While I do not mean to suggest that this list of desiderata is comprehensive, it does set out what I take to be the most important criteria for a satisfactory theoretical account of political obligation, and against which, therefore, the account set out later in this book should be assessed.

Theorizing political obligation

In this section, and in the light of the comments in the previous section, I shall seek to say a little more specifically about political obligation by making a few initial clarificatory points. First, as indicated earlier, the term 'political obligation' is not much used outside philosophical discussion, and is thus something of a term of art. However, although the term is itself a construct of political philosophers, I hope enough has been said already to indicate that it refers to something real and important: that is, the kind of bond that exists between people and the polity of which they are members. But what is it exactly that political theorists and philosophers have been trying to do in exploring this relationship?

There have been at least three questions that have been regarded as central to modern philosophical discussions of political obligation. These are:

1.   To whom or what do I have political obligations?
2.   What are the extent and limits of these obligations?
3.   What is the explanation or justification of these obligations?

While it is the first two questions that are usually most practically pressing, it is the third that is philosophically fundamental. The first two largely presuppose an answer to the third, in that what we think explains our political obligations, or if indeed whether we have any such obligations at all, will clearly be crucial in answering them. This book focuses almost exclusively on the third question: how it has been interpreted, the kind of answers that have been thought appropriate, and the actual answers that have been given to it. The second question will be largely ignored, although, as I shall explain in Chapter 7, this is at least in part because it is doubtful if very much that is illuminating can be said at a general level in answer to it. At least a partial answer to the first question is implicit within the associative account of political obligation that I go on to defend in Chapters 6 and 7.

Second, I take it that the idea of political obligation is understood to express, in the broadest sense, a *moral* or *ethical* relationship between people and their political community. This claim is not entirely uncontentious and has been denied by some philosophers (e.g. by McPherson, 1967 and, in a more nuanced and qualified way, by Gilbert, 2006). I shall discuss and reject this denial in Chapter 6, but it is very much the exception and, for the most part, I shall simply assume it to be mistaken. Thus, political obligation is understood here to concern the moral or ethical bonds between individuals and their political community. To understand one's relationship to the political community of which one is a member in ethical terms is not to see it as simply involving submission to the arbitrary imposition of force or to see it in exclusively narrow, instrumental terms. Thus, for example, to conform to the requirements of one's polity *only* through fear of punishment if one does not, or *only* when doing so happens to be in one's self-interest, is not to act in a way that involves acknowledging one's political obligations. While the dictates of self-interest and morality may often coincide, as with other moral requirements, political obligation may require us on occasion to act in ways contrary to our self-interest.

Although I shall mostly use the term 'political obligation' in discussing this moral relationship, such usage should not be taken to imply a narrow sense of 'obligation', rather than duties, as some philosophers have distinguished these terms (e.g. Brandt, 1965; Hart, 1967). No systematic distinction will be made between obligations and duties: both terms, along with others like 'moral bonds', are used to indicate general moral reasons for acting, although of course none of them refer to an *absolute* moral claim on our actions. Because obligations, understood here as general moral considerations, can conflict with each other, they do not necessarily identify a *conclusive* reason for action. For instance, if I have promised to meet a friend for lunch at a particular time, I have an obligation to do so, but I ought not to act on that obligation if to do so would prevent me from taking a seriously sick child to hospital. This does not mean that obligations can be overridden as or when we like, but only that, at the very least, they can be overridden by other conflicting moral claims on us. Even if they are overridden in a particular case, this does not mean that they should not be acknowledged in some other way, as for instance in the case of the promise by explaining to my friend why I had to break it. The simple point is that particular obligations provide us with moral reasons for acting that are not yet 'all things considered' reasons. In deciding how to act on a particular occasion we have to take account of *all* the relevant reasons, which will often mean that some obligations are overridden by others. Thus, to identify an action as being required by our political obligation is not to show that we must always perform it, though it is to indicate one (moral) reason that we have to so act. We should not forget that political obligations exist in a wider moral context and are far from exhaustive of the moral claims that are made on us.

A third point to be noted is that the obligation is 'political'. In this context, what is meant by 'political' is that the moral obligation has to do with a person's membership of a particular *polity*. While it might well be linguistically unobjectionable to refer, for example, to membership of a political party or commitment to a cause as involving or creating a political obligation, these are not what is intended here. Throughout the subsequent discussion, the use of 'political' in political obligation refers exclusively to whatever obligations are owed to the polity by its members. The key features of a polity, as understood here, are that it is the most comprehensive and inclusive structure of social organization within a territory; that sovereign power is exercised by an authority, usually a government; and that its members are systematically related to each other through the terms of their membership. Many important questions could be raised about this brief characterization of a polity, but it should provide sufficient guidance at this stage.

This leads naturally to the fourth point, which is specifically about the scope of the argument. For the most part, I use the slightly archaic term 'polity', or occasionally the less forbidding 'political community', rather than 'state', except where a state is specifically meant, so as not to prejudge the question of how far the arguments apply to other forms of polity. However, I have no very clear view about the relevance of what I have to say to forms of political society which are radically different from that of a modern state. The circumstances that I principally reflect on are those of a world of largely independent states and most of the subsequent discussion is directed towards them, without considering how far what is said applies to other forms of polity. States, as understood here, do not have to be entirely separate one from another, in that there is room for overlapping jurisdictions or for principles of subsidiarity, but they will normally possess a significant measure of at least formal sovereignty. *Mutatis mutandis*, the argument may well apply to other forms of polity, but I would not want to hang too much on whether, or how far, that is so. And while states are certainly the most common and obvious examples of polities – and in the modern world provide by far the most familiar setting in which the defining features of a polity, as set out above, are to be found – how far other kinds of political society can be incorporated within the argument is something about which, as indicated earlier, it is appropriate to keep an open mind: it is certainly not an issue that can be satisfactorily resolved by definitional fiat.

Finally, there is one further preliminary point that is especially important in relation to the subsequent discussion. This concerns the common reduction of the problem of political obligation to the question of whether or not a person is obligated to obey the law. Such reduction, however, tends to result in an inadequate characterization of political obligation. The question of the grounds of an obligation to obey the law is open to two broad lines of interpretation, neither of which necessarily coincides precisely with the problem of political obligation. First, if the question is understood quite generally to be asking about reasons that obligate us to obey any law then it is too broad, for it fails to focus with sufficient specificity on the particular relationship between persons and the political community of which they are members. Reasons that justify an obligation to obey the law, independently of whether or not the law is that of the polity of which a person is a member, are not reasons that can explain political obligation: they do not satisfy the particularity requirement as set out in the previous section. Second, however, if the question is taken more narrowly to ask why a person is specifically obligated to the law of his or her polity, then this is too narrow an interpretation. Although certainly part of the problem of political obligation, this way of formulating the question fails to encompass other aspects of it. Political obligation is not necessarily reducible simply to an obligation to obey the law of the polity of which one is a member. There may be other obligations or responsibilities specifically deriving from one's membership of a particular polity, such as a duty to vote, to serve one's country in times of crisis or even to oppose injustice perpetrated by one's own government, which are not enshrined in the law and, which if not observed, do not incur a legal penalty. As we shall see later, the relationship between political obligation and the law is more complex than simple reference to an obligation to *obey* the law suggests.

There are, it need hardly be said, entirely legitimate and interesting questions that can be asked about the nature of legal obligation and the moral claims that law per se has on us. Some of the issues and arguments to which these questions give rise are certainly relevant to a consideration of political obligation (see, e.g., Carnes, 1960; Wasserstrom, 1968; Pennock and Chapman, 1970; Smith, 1976; Mackie, 1981). However, the failure to recognize that questions about political obligation are not necessarily identical with, or simply reducible to, questions about the obligation to obey the law has sometimes resulted in confusion. In consequence, political philosophers have often been concerned with subtly but importantly different questions. In so far as this is the case, there will be something of a mismatch between the concerns of those who equate the two sets of issues and the point of view adopted in this book. Hence, there is occasionally some uncomfortable but probably unavoidable shifting between these viewpoints in the ensuing discussions, resulting in a blurring of focus.

Conclusion

The principal purpose of this chapter has been to introduce the problem of political obligation; to attempt a preliminary exploration and clarification of some of the many questions to which it gives rise; and to articulate the kind of inquiry into it that is to be undertaken in what follows. I have also indicated some of the questions and issues with which the book is not concerned. In Chapters 2 to 4, I consider each of the more philosophically resilient and influential accounts of political obligation that have been advanced and continue to have some appeal. My approach in these chapters is to distinguish three broad types of theories of political obligation, which I label 'voluntarist', 'teleological' and 'deontological', and to explore the strengths and weaknesses of each of these types. It is only right to acknowledge from the start that this kind of approach, especially one that attempts to cover such a large amount of ground in brief compass, has its limitations. In particular, the classification of theories can be somewhat Procrustean, both in neglecting the richness and complexity of even those theories that fit reasonably comfortably within the classification, but especially in its treatment of those theories that are inclined to escape such easy classification. It should also be noted that it is inherently biased against pluralist theories that seek to combine elements from different types of theory. Thus, while I continue to believe that this threefold classification has its uses, especially for expository purposes, it should also be treated by the reader with some caution and a degree of scepticism.

Having surveyed the principal theories, the main task in Chapter 5 is to consider, and ultimately to reject, the claim that because none of the traditional justifications of political obligation is very convincing, this shows that (ordinarily at least) most people lack any political obligations. This is the view associated with anarchism in one form or another. However, the full vindication of the case against anarchism, and especially philosophical anarchism, depends upon the cogency of the arguments in Chapters 6 and 7, particularly the former. Thus, in Chapter 6, after considering the conceptual argument, which denies that political obligation stands in need of any justification, I briefly sketch in very general terms the contours of an alternative account of political obligation, which I claim is more satisfactory than the theories so far considered: this is the associative account. I note one sophisticated version of this account – Margaret Gilbert's plural subject theory – but for the most part the chapter is taken up with defending the associative approach against a raft of apparently powerful criticisms. Chapter 7 then sets out and seeks to elaborate in a little more detail one particular version of the associative account. The key aspects of this account involve explaining how an effective polity has value for its members and how those members can come to identify themselves with it. Taken together, the primary aim of Chapters 6 and 7 should be seen as attempting to vindicate the widespread sense of people that they do indeed have political obligations to their polity, and thus rejecting the charge that such views are merely mistaken. In doing so, I try to show that it is the denial that almost anybody has or has had any political obligations that is problematic, although I do not claim that such a denial is always and necessarily confused.

Finally, in the Conclusion, I briefly return to two questions that can be seen to run through the various arguments of the book. First, why does political obligation matter? That is, what hangs on whether or not we are thought to have such obligations? Second, what kind of account of political obligation should we be looking for? And, connectedly, what account best fits with what we are looking for? As I make clear, I do not for a moment believe that the particular version of the associative account of political obligation that I set out in Chapter 7 is the last word on the subject. However, I do hold that some version or other of a broadly associative account, as defended in Chapter 6, is best equipped to explain the widespread sense that we do have political obligations. I also firmly believe that for both theoretical and practical reasons we have to take the ordinary sense of our having political obligations seriously, as a good place to start. Taking it seriously does not, though, mean that we cannot be led to reject that ordinary sense of our having political obligations, because there is no guarantee that we can come up with an intellectually and morally satisfying theoretical account of it. However, my claim is that an associative theory does succeed in coming up with just such an account.

The argument of this book is that, at least for the standard case of someone who is born into their polity, something like the ordinary sense of political obligation can be convincingly vindicated through an associative account, which understands political obligation as a concomitant of membership of a valuable association with which its members have come to identify. Indeed, most of those people fortunate enough to live in an at least minimally decent polity have good reason to develop such a sense of political obligation. However, there is a long journey to be undertaken before we arrive at this destination. It begins in the next chapter, which takes up what is, perhaps, the most popular and, if it works, potentially convincing kind of explanation of political obligation in the modern era: the idea that people are bound to their polity as a result of some voluntary choice or action of their own.

2 Voluntarist Theories

In this chapter I seek to offer an overview and critical assessment of one broad and potentially attractive class of accounts of political obligation. These accounts, following terminology which has become quite familiar, can be labelled 'voluntarist' (Riley, 1973; Pateman, 1985), and many of them can also be covered by the even more familiar idea of consent theories. Such theories have proved consistently appealing in the long history of discussions of political obligation, but especially so in the modern world to theorists of a broadly liberal persuasion. Central to these theories is the role that they attribute to individual choice or decision, to some specific act of voluntary commitment, in explaining or justifying political obligation. Their essential and common feature is simply that they seek to explain political obligation in terms of some freely chosen undertaking through which persons act so as to bind themselves morally to their polity. It is through this act or decision that people are thought to acquire their political obligations. However, the particular form of this act or decision; the conditions that are taken to be sufficient to render it freely chosen; the precise nature of the relationship implied; the extent of the obligation incurred; and to whom or what the obligation is owed – are all variously articulated within differing voluntarist accounts. Often these differences are important and for some purposes may be regarded as more significant than the features that these accounts share. Without, though, seeking to deny or underestimate those differences, the discussion that follows is premised on the assumption that it is legitimate and instructive to treat such differences for the most part as variations within one broad class or type of views.

The ensuing discussion, therefore, will for the most part be concerned with what is common to these accounts, or at least to features sufficiently similar for the differences not to matter much, rather than with what differentiates them from one another. One advantage of this strategy is that it enables us to focus on one logically distinct type of argument without becoming diverted by peripheral or secondary detail. Another advantage in considering one broad type of argument, rather than the complex ideas of particular political theorists, is that the latter often contain several logically distinct arguments that coexist in uneasy, ambiguous and sometimes even confused relation to each other. Locke is a good example of a political philosopher who employs the notion of consent in his account of political obligation, yet leaves it unclear precisely how much weight it is supposed to bear within the overall theory that he articulates (Locke, 1967). However, this approach also has some significant limitations, principal among which is that it is inclined to drain the actual accounts offered by individual political theorists of their richness and imaginative complexity. At worst, it risks charges of setting up the proverbial 'straw man', although some simplification is probably unavoidable. Thus, the discussion here is principally directed towards one type of argument and its central features, and the ideas of particular political philosophers or theorists only in so far as they employ this type of argument.

Voluntarism and political obligation

Voluntarist accounts, it has been suggested, explain or justify political obligation in terms of some freely chosen act, undertaking or commitment which morally obligates a person to his or her polity. Most commonly this view has been associated with the claim that the majority, if not all individuals, have political obligations in at least some polities, and that these are to be explained by reference to an individual's voluntary act of commitment. However, some political philosophers have used voluntarist arguments in a much more radical way, in order to subvert the claim that most people, either now or in the past, have, or have had, any obligations to their polity. They argue that while a voluntarist theory gives a fundamentally correct account of political obligation, the vast majority of people have and have had no such obligations. Political obligation exists only when people have freely chosen membership of their polity, but since most people do not freely choose they are not obligated (e.g. Pateman, 1985). Somewhat crudely, the distinction is between voluntarist accounts, which purport to explain or justify a relationship that has actually obtained between many people and their polity, and those which claim that the requisite conditions for the proper ascription of political obligation have, as a matter of fact, at best only rarely existed. In short, both are voluntarist accounts in that they endorse the claim that some voluntary undertaking is needed to provide the justification for political obligation, but they disagree as to whether or not most people have made such an undertaking. This disagreement results from a difference about either what the conditions are that have to be met for an undertaking to be genuinely voluntary, or whether or not in fact the appropriate conditions of a voluntary undertaking have been met. The first is certainly a theoretical dispute, whereas the second may be at least partly empirical, in that disagreement revolves around factual rather than theoretical claims.

The distinction between the two views is not a sharp one at the margins, but it does reveal a real and significant gulf between different voluntarist accounts of political obligation; a gulf which is often reflected in its most acute form in differing judgements about whether or not people have political obligations in liberal democratic states. It also means that, to some extent, distinct criticisms are appropriate to voluntarist accounts divided on this basis. Although later in this chapter I will address specifically those theories that endorse voluntarism but which claim that the conditions for political obligation have rarely if ever been met, most of the discussion here is concerned with what those conditions are or should be, and whether they have obtained (at least in some polities for most people). With respect to this last point, I shall be particularly concerned to assess the claim that liberal democratic polities have so successfully incorporated the requirements of voluntarism that the ascription of political obligation to their citizens is justified within the terms of a voluntarist theory. My conclusion about this, and also about voluntarist theories of political obligation more generally, is to a large extent sceptical.

First, however, more needs to be said about the structure and content of voluntarist accounts of political obligation. The most familiar of these accounts are those that deploy concepts such as a 'social contract', 'express consent' or 'tacit consent'. The role of these concepts in voluntarist accounts is to provide the relevant connection between the individual and the polity that explains or justifies the claim that people have a political obligation to their particular polity. What makes these accounts voluntarist is that they all regard the political relations constituted by membership of a polity as in some way the result of voluntary, freely chosen undertakings by those so related. Where they differ, however, is in the specific accounts that they give of how such relations are instituted. Thus, political obligation is variously understood to arise from, for example, a contract between many individuals to establish a political community, or a contract between individuals and their government, or the express or tacit consent of individuals to the government or the constitution or political system. While these do not exhaust the possibilities, they are indicative of the kind of claims that are characteristically made by voluntarist theories. The more or less explicit, but essential, background assumption of voluntarist theories is that no person has any political obligation unless he or she has voluntarily bound him or herself to a particular polity. Furthermore, in explaining how individuals come to acquire this obligation, voluntarist theorists also attempt to explain the precise substance of the obligation, its extent and to whom or what it is owed, although the answers given to these more specific questions inevitably vary according to the details of different voluntarist accounts.

Voluntarist theories of one kind or another have a long and complex history with roots dating back at least as far as classical Athens (Gough, 1967; Lessnoff, 1986), although the term 'political obligation', as noted in Chapter 1, does not as such appear in the writings of any thinker prior to the late nineteenth century. In the *Crito*, Socrates considers escaping from his imprisonment and avoiding the death penalty but argues that the Laws (the embodiment of political authority in Athens) could legitimately ask of him: 'Are we or are we not speaking the truth when we say that you have undertaken, in deed if not in word, to live your life as a citizen in obedience to us? ... It is a fact then that you are breaking covenants and undertakings made with us, although you made them under no compulsion or misunderstanding' (Plato, 1969, p. 93). Here, as Plato reports him, Socrates clearly expresses the thought that he has, through his own voluntary actions, entered into a covenant or agreement with the Laws of Athens, and in doing so has thereby acquired an obligation to obey them. Although this is not the only, or even perhaps the most important, line of argument advanced in the *Crito*, it is a significant voluntarist strand in the broader position Socrates elaborates (Woozley, 1979). Subsequently, elements of voluntarist theories have been detected in other Greek thinkers, although not Aristotle, and in Roman law, as well as in Hooker, Grotius and Milton, before what is generally considered to be their full flowering in the work of Hobbes and Locke in the seventeenth century.

Thomas Hobbes famously asserted in his *Leviathan* 'that life in a state of nature [i.e. without political authority] would be solitary, poor, nasty, brutish and short' (Hobbes, 1968, ch. 13). In order to escape from this condition, he argued, the rational response is to covenant (i.e. contract) with each other to give up our natural right to whatever we want in return for the protection of an all-powerful sovereign (which could be a single person or a body of people, such as a Parliament). The purpose in establishing political authority is peace and security, but its ground is our voluntary submission. We thus agree to obey the sovereign, who is not himself a party to the contract, and abide by his commands, subject only to the residual right that we each have to protect our own life when it is directly threatened, whether that threat comes from the sovereign or some other person or persons from whom the sovereign is unable or unwilling to protect us. In this way we both establish the authority of a particular sovereign and simultaneously acquire the obligation to obey him. The many details of Hobbes's subtle arguments are complex and controversial, which has resulted in a wide variety of interpretations of his exact views, from the theistic to the game-theoretic, but it is neither possible nor necessary to pursue these further here (see Newey, 2008, chs 5, 6).

There are, though, features of Hobbes's argument that have looked unconvincing to most of his readers. Particularly relevant to the argument here is his latitude about what is to count as a *voluntary* act, which for Hobbes was quite consistent with acting under duress – being offered the choice between your money or life is still a choice, for Hobbes, and if you give up your money in such circumstances then you do so voluntarily. (The conditions of voluntariness are an issue to which we will return later.) Unsurprisingly, many subsequent thinkers have doubted whether Hobbes's cure – the absolute authority of the sovereign and the (almost) unlimited obligation of the subject – was really any better than the disease of the state of nature which it was supposed to remedy. Thus later in the seventeenth century, in his *Second Treatise on Government*, John Locke, though making the social contract central to his theory, argued for a more limited political authority (Locke, 1967). He also afforded an explicit place in his account of political obligation to the notion of consent.

Locke, like Hobbes before him, explained the origin of political obligation in a contract made in a prepolitical state of nature. However, Locke's conception of the state of nature is considerably more benign than that of Hobbes, and the process by which political authority is instituted is more complicated. According to Locke, political authority arises in two stages: first through a unanimous contract to form political society, and then by a majority decision to entrust a government with legislative, executive and judicial powers. Throughout this process people retain their natural rights to life, liberty and property: the purpose of forming a political society with a government is to provide for the better protection and impartial enforcement of these rights than is possible in the state of nature. In the absence of any authoritative interpretation of these rights and any impartial body charged with their protection, there is inevitably scope for some arbitrariness of judgement and unpredictability of enforcement. Subsequent generations, not party to the original contract, acquire their political obligations through their consent: either in the form of an explicit oath of allegiance or through what Locke calls their 'tacit consent'. The idea of tacit consent has proved an enduring contribution to voluntarist theories of political obligation and, although Locke is not always clear about what is necessary for tacit consent, it includes enjoying or making use of any property under the jurisdiction and protection of the state; but it is also capable of being developed in ways that Locke himself did not anticipate. Again, the problems involved in the idea of consent, whether express or tacit, provide a major focus of discussion later in this chapter and, therefore, will not be pursued further at this point.

The most politically important feature of Locke's account of political obligation, in contrast to that of Hobbes, is that it allows for a right of resistance to a tyrannical and oppressive government; though how and by whom this was to be judged was also left somewhat unclear. It also gives rise to doubts about the real importance of consent within Locke's theory, for it sometimes seems that the significant question for political obligation becomes not whether a person consents, but whether the government is acting justly (Dunn, 1967). Indeed, we can understand Locke as embracing two quite different kinds of arguments about political obligation, both of which are necessary to support his case: those that focus on the activities or moral qualities of the state and those that look to some voluntary act of commitment on the part of the citizen. A. J. Simmons has made an influential distinction in this regard between 'justification' and 'legitimacy', although for reasons that I will not expand on here I do not adopt this terminology (Simmons, 2001, ch. 7). In any case, it is only the second argument that will be considered in this chapter.

Although, as we have seen, voluntarist arguments can be found as early as Socrates, it is probably true to say that it is in Hobbes and Locke that modern voluntarism has its roots. Given the diversity of circumstances in which voluntarist ideas have surfaced, it would be implausible to claim that voluntarist theories of political obligation are only articulated within a very historically specific set of socio-economic conditions; yet some particular historical circumstances may indeed favour, or be especially conducive to, their development. For example, it seems likely that the prominence of voluntarist theories in the seventeenth century owes a good deal to the peculiar social, economic and ideological changes that Europe was then undergoing; in particular, those consequent on the Reformation, the rise of Protestantism and the emergence of market capitalism (MacPherson, 1962). These historical developments did much to undermine the theory of the divine right of kings, which had helped to justify the political authority of secular rulers during the period of the increasing separation of Church and state. This theory, which perhaps receives its most articulate statement in the writings of Sir Robert Filmer, maintained that God had directly ordained the authority of secular rulers, and that therefore their subjects were morally obligated to obey the ruler's commands (Filmer, 1991). The theories of Hobbes and Locke, in their different ways, were both conscious attempts to develop a justification of political authority more suited to the changing material and ideological conditions. Indeed, though I shall not attempt it here, an exploration of the historical context of seventeenth-century contract and consent theories can be especially illuminating about some of the merits and limitations of such theorizing (Herzog, 1989). It is also possible to conjecture more generally that voluntarism is likely to prove particularly attractive when established authority and its traditional justifications are under attack, and where there is no settled moral consensus to which appeal can be made. However, whatever the merits of such a speculation, there can be no doubt that, in one form or another, voluntarist theories continue to have a considerable attraction for political theorists; an appeal that survives into our own time, as is illustrated in particular in the work of several liberal political philosophers (Tussman, 1960; Plamenatz, 1968; Beran, 1977, 1987).

It is appropriate, therefore, briefly to consider what it is about voluntarist theories of political obligation that accounts for their persistent and continuing attractiveness. Why have political philosophers shown such remarkable tenacity and ingenuity in trying to reconstruct or rehabilitate such theories, despite what appear to be, as we shall shortly see, some obvious and deep-rooted objections to them? These attractions have both moral and philosophical dimensions. Probably the principal feature of voluntarist theories that accounts for their appeal is the crucial role that they assign to people's voluntary choices or commitments. For, on this view, a person only becomes obligated to his or her polity through some act (a contract, a promise, a form of words, or an action or actions expressing or implying consent) that is voluntarily performed by that person. The individual is recognized as a morally free agent, only legitimately bound by the demands of the polity because of a free and voluntary undertaking to be so bound. As the individual is the author of his or her own obligation, such an obligation in no way undermines or impairs the moral autonomy of the person. The lucid summary of the attractions of consent theory by A. J. Simmons serves equally for pretty much any voluntarist theory:

> 'It respects our belief that the course a man's life takes should be determined, as much as possible, by his own decisions and actions. Since being born into a political community is neither an act we perform, nor the result of a decision we have made, we feel that this should not limit our freedom by automatically binding us to the government of that community. And these convictions serve as the basis of a theory of political obligation which holds that only the voluntary giving of a clear sign that one finds the state acceptable (and is willing to assume political bonds to it), can ever obligate one to support or comply with the commands of that state's government.' (Simmons, 1979, p. 69)

On this view, the polity is an association of individuals much like other voluntary associations, such as sports clubs, political parties and trades unions, created and maintained by the freely entered into commitments of the multiplicity of individuals who compose them. In the modern world, at least, the voluntary membership of an association is usually thought of as a necessary condition of its having authority over its members, and correspondingly of their acquiring obligations to it. If this is true of other associations, then why is it not true of the polity? Clearly, if some account of political obligation along these lines were plausible, it would satisfy a widely held conviction that the moral authority of a polity, and in particular its right sometimes to coerce its members, resides in the voluntary agreement of its members, a conviction which is especially attractive to those of a broadly liberal political persuasion. Such an account would also have the benefit of rendering political obligation intelligible in terms which, if not entirely unproblematic, would at least identify it as belonging to that familiar category of moral obligations of which promises are the paradigmatic example. Hence, if it were possible to formulate a convincing voluntarist account of political obligation, it would have considerable moral and philosophical appeal, being both morally attractive and philosophically fairly straightforward. What, then, are the most important objections to such an account? And why is it not possible to arrive at a convincing voluntarist theory?

   The most obvious and apparently decisive objection that has confronted voluntarist theories from the outset has been an inability to discover anything in practice that could reasonably be interpreted as the type of act required to create a political obligation. We have a good idea, for example, of what acts are required to become a member of a club, but what comparable act is there that accounts for membership of a polity? Indeed, for those voluntarist theorists who claim to give an explanation or justification of political obligation in any existing polities, this problem appears insurmountable. This perhaps banal and obvious point is no less important for its familiarity and simplicity. In the case of a supposed contract the embarrassing questions to which this objection gives rise are easily apparent. When was this contract made? Who are the parties to the contract? What are the terms of the contract? Where are we to look to resolve any disputes about the contract? It does not seem that any social contract theory of this very simple form could possibly provide remotely plausible answers to most of these questions. It is true that in some times and places oaths of allegiance and declarations of loyalty have been common, but how plausible is it to regard these as meeting the conditions of a contractual basis for political obligation? First, even if they were thought to fit the bill, this would only explain the political obligation of those who had entered into such commitments. Second, such oaths and declarations would need to have been freely entered into if they were to count as a truly voluntary contract. (This is a point that will be developed more fully later when considering the conditions that the weaker notion of consent requires to be met, if an act or utterance is to count as a genuine expression of voluntary agreement.) Third, the content of these oaths and declarations is often either too vague or too narrow to license a general political obligation, although there is no compelling reason why they could not be made more determinate. Finally, while not perhaps crucial, such oaths and declarations typically lack features that are usual to contracts: for example, only one party undertakes an obligation with the other, offering little, if anything, explicitly in return.

These objections, though, might give rise to the reply that they take the idea of contract far too literally. Perhaps a more informal analogue of a contract such as a promise, bargain or agreement is involved. Indeed, it might be argued that what such oaths and declarations, as well as other acts, should be understood as expressing is rather a person's consent to the authority of the government. Thus, as it seems likely that the concept of consent will prove to be more defensible than that of the more formal contract, subsequent criticism will be directed to voluntarist accounts that focus on consent. Any criticisms of consent theories are likely to apply *mutatis mutandis* to all genuinely voluntarist contract accounts (although, as will be explained later, the most powerful versions of contract theory are in fact not genuinely voluntarist, as defined here). It is, therefore, more profitable to concentrate on consent theories as the most plausible and sophisticated of genuinely voluntarist accounts of political obligation.

Consent

Consent, it has been suggested, is a more informal and less legalistic concept than contract. We give and refuse consent in a wide range of contexts, for a multiplicity of purposes and in a variety of forms: a patient consents to a surgical operation; a woman consents to allow a friend to borrow her car; a father consents to the marriage of his daughter (where such consent is necessary); an employer consents to her employee taking the day off; a famous author consents to the use of his name in a charitable cause; homosexual acts are legal in Britain if performed in private by consenting adults; heterosexual rape involves sexual relations between a man and woman without the consent of the woman; and so on. Precisely because consent is a diverse, multifarious and informal phenomenon, however, it is quite difficult to articulate an exact set of necessary and sufficient conditions for its proper attribution; and there is more than one way that such conditions can be formulated (Higgins, 2004, ch. 3). Fortunately, though, for our purposes it is not necessary to become too embroiled in these philosophical subtleties, as the key conditions are relatively uncontroversial and fairly easily specified. Richard Flathman has helpfully identified three such conditions. On Flathman's account, for a person to consent, he must, when the appropriate background conditions of freedom of choice obtain (about which I shall say more shortly):

'(a) Know what he consents to;
(b) Intend to consent to it;
(c) Communicate his knowledge of what he is consenting to and his intention to consent (that is, communicate his consent) to the person or persons to whom the consent is given.' (Flathman, 1972, p. 220)

These seem plausible conditions, if an action or utterance is to be legitimately interpreted as an expression of consent, at least in most circumstances, in anything like our ordinary understanding of the term. I shall subsequently refer to these three conditions as, respectively, the 'knowledge', 'intention' and 'communication' conditions. Although it is not possible here to explore these conditions in great detail, there are a few preliminary observations that can usefully be made.

First, the knowledge condition, which requires that a person know what it is that he or she consents to, is more complex than it perhaps appears. For, sometimes, due to what is called the opacity of belief or knowledge, it can be reasonably claimed that a person has consented to something even though he or she did not know or fully understand what had been consented to. For example, if a mother consents to her young son going to the theatre one evening she may also consent to his coming home late. This may be true even though the mother did not know she was consenting to her son's coming home late, perhaps because she mistakenly thought the play finished earlier. (The implications would be different if her son had deliberately misled her about the time at which the performance finished.) Thus, the 'knowledge condition' must not be interpreted in too narrow or strict a way, though it is obvious, despite these complexities and indeterminacies in its application, that it is an indispensable condition in deciding whether or not, in any particular case, consent has been given. Indeed, and this is the second point, it should be noted that, notwithstanding the apparent clarity of the three conditions, it can be in practice very difficult to be confident about whether or not they have been met: it is sometimes as a matter of fact very difficult to determine whether or to what a person has consented. This is especially true of the intention condition. Sexual intercourse and some kinds of medical circumstances provide two notorious contexts in which the difficulty of establishing whether or not consent has been given may be considerable. Of course, such difficulties do not preclude there being many instances in which the presence or absence of consent is clear and entirely unproblematic. The third observation is that all three conditions apply equally to tacit consent as to express or explicit consent. As this point is more controversial, yet is highly relevant to what may seem to be the most plausible version of consent theory, it is worth considering it further.

The notion of tacit consent is principally familiar from situations in which an individual, on being given an opportunity to express dissent from some policy, proposal or other course of action, does not do so remaining silent or impassive. Here it would be natural to say that, although the individual does not do or say anything in response to the proposal, he or she tacitly consents to it. Such situations are especially familiar in committee meetings, though they also exist in more informal and less structured settings. For example, in getting into a taxi and stating my destination, though no explicit mention is ever made of a fare, under normal circumstances I am taken to be tacitly agreeing to pay the fare that shows on the meter. It would be disingenuous for me to claim that I never consented to pay. Or, if we are discussing where to have dinner this evening, and someone proposes a particular restaurant, and I do not express dissent or propose an alternative, then again this will normally be taken as expressing tacit consent to the proposal. What distinguishes tacit from express or explicit consent, in these as in other instances, is only the *manner* or *form* in which it is indicated. Tacit consent is expressed through silence or passivity. However, it is obvious that not just any instance of passivity or silence can reasonably be interpreted as an act of consent, or else each of us would be unintentionally consenting to all manner of things all the time.

What singles out a particular instance of silence or passivity as an act of consent is precisely those conditions that Flathman identifies. The person must know what it is he or she is consenting to, subject to the qualification mentioned earlier; must intend to give consent; and most importantly in this context must know that silence or passivity will be understood as an expression or sign of consent. These conditions need not imply any sustained or complicated process of explicit reasoning on the part of the person consenting, but it is only when they are met that it is appropriate to impute tacit consent to someone. Thus, tacit consent is distinctive only in the form in which it is expressed and in other respects is essentially similar to express or explicit consent. In particular, it should be emphasized that the qualification of consent by the adjective 'tacit' does not imply a radically different type of consent, logically distinct from other forms of consent. Indeed, if one can honestly say that one would not have expressly consented at the time, had one been asked, then this is generally a very good reason for denying that there was tacit consent. In sum, therefore, this is to say no more than that tacit consent is an instance of *consent*; but to say that much may prevent one being misled when the emphasis is placed on its being *tacit* consent. The difference between tacit and express consent is of the same order as the difference between consent being indicated by raising a hand or by saying yes. The nature of silence and passivity may make such consent more difficult to identify and more disputable in practice, but the logic of tacit consent is no different from that of express consent.

The intention, knowledge and communication conditions are all necessary for an act to count as a genuine expression of consent; but they are not sufficient. There also have to be present what were earlier referred to as the appropriate background conditions of choice. These need to be explained more fully, though they are both vaguer and more controversial than Flathman's three conditions. However, their necessity can easily be shown from the following example. If presented with a choice between our money or our life, most of us (although not Hobbes) would accept that we cannot be said to have genuinely consented to the taking of our money, even though we do allow it to be taken and the intention, knowledge and communication conditions have all been met. The reason for denying that genuine consent is involved in this example is that we did not have the appropriate kind of choice as to whether or not to refuse our consent. It would be natural to say that we had no real alternative to consenting, though it would not be literally true to say that we had *no* choice at all: we could have chosen death. The problem here is one of establishing how much, or, better, what sort of choice is necessary for an expression of consent to be genuine. This is particularly important for voluntarist theorists of political obligation, who need to show that people do have a genuine choice if consent is to play the role required by their theories.

Matters are complicated further, however, if we consider a rather different example. If a woman is faced with a choice between a surgical procedure to save her life and the inevitable consequences of a terminal illness, it would be quite proper, if she agrees to the surgery, to say that she gives her consent. Indeed, under normal circumstances her consent is just what is required before the operation can legally be performed. In both this example and that of the man faced with the choice between his money and his life the person will die unless he or she gives consent to one course of action, though in the latter example the attribution of consent is strongly counter-intuitive, while in the medical example it would seem uncontroversial. How, then, are these cases to be distinguished? Why is one case normally understood as involving an expression of consent and the other not?

The different responses to these two examples can only be fully explained in normative terms. The difference cannot be satisfactorily accounted for simply in terms of the number of choices available or in terms of their attractiveness, though in some instances these may be relevant considerations. In the two examples under discussion, if they are filled out in appropriate detail, both the number of choices and their utilities or values could be equivalent, yet the difference in judgement about whether or not consent had been given would remain. The normative feature of these two examples that most plausibly explains this difference of response is the presence or absence of coercion by another person or persons. In the first example it is the clearly coercive element of the threat that invalidates the imputation of consent, whereas in the medical example no coercion is either exercised or threatened.

Unfortunately, though this distinction between the presence and absence of coercion is easily observed in these particular examples, in many circumstances, what is to count as an instance of coercion can be a matter of vigorous dispute. For example, when are the unpleasant consequences of an action to be understood as simply following from the action and when as coercively induced? When does persuasion become coercion? The point is not that answers cannot be given to these questions but that such answers will often be both lacking in precision and also controversial. Many cases will be clear, such as in the two examples cited, but some of the most interesting and important in political contexts are likely to be contested. For instance, Marxists characteristically view labour contracts within a capitalist economic system as coercive exchanges, while by contrast defenders of the free-market typically see them as paradigmatic instances of free exchange. Similar disputes are liable to pervade discussions of consent in the context of voluntarist theories of political obligation. As we have seen, Hobbes argued that even contracts entered into under extreme duress, such as those made by people whose lives were directly threatened by an external aggressor, were no less voluntary and hence equally obligatory as those made under much more auspicious circumstances (Hobbes, 1968, ch. 20). While this view has some justification within Hobbes's metaphysical system, it has not won much favour with other philosophers, and generally it has not been thought to meet the conditions of an authentically voluntarist theory of political obligation. However, even among those who accept that the background conditions of choice require that genuine consent must not be coercively induced, there is still an important area of disagreement as to what exactly is to count as the absence of coercion. This is not in itself an objection to consent theories, but a reminder that their application will not be without difficulties.

At this point, it may be appropriate to advert briefly to another area of contention. This concerns the claims of some feminist theorists, who have argued that the way in which the notion of consent is characteristically employed within the theories of political philosophers, and indeed the entire social contract tradition, is riddled by patriarchal assumptions (Pateman, 1988, 1989; Hirschmann, 1992). These assumptions have been such as effectively to exclude women from consent or participation in the social contract; for either it has been tacitly implied that the relevant parties are male heads of households or, as with Rousseau, it is explicitly stated that women are excluded for other reasons. Historically, there can be no doubt that there is much justice in the feminist complaint, and consent theory, like much of the rest of the history of political theory, has been thought about and presented in gendered terms.

The more difficult and philosophically interesting issue, however, concerns the extent to which such patriarchal bias is ineliminably embedded within voluntarism; whether, in the words of Nancy Hirschmann, it is 'not merely *contingently* sexist but *structurally* sexist as well' (Hirschmann, 1992, p. 11). If it were, then this would seem to constitute a compelling objection to the entire enterprise of developing a voluntarist theory of political obligation. However, the issues are complex, and while I sympathize with many aspects of Hirschmann's and Pateman's critiques of consent theory, not least Hirschmann's often penetrating rejection of the voluntarist paradigm for conceptualizing the problem of political obligation, I am not convinced that they have shown voluntarist theories to be irredeemably gendered. It is probably true that some implicitly patriarchal assumptions have in fact helped to shape the whole idea of the social contract and of consent. Moreover, I believe that they are right in rejecting the picture of what political obligation must be like, and which seems to underlie voluntarism; and I shall have more to say about that in the final section of this chapter. However, there does not seem to be anything in the logic of voluntarism that *necessitates* a distinctively gendered perspective; and there is no compelling reason why such theories cannot be reconstructed along non-patriarchal lines, as contemporary consent theorists have sought to do. In short, while there is much that is, in my view, compelling in the feminist critique, what is valid in that critique can be advanced without being grounded in a specifically gendered perspective. At least, for the sake of the argument that follows, this is what I shall assume, although the whole issue clearly merits a more detailed discussion than is possible here. It remains, then, to consider whether there are good reasons, independent of specifically feminist critiques, for rejecting an account of political obligation in terms of consent.

Political obligation and consent

The central problem for consent theorists, as with all voluntarist theories, has been to identify any action in the personal history of most individuals that successfully meets the conditions necessary for the ascription of political obligation. As with contract theories we can ask: Who has consented? When and how have they consented? To what have they consented? To whom have they given their consent? Although many different answers could be, and indeed have been, offered to these questions, it is tacit consent that, in the words of Ruth Higgins, 'has been both the refuge and ridicule of status quo consent theories that seek to insist both that consent is a necessary condition of legitimate government authority and that at least some existing states are legitimate' (Higgins, 2004, p. 102). And, in particular, two interpretations of tacit consent have proved especially popular among consent theorists. First, it has been claimed that continued residence within a polity, or the enjoyment of the benefits consequent upon continued residence, provides sufficient evidence that an individual consents to its political arrangements. Although the two formulations of this interpretation are not strictly equivalent, and the expression 'political arrangements' for indicating what is consented to is deliberately vague, the differences that are blurred by this general formulation can be safely ignored for present purposes; for the objections that follow apply irrespective of these differences. The second interpretation of tacit consent is of more recent provenance and involves the claim that voting in a genuinely democratic election is an expression of consent to the authority of the duly elected government. This suggestion is obviously much more restricted in its scope, being limited to polities that have authentically democratic constitutional and political practices. Although it should be noted that there is likely to be some dispute about what constitutes a genuinely democratic election and also about whether any, and if so what, limits are implied upon what a government may legitimately do, it would be wrong to make too much of these, and thus the details of these disputes will be ignored. I begin by considering the first interpretation of tacit consent.

Does the claim that residence, or the enjoyment of the benefits of residence, implies consent meet the conditions necessary for an act to count as an expression of consent? It seems highly implausible to think that it does. There are no commonly understood conventions by reference to which continued residence or the enjoyment of its fruits can be reasonably interpreted as implying consent. Moreover, it is not at all clear what individuals are consenting to; or that they know they are consenting; or that they intend to do so. There may of course be other arguments, for example from fairness, justice, gratitude or utility, as to why individuals *should* consent; but these are not to the point here. The question is rather whether people, through such actions, *do* signify or imply their consent; and to this the answer must surely be negative.

Additionally, there is further reason why residence or the benefits of residence are likely to be thought dubious candidates as genuine indications of consent. It might reasonably be doubted in many instances whether the background conditions of choice obtain. In many circumstances there is simply no realistic alternative to continued residence. Some polities do not permit emigration or radically constrain it, and even when it is neither legally proscribed nor actively discouraged it is often likely to be a prohibitively costly option. As David Hume wrote in a justly famous passage:

> 'Can we seriously say that a poor peasant or artisan has a free choice to leave his country, when he knows no foreign language or manners, and lives, from day to day, by the small wages which he acquires? We may as well assert that a man, by remaining in a vessel, freely consents to the domination of the master; though he was carried on board while asleep, and must leap into the ocean and perish, the moment he leaves her.' (Hume, 1953, p. 51)

Even allowing for Hume's concluding rhetorical flourish, there is much force to his observation. It is still more telling when, even for those for whom emigration might be a real possibility, the choice they face is often only between polities more or less like their own (and in any case, in a world where immigration is yet more tightly controlled than emigration, there is no guarantee that they will be accepted). Furthermore, unlike the time when Locke wrote, there is no longer any refuge for a person who wants to escape political relations altogether; and hence the choice facing a non-consenter will not include such an option. Together these considerations comprise a powerful case against mere residence, or the enjoyment of the fruits of residence, being regarded as implying or signifying consent. The nature of the acts involved are insufficiently voluntary; their connection to the political obligation to which they are supposed to give rise is too diffuse and indeterminate; and there are no generally accepted conventions by reference to which it can be reasonably argued that the 'knowledge', 'intention' and 'communication' conditions have been met.

It may be, however, that we could conceive of political arrangements being so changed that many, and perhaps all, of these objections would no longer have any force, and this is a possibility that is explored with no little ingenuity and imagination by Harry Beran (Beran, 1987). He advances what he calls a 'membership' version of consent theory according to which 'consent consists in accepting membership of the state'; and this requires the actual personal consent of individuals (Beran, 1987, ch. 3). His is a 'reform theory' in that he concedes that no existing states meet the conditions for such consent, but where his account is unusual is in his claim that the reforms that are needed are comparatively modest, and that 'consent-based political authority and obligation is possible without utopian changes to existing liberal democracies' (Beran, 1987, p. 153). In particular, he argues that people should be given a formal opportunity on reaching maturity to accept membership of the state, or there should be some clearly established convention according to which continued residence (or perhaps the assumption of the rights of citizenship) will be generally understood to indicate consent. Furthermore, if the proportion of people living within a state who are under consent-based political obligations is to be maximized then the following conditions should also obtain:

'(a) There is a legal right to emigrate and to change one's nationality.
(b) Secession is constitutionally permitted if desired and feasible.
(c) A dissenters' territory is created.' (Beran, 1987, p. 125)

While such conditions would not necessarily establish that everyone within a state consented or needed to – there might still be a place for a status similar to 'resident alien' – they would be sufficient to establish the political obligation of most people. So, how successful is Beran's reformist, membership version of consent theory in meeting our earlier objections?

Certainly, the kind of changes to the liberal democratic state that Beran recommends would do something to make it more of a 'voluntary association' in accordance with the requirements of a genuinely voluntarist consent theory. However, there remain several serious problems. First, it is highly doubtful whether these proposed reforms are really as modest as Beran claims. For example, the theory of secession and even more the idea of dissenters' territories (places where those who do not consent can move) are full of both theoretical and practical difficulties. While Beran has at least tried to deal with some of the problems of secession, he has almost nothing to say about dissenters' territories. It seems quite bizarre to think that a dissenters' territory, whose occupants may only be united by their refusal to consent to any actual polity, represents a viable option, let alone one that is likely to attract many dissenters. And, would they have to consent to be 'members' – whatever exactly that might mean – of any dissenters' territory, or could they also opt out of those? Second, even if liberal democratic states were reconstructed broadly along the lines Beran describes, would that be sufficient to make membership of the state voluntary? Beran concedes that the choices available would still be limited, but he denies that this limitation is in any way coercive.

However, this is to be insufficiently attentive to the extent to which the choices available to a person in such circumstances are structured by the state. This would not be a problem if one already accepted the authority of the state over such matters, but as that authority is precisely what consent is supposed to establish this seems to beg an important question. For the person who does not consent, and therefore does not recognize its authority, the state will be understood to be behaving coercively in so restricting the available options. Nor is this only a problem for the non-consenter, because many people may consent who would not otherwise do so, if they were offered a different set of options from which to chose. As, on Beran's account, 'the state is not a naturally occurring phenomenon' (Beran, 1987, p. 149), the question at least arises as to why the range of choices with which the state confronts us provides an appropriate situation for deciding whether or not to consent to its authority. Thus, I suggest, for all its ingenuity, Beran's attempt to re-establish the credentials of consent theory is less than successful.

Does, then, the second interpretation of tacit consent – that of voting in a democratic election – fare any better? It might seem to, for as John Plamenatz writes:

> 'Where there is an established process of election to an office, then, *provided the election is free*, anyone who takes part in the process consents to the authority of whoever is elected to the office. This, I think, is not to ascribe a new meaning to the word *consent* but is only to define a very ordinary, and important political, use of it. The citizen who votes at an election is presumed to understand the significance of what he is doing, and if the election is free, he has voluntarily taken part in a process which confers authority on someone who otherwise would not have it.' (Plamenatz, 1968, p. 170)

As Plamenatz himself agrees, it is no doubt a difficult task to specify precisely those conditions that make an election free, but some latitude should be allowed on this matter; though it should perhaps be remarked that radical critics of liberal democracy have argued that elections within liberal democracies do not meet the required conditions. Sometimes, taking a lead from Rousseau, they have maintained that only direct participatory democracies would meet the conditions for consent (Rousseau, 1973; Pateman, 1985). However, leaving aside this line of argument, on Plamenatz's own account we should presumably have to exclude not only elections in many parts of the world where the conditions for genuinely free elections do not obtain, but also those in countries such as Australia, where voting is legally compulsory. This last exclusion might itself make us somewhat sceptical of Plamenatz's contention, for it may seem odd to think that the legal compulsion to vote makes such a fundamental difference to the political obligation of the citizens of Australia and, say, the USA, where voting is entirely optional, as his account implies. But, perhaps this is no more than a curiosity; and there are, in any case, much more serious objections.

First, there is the obvious point that on this account only those who vote can be said to consent to the authority of the duly elected government. This will, as a matter of fact, leave a large minority, and sometimes even a majority, of the citizens of any existing state that could reasonably be thought to have free elections without any political obligations. The attempt to claim, as some have, that abstainers in such elections have also given their consent, is so implausible as not to merit serious consideration. If both voting and not voting are interpreted as expressions of consent then it is obvious that consent cannot be distinguished from refusal to consent: if it is impossible not to consent then consent cannot seriously be regarded as voluntary. This is recognized, for example, by Tussman who accepts that many '"citizens" have in no meaningful sense agreed to anything'. They are like 'political child-brides who have a status they do not understand and which they have not acquired by their own consent', and such 'non-consenting adult citizens are, in effect, like minors who are governed without their own consent' (Tussman, 1960, pp. 36–7). At the very least, if voting is to be a genuine expression of a person's consent, then that person must vote.

Second, Plamenatz's account of what is involved in or implied by a democratic election is open to dispute. Some people may participate in elections in an entirely pragmatic or instrumental spirit and not regard themselves or others as *morally* bound by the result. And it is not clear that there is any logical or conceptual mistake in denying that voters are morally bound to recognize the authority of whoever wins the election. One reason for this relates to a general failing in Plamenatz's account, which is that elections may be understood simply as mechanisms for deciding who will rule rather than conferring authority on those who are elected. The former need not imply the latter, nor is there anything intrinsic to democratic elections that compels anyone who participates in them to adopt the latter understanding of them. For example, an anarchist, who denies authority to any government, may vote in an election, believing some governments to be worse than others, in an attempt to ensure that the least bad government is elected. The decision to vote may be based on a strategic or tactical judgement about what is for the best in the circumstances without any belief that the election secures the authority of the government or entails any obligation towards it. It is simply not true, therefore, that participation in an election necessarily expresses or implies consent to the authority of the elected government. Of course, some people do believe that being democratically elected is what confers authority on a government, and for them voting in an election may entail a political obligation, but the point is that this belief cannot be inferred merely from someone participating in a democratic election. It is this illegitimate inference that appears to underlie Plamenatz's account of democratic elections as expressing or implying consent on the part of those who participate in them.

The conclusion of the argument so far is that voluntarist theories, to the extent that they attempt to provide an account of political obligation in existing or previously existing polities, generally fail. The principal reason for their failure is that no such theory can give a satisfactory account of the undertaking that supposedly generates the obligation. Whether it is contract, express consent or tacit consent that is said to be the basis of political obligation, there is no warrant for these claims in the personal history of most people. Participation in democratic institutions and some oaths of allegiance, provided they are genuinely voluntary and have the appropriate content, may do something to explain the political obligations of some citizens. However, the numbers involved are likely to be small and the obligations incurred highly circumscribed. At best, therefore, consent theory may have a limited role to play in explaining the genesis of some specific political obligations for some people. These considerations, however, might be thought to be less than compelling because they treat voluntarist theories of political obligation too literally; and that in doing so they miss the real point of such theories. Not surprisingly, my argument will be that they do not, and indeed it will be further suggested that it is only by transforming voluntarist theories into a logically different kind of account of political obligation that these objections can be circumvented. In order to show this we must examine some other interpretations of consent theory.

First, it should be noted that in discussing consent theory it was simply assumed, without argument, that consent must mean straightforward 'personal consent'. A. J. Simmons distinguishes theories of personal consent, defined as those where 'political obligations are grounded in the personal consent of each citizen who is bound', from both 'historical consent' and 'majority consent' theories (Simmons, 1979, pp. 60–1, 71–4). The 'historical consent' theory holds 'that the political obligations of all citizens (of all times) within a state are generated by the consent of

the members of the *first* generation of the political community'
(Simmons, 1979, p. 60). As Simmons observes, this theory has little to
commend it and it can be briskly dismissed. There is no reason to think
that any actual states were in fact created by the initial consent of the
members of the first generation. Moreover, it is only in special circumstances, such as where one person is authorized to act on behalf of
another, which clearly do not obtain in this case, that the act of one individual can morally bind another. But, even if those circumstances did
obtain, the 'historical consent' theory could not be regarded as a
genuinely voluntarist account of political obligation, for all later generations would have no choice whether or not to be so bound.

The 'majority consent' theory, on the other hand, claims that citizens
are all obligated to their polity when a majority of their number consent
to it. This theory too is vulnerable to compelling objections and need not
detain us for long. First, it is clearly parasitic upon the theory of
'personal consent', as a majority must personally consent; and this has
already been found to be an untenable claim. Second, it is necessary to
give some account of how a majority could morally bind a minority who
have not consented, and it is not easy to see how this is to be done. Third,
supposing that some such account is offered, the 'majority consent'
theory could not be regarded as a fully voluntarist account of political
obligation as it would entail that the minority could be morally bound
without their consent and even, presumably, against their will. The
second and third objections could be met if there were some prior agreement of all to be bound by majority decisions, but then this prior agreement would involve an eventual regress to personal consent and be
subject to the same objections as those made earlier to personal consent
theories. Thus, neither the doctrine of 'historical consent' nor that of
'majority consent' looks remotely attractive as an alternative to 'personal
consent'. Indeed, both theories are either parasitic upon 'personal
consent', and are hence open to the same objections as personal consent
theories, or are not genuinely voluntarist at all.

A rather different approach that has been adopted to reconstructing
consent or contract theories involves the thought that such ideas should
be understood as logical constructs. Such an approach has been claimed
to have its origins in the political philosophy of Immanuel Kant (Kant,
1991). One recent version of it is that of Hanna Pitkin, who writes:

'Your personal consent is essentially irrelevant to your obligation to
obey, or its absence. Your obligation to obey depends upon the character of the government – whether it is acting within the bounds of *the*

(only possible) contract . . . So, not only is your personal consent irrelevant, but it actually no longer matters whether this government or
any government was really founded by a group of men deciding to
leave the state of nature by means of a contract. As long as a government's actions are within the bounds of what such a contract hypothetically *would have* provided, would have *had* to provide, those
living within its territory must obey. This is the true significance of
what we have all learned to say in political theory: that the historical
accuracy of the contract doctrine is basically irrelevant – that the
contract is a logical construct. The only "consent" that is relevant is
the hypothetical consent imputed to hypothetical, timeless, abstract,
rational men.' (Pitkin, 1972, p. 57)

Pitkin recognizes that this reconstruction involves an element of transformation in the usual understanding of consent, but she still claims that
her doctrine of 'hypothetical consent' can legitimately be understood as
a version of consent theory. Thus she writes:

'In one sense this "nature of the government" theory is thus a substi-
tute for the doctrine of consent. But it may also be regarded as a new
interpretation of consent theory, what we may call the doctrine of
hypothetical consent. For a legitimate government, a true authority,
one whose subjects are obligated to obey it, emerges as being one to
which they *ought to consent*, quite apart from whether they have done
so. Legitimate government acts within the limits of the authority
rational men would, abstractly and hypothetically, have to give a
government they are founding. Legitimate government is government
which *deserves* consent.' (Pitkin, 1972, p. 62)

Whatever the merits of the substance of Pitkin's theory of 'hypothetical
consent', and these are considered in Chapter 4, it is, I suggest, highly
misleading to present it in the language of consent: this kind of account
is very different from that of voluntarist theories. For the theory does not
require that I actually consent, explicitly or tacitly, or even that I would
in fact consent if I had the opportunity to do so; rather, the theory claims
instead that a rational person would or should consent. However, it is
hard to see how the idea of consent is doing ant real work now.

It is, though, briefly worth noting that there is one sense of hypothetical consent (perhaps better conceived as counter-factual consent) that
does conform more closely to the logic of voluntarist theories: this is
where consent would *as a matter of fact* have been given but for some

reason was not. A good example of this is where a person is unconscious and needs medical intervention to restore his or her consciousness. In such a case we would typically *assume* that consent would have been given if the person had been able to do so. Of course, we could turn out to be mistaken about that – perhaps the person was trying to commit suicide and will subsequently reproach us – but the fact that we may occasionally be mistaken to assume consent does not mean that there will not also be many cases in which we would be right to do so. However, outside of medical contexts, such cases are quite unusual and would seem to have little bearing on the problem of political obligation; but they are considered more fully in Chapter 4 in the context of a more extended discussion of Pitkin's arguments.

At the risk of labouring the point, the mere word 'consent' is not the issue but rather the confusion that is created when it is used to cover what are at root logically different types of argument. The logic of 'hypothetical consent' is quite different from the personal or actual consent of voluntarist theories; and arguments from hypothetical consent direct our attention to entirely different sorts of considerations. Genuinely voluntarist theories require us to look to the personal history of individuals to establish whether or not they have consented, whether expressly or tacitly, and not, for example, to assess whether it would have been prudent or right for them to do so. By contrast, hypothetical consent theories direct our attention to the reasons why it would be rational or right for an individual to consent, whether or not an individual has in fact consented. In short, the doctrine of 'hypothetical consent' is not a voluntarist theory of political obligation at all and should be acknowledged to be a logically different type of theory. Furthermore, similar arguments would show that the same is true of various games-theoretical interpretations of social contract theory (see Taylor, 1976). Of course, to say this is not to show that such accounts are mistaken; it is only to identify them as not being truly voluntarist in character.

The limits of voluntarism

So far, my argument has been that voluntarist accounts, notwithstanding their obvious attractions, suffer from crippling defects as an attempt to explain or justify political obligation within any known polities. And it has been further argued that attempts to reformulate these accounts to avoid the defects fail in one or both of two ways. Either the objections are only apparently avoided, mostly through conceptual obscurity or empiri-

cal implausibility, or the objections are successfully avoided, but only at
the cost of subverting the voluntarist nature of the account and transforming it into a logically different type of theory. However, it is at this
point useful to consider, admittedly in a rather more speculative and
tentative spirit, some of the underlying or background assumptions and
beliefs that appear to inform voluntarist accounts of political obligation.
Such a consideration also takes in the more radical voluntarist theories
that claim that the conditions for the justified ascription of political obligation (to more than a few individuals at best) have yet to be historically
realized. In particular, three issues are especially worth examining. First,
there is the basic assumption that political obligation must be explicable
in terms of a voluntary undertaking of some kind, because there can be no
other valid alternative account. Second, there is the underlying model of
a polity as essentially a form of voluntary association. Third, there is the
conception of the person implied by voluntarist theories. Unsurprisingly,
these three issues are also interconnected in a number of ways.

As we have seen, voluntarist theorists claim that political obligation is
generated by some voluntary act, the performance of which *creates* the
obligation for the person who so acts. Proponents of such accounts, at
least with respect to political obligation, often seem attracted by
Hobbes's view that there is no 'obligation on any man, which ariseth not
from some act of his own' (Hobbes, 1968, p. 268). Michael Walzer
expresses a similar view when, after quoting Hobbes and explaining his
own adherence to consent theory, he writes: 'nor do I want to offer a
theoretical defence of the proposition that obligations derive only from
consent. I am simply going to assume of the many obligations I discuss
that they can have no other origin, and the reader must judge for himself
whether descriptions and arguments rooted in that assumption are at all
helpful' (Walzer, 1970, p. x). Pateman, perhaps surprisingly given her
feminist credentials, is another who is sympathetic to this view
(Pateman, 1985). A similar view seems to be embraced by A. J.
Simmons, although he draws sceptical conclusions about political obligation from the voluntariness requirement. However, he agrees that it is
only some voluntary act that could bind the individual to his or her polity
in the appropriate manner.

Generally, voluntarist theorists have readily accepted that a voluntary
undertaking, such as consent, cannot be a complete explanation of the
basis of a person's acquiring a political obligation, even where the conditions for such an obligation being voluntary are fully met. This is in part
because a voluntarist theory cannot explain its own foundations. Any
voluntarist account of obligations must rest on the prior acceptance of

the proposition that people have an obligation to act in accordance with their voluntarily commitments; this obligation itself cannot in turn be based on any voluntarily acquired obligation, or else that obligation too would have to be voluntarily acquired, and we would be faced by a potentially infinite regress of voluntary obligations: every voluntary obligation would require a preceding voluntary obligation, and so on indefinitely. Voluntarist theories cannot be voluntarist all the way down, so to speak. Furthermore, there are some actions that a person does not have the right to do, hence could not have an obligation to do, even if that person promises, contracts or consents to do them. Consent cannot normally create an obligation to do that which is seriously morally wrong: for instance, one is not obligated to commit a murder even if one has voluntarily agreed to undertake it. Such commitments have no moral force, because one has no right to make such a commitment in the first place. Thus, it would be a mistake to focus too narrowly or exclusively on a supposed obligation-creating act. For example, an oath of allegiance requiring one unconditionally to obey the government, no matter how voluntarily entered into, cannot reasonably be thought to issue in an obligation to obey the government *whatever* in fact it requires one to do; as most voluntarist theorists have, of course, been keen to stress. The circumstances in which a voluntary undertaking can give rise to an obligation to perform what one has undertaken to do, therefore, are always limited by broader moral considerations. Voluntarist theories of political obligation, as is widely recognized by their proponents, need to be part of a more complex moral picture, which charts the legitimate contours within which it is possible for voluntary acts to create obligations. And, for this reason, voluntarist theories are often typically supplemented or supported by elements drawn from at least one or other of the approaches discussed in the next two chapters.

Much more controversially, though, I also want to suggest that not only is such a voluntary act not a sufficient condition for political obligation; it is not necessary either. This is a contention that will be argued for more fully later, but it is at least worth briefly introducing the point here, as it is at the heart of my rejection of the voluntarist approach. In particular, it is worth noting that there are many commonly recognized obligations that are not owed equally to everyone (such as respecting human rights) and which do not have their origin in any voluntary undertaking on the part of the person obligated. These include, most conspicuously, obligations to parents and siblings. It is very unclear how we could possibly envisage some of these obligations as arising from voluntary acts such as promises, contracts or consent. Nor, even were this, *per impossible*, something that we could do, it is far from obviously morally attractive that we should try to do so. Such obligations, I shall argue, grow out of forms of involuntary association – membership of groups that we did not choose to join, but that nonetheless have real and substantial moral significance for us. These are what I shall later term 'associative obligations'.

A voluntarist theory of political obligation, however, does not entail a rejection of all associative obligations. It may be conceded that, say, familial obligations are indeed an example of such obligations, whilst still denying that political obligations are of a similar type. However, at the very least, these reflections may help to loosen the hold that those theories have on us. This seems particularly true of the idea that consent is a necessary condition of political obligation; for if we come to see that something is not necessarily so, this may be a decisive step towards seeing that it is not so at all. Thus, if a voluntary obligation-creating act is seen not to be necessary for the ascription of some other non-voluntary but also non-universal obligations, which we are wholly convinced are obligations, such as those to members of our family, then this may make us more receptive to the idea that such an act is not necessary to the acquisition of political obligations either. It may prevent us from becoming unduly fixated on what is only one among several possible models of how we can acquire an obligation. Granted the difficulties with voluntarist theories outlined earlier, it may even incline us to look more closely at some of our other, non-voluntarily incurred, obligations for a better understanding of political obligation. And this is a suggestion that will be explored more fully in Chapter 6.

The second aspect of voluntarist accounts to be considered is the more or less explicit model of the polity as a voluntary association. Characteristically, on this view, the polity, or at least a legitimate polity, is conceived as an association constituted (and to some extent sustained) by the voluntary choices of those individuals who compose it. Although no doubt much more complex, a polity is not viewed as *essentially* different from those many other voluntary associations that we may choose to join or leave, more or less as we please. As one defender of this understanding of a polity writes:

'A body politic, on this view, is a group of persons related by a system of agreements; to be a member of a body politic is to be a party to the system of agreements. The model is obviously the voluntary group or organization. A voluntary group is composed of a number of individuals who, in pursuit of a common purpose, agree to act in concert, putting themselves under a common discipline, authority and obligation.' (Tussman, 1960, p. 7)

Although far from conclusive, one immediate reflection on this claim is that it does not seem to conform to the understanding that most of us have of our relationship to our polity, as in fairness Tussman is himself well aware. People do not characteristically see themselves as having much choice in the matter of the polity of which they are members. Furthermore, if the arguments of the earlier part of this chapter are correct then this discrepancy is easily explained. The reason is that people do *not* voluntarily join their polity; usually citizenship is more like a status that they acquire rather than something that they choose for themselves. It is, therefore, unsurprising that people should be aware that it is not something that they have chosen. By contrast with Tussman, Neil MacCormick forcefully, and surely correctly, observes:

'Human societies are not voluntary associations. At least so far as concerns national societies and states, most human beings do not have a choice which one they will belong to, nor what shall be the law and the constitution of that to which they do belong; especially their belonging to a given state is not conditional upon their assenting to the basic structure of its organization.' (MacCormick, 1982, p. 84)

This is a point of considerable importance. At least so far as existing political communities are concerned, to conceive them as voluntary associations is fundamentally to misrepresent their character.

Naturally, this observation has no force against those theorists who hold that only if the polity were reconstituted as a voluntary association would its members have genuine political obligations. What, if anything, can be said about this view? Certainly, we need to ask what polities would have to be like if they were to be voluntary associations (see Johnson, 1976). For example, what would be the position of those who did not wish to join? Would they be permitted to reside in the territory of a polity they did not wish to join? What would their relation be to those who were members? What would they be allowed to possess? On what terms could members 'resign' from the polity? What should be done about those who wished to become members, but whom others, already members of the polity, did not want to allow to join? As we saw earlier, when discussing Beran's work, some voluntarist theorists have attempted to answer some of these questions, and they might reply, therefore, that while these, and other similar questions which could be asked, do raise genuinely difficult practical problems, it is still possible that with sufficient ingenuity they could be satisfactorily resolved. It might be denied, therefore, that such problems are in any sense fundamental objections to the voluntary association model of the polity. But how adequate is this reply?

There are at least three points that can be made in response. First, it is surely not the case that scepticism about the feasibility of transforming the polity into a genuine voluntary association is simply a manifestation of complacent attachment to the status quo. It really is extremely difficult to see how these questions could be satisfactorily answered, given even remotely plausible assumptions about human beings, political institutions and the world in which we live. In part, this difficulty is a consequence of the sheer size, scale and complexity of modern advanced technological societies; but it is also a function of the more general conditions of social order and the problems involved in securing sufficient agreement about the terms of political association among even a small number of socially and culturally homogeneous people. Second, even if we suppose that tolerably practicable answers could be given to these questions, it is not obvious that they would be as morally attractive as voluntarists are inclined to assume. Indeed, there is some reason to believe that if a polity were to be transformed into a voluntary association it would have some harsh and unwelcome consequences, at least for some people. For, as has been aptly remarked, while 'voluntary association is a fine principle for those with whom others are eager to associate, it is a disaster for those whom others instinctively avoid' (quoted in Johnson, 1976, p. 18). Third, and perhaps most interestingly, if the conditions of a voluntary association could be met, we might wonder how far what resulted could be understood as a polity at all. The differences between a voluntary association and a polity can be seen as so fundamental that any attempt to transform the latter into the former might be thought to undermine those very characteristics of a polity that are essential to it.

This last claim is undeniably controversial and requires more justification than it receives here, but two particularly significant differences between voluntary associations and polities, as they are commonly experienced and understood, are worth observing. First, there is the role of legitimate coercion. Although voluntary associations may in some circumstances legitimately coerce or penalize their members, such a right is effectively circumscribed by the powers allowed them by the wider political authority to which they are subject. This is not in most respects true of a polity, which, as it constitutes that wider coercive authority, does not have its authority defined or circumscribed by any external body, for it is thus circumscribed only in so far as it agrees to be so bound, though this is not to deny that political authority is properly subject to some moral constraints. (The picture I am presenting here clearly needs to be finessed somewhat in the light of the growth of political organizations like the EU.) Second, voluntary associations characteristically have some more or less specific, determinate and substantive purpose which their members share. This is much less true of polities, though the contrast should not be overdrawn. It is not a distinction between complete unanimity and complete absence of agreement about ends, but there does seem to be a qualitative rather than a merely quantitative distinction. Disagreement about substantive political purposes seems a fundamental and ineradicable feature of polities, and in a manner that is not so with respect to voluntary associations; a point to which we shall have occasion to return later. Taken together, these considerations raise serious doubts as to whether the attempt to understand or reconstruct the polity as a voluntary association is practicable, desirable or, perhaps, even truly conceivable. Such considerations may not be wholly conclusive, but nor are they negligible.

The final feature of voluntarist theories of political obligation to be addressed is the understanding of the person that they generally presume. What follows on this issue is especially sketchy and tentative. There has been extensive discussion of personal identity in recent Anglo-American philosophy. Much of this work has focused quite narrowly on the problem of how bodily or psychological continuity relates to a person's persistence over time, though some of this has been interestingly connected to wider moral and social issues (Williams, 1973; Parfit, 1984). However, issues of selfhood have over the last few decades also assumed an increasingly important role in some areas of political theory, stemming particularly from the work of so-called 'communitarians', such as Charles Taylor (Taylor, 1989), Alasdair MacIntyre (MacIntyre, 1981) and Michael Sandel (Sandel, 1982). The question most to the point in this context concerns what makes a person who he or she is: the question, who am I? Characteristically, voluntarist theories assume, for the matter is rarely discussed in detail, a view of the person that may likely seem at first glance admirably commonsensical, robust, non-metaphysical and unproblematic. Persons are conceived as separately existing entities, only contingently related to each other and to their social context, possessed of natural freedom, at least, and some minimal measure of reason. However, this picture and, in particular, the portrait of persons as possessing natural freedom, in opposition to the constraints imposed by social life, is potentially misleading. It is not so much that the necessity of some social context for a person's development is entirely unacknowledged, but that the connection between the person and that social context is seen as essentially contingent rather than as partly constitutive of whom the person is.

Voluntarist theorists, at least in recent times, have been suspicious of attempts to connect a conception of the person in some deeper way with the social context in which persons are formed. Typically, they have preferred to ask, what sort of life shall I choose to lead? and to resist the question, who am I? This latter question is viewed as both metaphysically suspect and politically dangerous, often being seen as damagingly associated with the obscurity of Teutonic Idealist philosophy and the political fanaticism of totalitarianism or extreme nationalism. Moreover, such worries cannot simply be dismissed as without justification. However, even where this 'atomistic' conception of the person does not ignore the general point that a person is in part a product of society – and the pervasive attraction of the idea of a state of nature to voluntarist theorists is in some cases evidence of a reluctance to accept even this – there is a marked failure to appreciate the more specific point that *particular* persons are in part the products of *particular* societies. There is an obvious sense in which if we had been born and raised in a different place and/or at a different time we would be different people; not only because we would be a different genetic bundle, but because our formative experiences would be different. It is true that, the specific formative experiences of each of us are different, but there is also a significant discontinuity between different polities. One of our important formative experiences is the development of our sense of being a member of this particular political community. Selfhood, our sense of who we are, is partly constituted by where we are born, resident and educated; and it is partly a function of the history, culture and rules of our community that confer a particular status on us and from which we necessarily acquire some self-understanding. In part, our identity is bound up with the particular polity of which we are members, and it would not be surprising if this connection between the sense of who we are and the polity of which we are members were reflected in our conception of political obligation.

Much of the substance of these reflections on personal identity could be conceded, at least for the sake of argument, yet it might still reasonably be asked what specifically they show about political obligation. There seem to be at least two questions that need to be answered. First, how closely are the socially constituted elements of the person tied to distinctions between polities? There is, it has been suggested above, some connection, but it is not clear how deep or extensive this must be. Second, even if some deep connection is established between the identity of persons and the polity of which they are members, what are the precise implications of this for their political obligations? These are difficult questions that will be left until Chapter 6. As with the discussions of the nature of obligation and the voluntary association model of the polity, these reflections on personal identity are largely intended to prepare the ground for the account of political obligation that is advanced there. This I attempt to do in two ways. The first is through undermining the plausibility and appeal of the manner in which these issues are usually treated within voluntarist theories. Second, through intimating the kind of approach that might prove more satisfactory, I suggest that what is required is an account of political obligation in which the obligation (i) is not created by a person's voluntary undertakings; (ii) draws on a conception of the polity that is not modelled on a voluntary association; and (iii) involves a better understanding of the person more deeply.

Conclusion

This chapter has offered an assessment of one broad type of account of political obligation – those that I have labelled 'voluntarist theories'. Such theories have shown impressive resilience in the history of political thought, and in one way or another continue to have considerable appeal. However, the argument of this chapter has been that voluntarist theories do not give us a plausible understanding of political obligation, at least in so far as it is thought that such obligations actually obtain. At best, voluntarist theories could account for political obligations only in a few, exceptional cases. One inference that might be drawn from this argument, however, is that this does not show the theory to be flawed; rather, it shows that (with few exceptions) people are not under any political obligations and are simply mistaken if they believe that they are. This is the position of philosophical anarchists like A. J. Simmons; a view that I shall explore much more fully in Chapter 5. However, I have also tentatively argued that the way in which voluntarist theories conceptualize the problem of political obligation rests on highly questionable assumptions about the basis of political obligation, the nature of a polity and the conception of a person. This last point is especially worthy of note. It is widely agreed that, exceptions aside, voluntarist theories cannot explain how political obligation is owed to existing polities. However, it is also widely accepted that if there were a voluntary basis for polities then political obligation would be justified. However, without flatly refuting this claim, I have also sought to suggest that there are good reasons for thinking that a polity cannot be a voluntary association in the way that voluntarist theories suppose.

Given their popularity, however, it would seem unlikely that voluntarist theories are *entirely* mistaken; and in rejecting them I should not be understood as suggesting that voluntarism lacks any insight into political obligation, even if it misconceives what I believe to be the valid insight that inspires it. This insight is that political obligation does require a certain attitude towards the polity; an attitude that involves the acknowledgement or recognition by the citizens of its authority or legitimacy. Without something like that, I agree, there is only brute power. However, where voluntarist theories go wrong is in translating this into a theory that *derives* political obligation from some kind of voluntary commitment. Before pursuing these issues further, though, we need to examine some other theories. The next chapter, therefore, addresses an alternative approach to justifying political obligation – an approach in which voluntarism plays no significant part.

3 Teleological Theories

The preceding chapter examined one broad category of accounts of political obligation: voluntarist theories. In this chapter we look at another type of account: I label these 'teleological theories'. Whereas voluntarist theories seek to explain political obligation in terms of some putative voluntary undertaking by the person obligated – a specific utterance or form of action – which puts that person under an obligation, the theories discussed in this chapter approach political obligation from a different perspective. These theories seek to explain political obligation by looking to the future rather than to the past, and by looking to the likely consequences or the purposes of the obligation, rather than to some obligation-creating voluntary act. They are teleological theories because they explain political obligation in terms of some goal, end or purpose, a *telos*, which provides the explanation or justification of the obligation. Political obligation within teleological theories characteristically derives from a general requirement to act in a manner designed to bring about a particular state of affairs. Teleological theories, therefore, are typically consequentialist or purposive in structure: broadly, the rightness of an action (or type of action), practice or institution is to be judged in terms of the value of what it brings about. Where teleological theories divide sharply one from another is in their accounts of the nature and value of these purposes or consequences. Thus, while all teleological theories account for political obligation by reference to the beneficial purposes or consequences of there being such an obligation – the obligation ultimately deriving from these purposes or consequences – they differ about the point of the obligation.

In the previous chapter, it was argued that voluntarist theories of political obligation essentially conceive of political relations in terms of individual choices or commitments, and of polities as a form of voluntary association. By contrast, teleological theories view polities as instruments: typically, the polity is conceived as the best means to achieve a valuable end or particular benefits. The relationship between the individual and the polity is understood in instrumental terms, although according to some teleological theories membership of a polity may also be partly constitutive of the good that is to be achieved. While it would be a mistake to overdraw this contrast, not least because the reasons for joining a polity on a voluntarist view are also likely to be instrumental, it remains the case that the two types of theory differ significantly in their approach to political obligation. According to voluntarist theories, as we have seen, it is a voluntary undertaking, an act of consent or allegiance, which is fundamental to grounding political obligation. According to teleological theories, however, there is no need for any such voluntary undertaking; for what grounds political obligation are the ends that it serves, and these do not depend upon any voluntary act on the part of the person obligated. Political relations are not to be explained or justified by their being the subject of a voluntary agreement, but by their being instrumental to the achievement of valuable ends. Thus, a polity is not a voluntary association – or, more accurately, need not be one – and if it were, the obligation deriving from it would not arise from its being voluntary, but from its being instrumental to the achievement of those valuable ends. In short, although voluntariness is not necessarily incompatible with a teleological account of the polity, it is neither a necessary nor a sufficient condition for political obligation.

Detaching political obligation from any putative voluntary undertakings by the person obligated has the obvious benefit that teleological theories avoid the besetting problem of voluntarist theories. Voluntarist theories, as we have seen, appear unable to overcome the problem of discovering or characterizing a plausible voluntary undertaking that is the basis for political obligations. As teleological theories do not depend for their validity upon such an undertaking, they do not face this difficulty. In this respect, therefore, teleological theories have a clear advantage over voluntarist theories. Furthermore, teleological theories typically possess what many will see as a second advantage: such theories are usually part of a comprehensive and more or less unified moral theory. Most teleological theories, including the most popular and fully developed of such theories, utilitarianism, purport to offer a complete moral theory in a way that voluntarism does not. For reasons mentioned in the last chapter, voluntarism is not a self-sufficient moral theory; at the very least it depends upon a logically prior belief that promises or consent obligate, which is necessarily non-voluntarist. Many teleological theories, however, are either single-principle theories, such as utilitarianism, or clearly prioritize different principles and hence furnish a comprehensive and unified moral theory. This is not, though, a necessary feature of such theories, for it is possible to specify ends that are both plural and ultimately in conflict and/or incommensurable with one another. Where there is no hierarchy of values, or where values are incommensurable, the place of political obligation may be much more complex and difficult to elucidate with any precision. Arguably, though, it could also be said that theories that acknowledge deep conflicts and incommensurability reflect our own moral experience more accurately than those that seek to airbrush them out of existence.

In this chapter the focus will be on two broad, but reasonably distinct, types of teleological theory. This is not to imply that these two types exhaust all the possibilities, and each admits of a variety of interpretations, but they seem to be the most plausible and are certainly much the most widely canvassed of teleological theories. These are the 'utilitarian' and 'common good' accounts of political obligation, and each will be discussed in turn. More attention in this chapter will be devoted to utilitarianism, but not because it furnishes a more interesting or more convincing account of political obligation: indeed, I shall suggest that it is the common good approach that has more of value to offer. Rather, the principal focus will be on utilitarianism because it is a highly sophisticated and much elaborated moral theory, which continues to attract a substantial body of support among philosophers. Common good accounts on the other hand have been less fashionable, especially of late, and have also received less theoretical development. Both theories, it will be argued, fail to provide convincing general accounts of political obligation.

However, it should be noted that, in the case of utilitarianism in particular, the failure to provide such an account may not be viewed as a failure of the moral theory itself, and nor typically will it be so viewed by utilitarians themselves. For, it can be argued, a satisfactory account of political obligation is not essential to the adequacy of a moral theory; but, as our interest is in political obligation rather than the wider question of the adequacy of utilitarianism as a comprehensive moral theory, it is only utilitarian accounts of political obligation that will be of concern here. In fact, utilitarianism has been subject to extensive theoretical criticism (see e.g. Williams, 1985, esp. ch. 6; Rawls, 1999, esp. ss. 5, 6), but much of that, while important, will not be addressed in what follows. Only criticisms that bear specifically on political obligation will be discussed here, although it is perhaps inevitable that one's view of this issue is likely to be closely connected to one's overall evaluation of the merits of utilitarianism. The important positive insights into political obligation that is to be found in common good theories will be discussed in the next chapter. Here, I shall be concerned primarily with the weaknesses of common good theories as complete accounts of political obligation. But, as I have already indicated and shall make explicit at the end of this chapter, such theories do have something important and positive to contribute to our understanding of political obligation.

The structure and forms of utilitarianism

Utilitarianism is a moral theory that, in its simplest and most straightforward form, judges the rightness of acts, practices and institutions exclusively by their tendency to maximize utility or happiness. Although this apparently simple idea lies at the root of utilitarianism in all its forms, it is one of the most complex, fully elaborated and widely discussed of all moral theories. This process of refinement has led to the development of significantly different strands within a broadly utilitarian approach, although there is also, as one would expect, some unity in the diversity. Thus, R. G. Frey writes:

> 'the term "utilitarianism" refers not to a single theory but to a cluster
> of theories which are variations on a theme. This theme involves four
> components:
> (1) A consequence component, according to which rightness is tied
>   in some way to the production of good consequences.
> (2) A value component, according to which the goodness or badness
>   of consequences is to be evaluated by means of some standard of
>   intrinsic goodness.
> (3) A range component, according to which it is, say, acts' consequences as affecting everyone and not merely the agent that are
>   relevant to determining rightness.
> (4) A principle of utility, according to which one should seek to
>   maximize that which the standard of goodness identifies as
>   intrinsically good.' (Frey, quoted in Miller, 1987, p. 531)

Utilitarianism, therefore, judges actions and practices in terms of their maximizing a particular kind of consequence. It is both consequentialist and maximizing in its structure.

Utilitarians, though, often disagree among themselves about how these elements are to be specified. For example, the nature of the value of the consequences to be promoted has been variously characterized as pleasure, happiness, desire or preference-satisfaction, well-being, welfare or utility. Clearly, these are not all equivalent to each other. There have also been disagreements about the scope of the theory: does it, for instance, apply to all sentient creatures (including animals) or only to human beings? And does it apply across time to different generations, therefore including people yet to be born? The way in which these questions are answered will likely have important implications for, say, what ecological and environmental policies should be pursued. Furthermore, utilitarians also disagree about the appropriate form that maximization should take. Should the aim be to maximize the sum total of utility (however conceived) or, instead, average levels of utility? Which of these principles is adopted is likely to have radically divergent implications for population policy. Thus, aggregate utility will promote a world in which there are a large number of people with relatively low levels of utility, if this maximizes total utility, while average utility will favour a world in which there is a much smaller number of people but with on average higher levels of utility, even if this means that total utility is much less. (Where the population to which the utilitarian principle is applied is fixed, there will be no difference between total and average utility.) These are merely some examples of a range of questions to which utilitarians have given different answers, and it is impossible here either to survey all these variations or to attempt to evaluate all the many differing strands within utilitarianism – some simplification, therefore, is unavoidable. In what follows, two axes of division that are especially significant will be discussed: the distinction between act- and rule-utilitarianism and the distinction between direct and indirect utilitarianism. However, as a preliminary, a few very brief remarks about the development of utilitarianism may be helpful.

Historically, utilitarianism emerged as a fully self-conscious moral theory with the work of Jeremy Bentham, but substantial elements of the theory significantly predate his work. The search for origins is not of itself an especially fruitful activity, and either Godwin or Paley might have claim to the primacy I have attributed to Bentham. There is, though, one predecessor of Bentham who particularly merits mention: David Hume. Writing in the mid-eighteenth century, he developed a broadly utilitarian account of political obligation (or 'allegiance' in his own terms) as an alternative to the social contract theory of which he was a most trenchant critic. Among the more important of his criticisms of social contract theories was his recognition that the basis of the obligation to keep the contract cannot itself be contractual. For Hume, the obligation that we have to keep our promises, of which the social contract is only one example, in turn rests upon an obligation to promote the general interest (and ultimately upon self-interest). Hence, he argued that reference to a social contract is redundant, because we can base our obligation to government directly on our duty to promote the general interest, without recourse to an, in any case almost entirely fictional, social contract (Hume, 1953; 1978, bk III, pt II, ss VII, VIII). He maintained that political arrangements were devices, historically evolved, to protect people against the exigencies of the human condition and aimed at securing the benefits of a stable political order. Hume's utilitarianism, however, was blended with a conservatism that inclined him to view existing institutions, merely by virtue of their evolution and convenience, as utilitarianly justified.

In this respect, Bentham, a radical reformer, seemingly ceaselessly engaged in designing new and better institutions, was of a very different cast of mind. However, perhaps surprisingly, he had very little of interest to say specifically about political obligation. Bentham's ridiculing of social contract theory was no less enthusiastic than Hume's, but he did not add much of substance to those criticisms and his positive account of political obligation is insubstantial. It consists of not much more than observing that the duty of subjects to their government means: 'they should obey in short so long *as the probable mischiefs of obedience are less than the probable mischiefs of resistance* . . . taking the whole body together it is their *duty* to obey, just so long as it is in their *interest* and no longer' (Bentham, 1988, p. 56). Political theorists are not required to be equally interested in all the many questions that they could address, but in his comparative neglect of it Bentham seems to have set something of an example for later utilitarians who, for the most part, have had little to say specifically about political obligation. This neglect, though, is not merely the result of a lack of interest. One reason why Bentham and other radical utilitarians have had little to say about political obligation is that many of them have wanted to deny that there is any general political obligation. They are not, therefore, seeking a general justification of political obligation but consciously trying to undermine it.

However, a more philosophical reason why utilitarians have not been much interested in political obligation relates to its structure, particularly in its simplest and most straightforward form; although whether or not Bentham was an exemplar of this form of utilitarianism is a matter of vigorous scholarly debate (Kelly, 1990, esp. ch. 3). Act-utilitarianism judges an action to be morally correct if it maximizes beneficial consequences, however such consequences are precisely defined. On this view, how a person ought to act in a given set of circumstances should be exclusively determined through a calculation of the likely general utility of the various courses of action available. And the act that is right that will have, given the best available knowledge, the largest net balance of beneficial consequences over harmful ones. Act-utilitarianism requires that the consequences of each act be weighed, and the decision as to how to act be based on a calculation specific to the particular choices and circumstances that face the agent at that time and in that place. Such an approach, however, will have obvious difficulty in generating a general theory of political obligation; at best it seems likely that it may issue in some rules of thumb or rough maxims of conduct (for example, obeying the law will usually be more generally beneficial than breaking it). The bottom line of act-utilitarianism is that articulated by Bentham: citizens should obey government when it is for the best, but not do so when disobedience is for the best; and there is little more to be said. In fact, this is how an act-utilitarian will approach any practice or institution, and the institutions of government are no different. However, whatever its other merits, this form of utilitarianism is singularly ill-fitted to provide an account of general obligations deriving from special relations, including a distinctively political obligation, which will be a recurring theme in the subsequent discussion.

The requirement of act-utilitarianism that each and every act be evaluated individually on its utilitarian merits, however, has seemed to some utilitarians to be too simple and to ignore both the uncertainty and the costs involved in having to make such calculations every time we act (or choose not to act). While perhaps defensible with respect to small-scale decisions, act-utilitarianism seems more problematic when applied to complex decisions – involving a wide range of possible actions – a complicated computation of probable consequences, and where any individual's knowledge is likely to be very limited and often inadequate. The difficulty of some of these calculations, their costliness in terms of time, energy and other resources, the propensity of people's calculations to give undue weight to their own interests rather than the social benefit, and above all the uncertainty induced in others who have to rely on such, possibly faulty, calculations has led some utilitarians to adopt the more sophisticated form of the theory: this is what has become known as rule-utilitarianism.

According to rule-utilitarianism, it is better in many circumstances that people do not rely on their own uncertain calculations in deciding what to do but instead should follow a general rule. Rule-utilitarianism dictates that people should be guided in how to act by a general rule about the best way to act in circumstances that fall under the rule. The rules should be devised in the light of generalizations about what action, or which kinds of action, in these sorts of circumstances, are most likely to maximize the beneficial consequences. According to rule-utilitarians, most utility will obtain not if each person asks him or herself whether or not the killing of another person in any particular instance may be maximally beneficial, but by requiring everyone to observe laws prohibiting murder, whatever the circumstances. Thus, the kind of calculation undertaken by Raskolnikov in Dostoyevsky's novel, *Crime and Punishment*, which apparently justified his murdering a rich but cruel and mean moneylender for the greater social good (including his own), would be precluded. Rather, we should all follow a rule prohibiting murder to avoid potentially disastrous miscalculations. Rule-utilitarianism, therefore, seems a more promising approach to political obligation because it is better able to accommodate the institutional dimension of political obligation. For political obligation has to do with the relationship between individuals and their polity, and whereas act-utilitarianism is tied to assessments of specific actions, rule-utilitarianism is able to give a more adequate account of practices or institutions, which are at least partially constituted by complex structures of rule-governed relationships.

One immediate question that arises about rule-utilitarianism, however, is whether it is a genuinely coherent alternative version of utilitarianism, or whether it is essentially unstable and, on closer inspection, simply collapses back into act-utilitarianism. This is not a question that can be pursued in any depth here but the nature of the issue should at least be sketched (see Lyons, 1965). Basically, rule-utilitarianism appears to confront a dilemma when faced with a situation where breaking a utilitarianly justified rule will clearly result in more utility than keeping to it. On the one hand, it can approve the violation of the rule in such circumstances, in which case it appears to be merely a disguised form of act-utilitarianism, and rules are not really obligatory but only to be understood as helpful guides to action. Alternatively, rule-utilitarianism can hold that the rules are obligatory even when violating them would be more beneficial; in which case it does offer a genuine alternative to act-utilitarianism, but one that seems, from the perspective of maximizing utility, to be irrationally concerned with following rules for their own sake. In short, the claim is that either rule-utilitarianism collapses back into act-utilitarianism or it engages in a kind of 'rule-worship', which appears to be utilitarianly unjustified. The problem here is that if the violation of a rule is more beneficial, particularly if it is obviously and uncontroversially more beneficial, then observing it in such circumstances seems irrational, given utilitarianism's overriding concern with maximizing beneficial consequences. The most plausible response to this problem has been to stress the additional beneficial consequences of the rules, the stability and predictability that they provide, which any sanctioned violation of the rules may effectively undermine. The weakness of this defence is that while it has some plausibility in marginal or uncertain cases, when the violation of a rule is clearly beneficial it seems to be justified only by placing an undue weight on the beneficial effects of observing the rules. Such a strategy appears to be motivated only by the desire to validate rule-utilitarianism and not by any empirical observation of the likely consequences of rule violations. In that respect, such a strategy is inconsistent with the guiding spirit of utilitarianism.

Before proceeding to consider further the relationship between these types of utilitarianism and political obligation there is another distinction that it is useful to introduce: this is the distinction between direct and indirect utilitarianism. This distinction does not straightforwardly map on to that between act- and rule-utilitarianism, though it is closely related to it. The distinction between direct and indirect utilitarianism is more concerned with questions of motivation than of outcome. In its simplest form, it might appear that utilitarianism requires that actions be motivated by a desire to maximize utility (in some form or other). However, it was recognized fairly early in the development of utilitarianism, Sidgwick being among the clearest exponents of the view, that it may not be true that utility will in fact be maximized if people directly and consciously aim at maximizing it (Sidgwick, 1874). It may be more productive of utility, at least in some circumstances, if people act on a motive other than that of maximizing utility itself. In such circumstances, utility will be maximized indirectly, as a consequence of pursuing some other aim, for instance, the desire to be truthful or honest. Thus, indirect utilitarianism severs any tight connection between the good (maximizing utility) and any particular motivational assumptions. In this respect it is easy to see how indirect utilitarianism is related to rule-utilitarianism, but it is also important to see that indirect utilitarianism is a more encompassing category than rule-utilitarianism. Indirect utilitarianism implies nothing specific about the way in which utility will be maximized, other than that it may not always be achieved through the direct attempt to achieve it: it may or may not be best achieved by following rules in the manner recommended by rule-utilitarianism. Thus, rule-utilitarianism can be understood as one form of indirect utilitarianism, but it is not necessarily the only one.

On first encounter, indirect utilitarianism may look to be a peculiar doctrine. It might seem that if the best situation is one in which utility is maximized then *a fortiori* it would be most likely to be achieved if people aimed at its attainment. However, this inference is fallacious, as can be seen if one thinks, for example, of personal happiness. It is far from self-evident, and indeed there is a considerable body of experience to contradict the claim, that personal happiness is maximized simply through its direct pursuit. It seems that it is often best achieved indirectly, as a by-product of the pursuit of other aims and with other motivations. Similarly, social utility may in fact be maximized through means other than its direct pursuit. For example, it may be that coordination problems mean that if everyone directly pursues the general good there will be resultant inefficiencies. In consequence, levels of utility may be less than would result by people aiming at different ends than maximization itself. Thus, the general good might be maximized as an unintended consequence of very different intentions and motivations. Indirect utilitarianism, therefore, claims only that the best state of affairs might not be brought about by people directly aiming to achieve the best state of affairs.

Utilitarianism and political obligation

This detour into some of the intricacies of utilitarian theory is important because these refinements provide the most promising materials for a response to perhaps the most powerful objection to any utilitarian theory of political obligation. This objection, which was briefly mentioned in the previous section, has been advanced most clearly and forcefully by A. J. Simmons (Simmons, 1979, pp. 45–54). He argues that there is a structural feature of act-utilitarianism that precludes its providing a satisfactory theory of political obligation. Act-utilitarianism, as we have seen, requires us to act in whatever way will in fact maximize utility, and this requirement is entirely general. There is, therefore, within this perspective, no place for such particularized bonds as political obligations – the special relationship between individuals and their own polity. In discussing Bentham's account of the citizen's obligation to obey the law, Simmons writes:

> 'Bentham's approach to problems of political obedience fails in obvious ways to yield an account of political obligation. Act-utilitarian calculations, as Bentham suggests, may lead us to conclude that we ought to obey but they may lead us as well to conclude that we ought to disobey on some other occasion (or perhaps support the political institutions of some other countries). Insofar as the conditions influencing the results of these calculations are by no means constant,

we can derive from the simple act-utilitarian approach no moral requirement to support and comply with the political institutions of one's country of residence. There will be no particularized bonds on this model; at best, it seems obligations will be to comply when doing so is optimific.' (Simmons, 1979, p. 48)

Simmons argues that act-utilitarianism is structurally ill-equipped to offer an account of the kind of obligation that is necessary for a theory of political obligation. At best, it can develop a rough rule of thumb that, by and large, it is right to support and comply with the institutions of one's country. However, act-utilitarianism has nothing specific to say about the nature of that relationship nor why there is, or should be, any special relationship between members and their polity. As stated earlier, this need not be an embarrassment to act-utilitarians; from their perspective any account of political obligation may be unnecessary or mistaken. But, if we are looking for an account of the kind of obligations of which political obligation is an example, act-utilitarianism is not at all well suited to the task.

Simmons's claim that act-utilitarianism is, by virtue of its structure, incapable of providing a theory of political obligation is similar to our earlier conclusion and is, in my view, convincing. However, his treatment of rule-utilitarianism is less satisfactory, and about indirect utilitarianism he is almost entirely silent. His rejection of rule-utilitarianism depends entirely upon the argument that, if it is to remain consistently utilitarian, it will necessarily collapse into act-utilitarianism. As he puts it, 'while the rule-utilitarian's principles of obligation will have the kind of force we want in providing an account of political obligation, these principles will not be capable of a utilitarian defense' (Simmons, 1979, p. 52). He offers no other arguments against a rule-utilitarian account of political obligation. He also fails sufficiently to distinguish 'rule' from 'indirect' utilitarianism: it is not self-evident that the standard objections to rule-utilitarianism apply to all indirect utilitarianisms; or at least, if they do, this needs to be argued for rather than assumed. Thus, it is both desirable and necessary to say a little more about the relationship between utilitarianism and political obligation. It is desirable in the case of rule-utilitarianism since, though the arguments against it as an independent form of utilitarianism may be convincing, it would strengthen the case against a rule-utilitarian account of political obligation if there were other arguments against it. It is necessary in the case of indirect utilitarianism because it is less evident that all forms of indirect utilitarianism must collapse into act-utilitarianism.

One feature common to all the familiar forms of utilitarianism is that they are 'maximizing' moral theories. Utilitarianism requires us to maximize the beneficial consequences of actions and practices, whether in overall or average terms. This is important because even rule and indirect utilitarianism would have to show that political obligation involves practices that do not merely have beneficial consequences but *maximize* those beneficial consequences. In short, whatever is understood by political obligation, if it is to be utilitarianly justified, it must be shown to be maximally beneficial. One point worth noting is that it is very rare for utilitarians of any sort after Hume to attempt to demonstrate the validity of this claim. Bentham, as we have seen, made no such attempt, nor have many of his successors. Usually, such attempts as have been made, for example that by R. M. Hare, point to the very real and considerable benefits that flow from having a system of law and a stable political order. However, it seems implausible to think that these benefits must always outweigh the benefits of other options, or that moderate levels of non-compliance with the law necessarily threaten such benefits. Moreover, to repeat an earlier point, nor is it at all clear to what extent these arguments establish particular obligations between persons and *their* polity. Thus, for example, the kinds of disutilities that are associated with disobedience to the law usually apply quite generally: that is, they do not typically relate in any specific way to disobeying the law of the particular political community of which a person is a member. The utilitarian argument will be that obedience to the law, in whatever polity, is likely to have considerable utility. But this is not enough to provide an account of political obligation.

Indirect utilitarians could argue that utility is best promoted by a world in which individuals recognize a special obligation to the polities of which they are members. While some of the particular acts that would be enjoined will not directly maximize utility, so the argument would run, overall utility could still be maximized indirectly through people meeting their political obligations to their own polity. This is not a line of thought that has been addressed by critics such as Simmons, but equally it is not a line of thought that is much favoured by utilitarians. For, while an account of political obligation in these terms would appear to meet the structural requirements of a theory of political obligation – especially the particularity requirement – it lacks persuasiveness from a utilitarian perspective. The claim that overall utility will be maximized through such an account of political obligation – not merely that certain valuable goods will be ensured – is likely to be an act of faith rather than based on any genuine calculation of consequences, and it would obviously be implausible for utilitarians to present political obligation as a blank cheque. The requirements of political obligation would need to be 'cashed out'; but doing so might once again leave little scope for a general political obligation. What would be the point of such an obligation, even within an indirect utilitarian theory? It may have some useful motivational role as political rhetoric, but as is often the case with indirect utilitarianism, it can function in this role only if people believe what from the perspective of utilitarianism itself is untrue: that is, it might be utilitarianly best if we acted as if we believed that there is a general political obligation, even though this belief would not be justified on utilitarian grounds. Other than simply as a defence of indirect utilitarianism, such dubious moral casuistry would seem to be highly problematic (Williams, 1985, pp. 106–10), although there have also been some recent defenders of utilitarianism, specifically as a morality for public policy, who have been willing to embrace something like this view (Goodin, 1995, ch. 4).

Hare's utilitarian account of political obligation

Some of the considerations we have been discussing can be brought together by examining in a little more detail the arguments of one of the most sophisticated of utilitarians. R. M. Hare is one of the few modern utilitarians who have specifically addressed the problem of political obligation. For Hare, political obligations are 'the *moral* obligations that lie upon us because we are citizens of a state with laws' (Hare, 1976, p. 2). He concentrates particularly on the obligation to obey the law, although he recognizes that this is not the only such obligation. He also acknowledges 'that this obligation may lie, not only on citizens, but also on anybody, even an alien, within the jurisdiction (most people think that foreign visitors too have a moral obligation not to steal)' (Hare, 1976, p. 1). It is important, however, to note the significance of this acknowledgement. First, and most fundamentally, it seems to transform the question that Hare originally asked. What began as a question about our obligations as citizens of a particular state becomes a question about whether or not there is a quite general obligation to obey the law. If even an alien has this obligation, then it is not specifically an obligation of citizenship, though of course it may be an obligation that citizens share with others. Second, a further source of confusion is introduced by his example of stealing, which he uses to illustrate his argument. It is likely that most people will think that there is a moral obligation not to steal, whether or not there is a legal prohibition on stealing. Hence, even the revised question of whether there is an obligation to obey the law may be muddled by choosing an action that is likely to be thought wrong, independently of whether there is a law prohibiting it (although in fairness to Hare nothing in his argument in the end depends upon this possible confusion).

Hare then briefly explains his own form of utilitarianism and how he has been led to it. He writes:

> 'To ask what obligations I have as a citizen is to ask for a universal prescription applicable to all people who are citizens of a country in circumstances just like those in which I find myself. That is to say, I have to ask – as in *any* case when faced with a question about what I morally ought to do "What universal principle of action can I accept for cases just like this, disregarding the fact that I occupy the place in the system that I do (i.e. giving no preferential weight to my own interests just because they are mine)?" This will lead me to give equal weight to the equal interests of every individual affected by my actions, and thus to accept the principle which will in all most promote those interests. Thus I am led to a form of utilitarianism.' (Hare, 1976., p. 3)

He recognizes that in fact we could ask the question he identifies above in each and every case, but if we do then, of course, no general principles beyond that of utility itself would be required. However, for Hare there are good reasons why we need general principles:

> 'In practice it is not only useful but necessary to have some simple, general and more or less unbreakable principles, both for the purposes of moral education and self-education (i.e. character formation) and to keep us from special pleadings and other errors when in situations of ignorance or stress. Even when we have such principles we *could* disregard them in an individual case and reason it out *ab initio*; but it is nearly always dangerous to do so, as well as impracticable; impracticable because we are unlikely to have either the time or the information, and dangerous, because we shall almost inevitably cheat, and cook up the case until we can reach a conclusion palatable to ourselves. The general principle that we ought to obey the law is a strong candidate for inclusion in such a list as I shall be trying to show; there may be occasions for breaking it, but the principle is one which in general there is good reason for inculcating in ourselves and others.' (Hare, 1976, p. 4)

In this way, Hare articulates briefly and lucidly the standard arguments for some form of indirect utilitarianism. He further intimates how the general principle – that we ought to obey the law – can be utilitarianly justified. There are, however, several observations to be made about the argument contained in the passages just quoted, though the wider issue about whether utilitarianism does indeed follow, as Hare claims, will not be addressed. This last point, while very important to any overall assessment of Hare's utilitarianism, is tangential to our concern with political obligation, and in any case could not be discussed without considering much more fully his detailed arguments for these conclusions (Hare, 1963, 1981).

The first point again concerns his equivocation about whether the duty to obey the law is an obligation specifically connected with citizenship or membership of a particular polity, or whether it is an entirely general moral requirement that applies to anyone within the law's jurisdiction. Second, and connectedly, much will depend upon how 'circumstances just like these' are to be identified and characterized. To what extent, for example, do they permit variations between polities? This is important in determining the scope of the obligations. Do they apply only to people living in 'liberal democratic' states much like the Britain in which Hare was resident when he wrote? Do they apply to anyone living in any polity? Would they apply equally, or at all, to illiberal, undemocratic or even totalitarian states? Third, it is unclear what the precise status is of the general principle that we ought to obey the law. Hare concedes that there may be occasions when the law should be broken, but how are such occasions to be identified unless some judgement is made about situations in which the law should not be obeyed? It is natural to assume that such judgements will be made according to utilitarian criteria. The status of the principle would then appear to be more that of a rule of thumb, a guide to conduct or a summary of experience, but no more. Yet, Hare maintains that such general principles are not mere rules of thumb and that, for reasons largely to do with moral education and the dangers of partiality, we ought to inculcate sentiments that will encourage people to feel badly about violating such general principles, even though, on his own account, such people may have acted rightly.

For Hare, political obligations are those 'which arise only because there is a state with laws' (Hare, 1976, p. 5), and in discussing a hypothetical example he identifies three reasons for obeying the law that are supposed to justify political obligations. His hypothetical example concerns hygiene laws requiring delousing to prevent the spread of typhus. There are several good moral and prudential reasons why one should do what the hygiene laws require, as Hare observes, but there are three moral reasons specifically related to the existence of the law. These are:

'1.   The fact that, because there is an enforced law, resulting in general delousing, failure to delouse myself will harm people's interests much more, by making them *very much* more likely to get lice or typhus.

2.   The fact that, if I break this law, it will cause trouble to the police in catching me, thus rendering necessary the employment of more policemen, who therefore cannot grow yams instead, and so harming the interests of the people who could have eaten the yams.

3.   The fact that if I break this law, it may encourage people to break this or other laws, thereby rendering a little more likely (a) the removal of benefits to society which come from the existence of those particular laws, and (b) the breakdown of the rule of law altogether, which would do great harm to the interests of nearly everybody.' (Hare, 1976, p. 7)

He further remarks that the second and third reasons 'are subsidiary, but have the important property that (except for 3a) they might survive even if the law in question were a bad or unnecessary one whose existence did not promote the general interest' (Hare, 1976, p. 7). Again, there are several points to be made about Hare's arguments.

At the risk of repetition, the first point is that none of these reasons applies especially to people who are citizens rather than to anybody who happens to be geographically proximate. In fact, the first reason applies more to geographically proximate persons, whether or not they are citizens, than it does, for example, to relatively isolated citizens having less direct contact with other people. The first reason also has two other distinctive features that complicate matters. One is that most crimes are not contagious in the manner of typhus; hence, it is a very special and unusual feature of this example that the cost of not observing the law is likely to be literally contagious (by contrast with what might be called the metaphorical contagiousness suggested by the third reason). The second is that the first reason also depends upon the law's being effective, not merely in the sense that it is generally observed, but in the further sense that it will actually prevent the spread of typhus. If the law required something that did not in fact decrease the likelihood of the spread of typhus, then the first reason would not provide a good justification for obeying it. This is important because it shows that the merits of the first reason are largely independent of there being a law, but depend instead upon two other considerations: that the 'advice' contained in the law is good advice and that most people follow it. This can be seen, for example, in the case of exhortations to take precautions to stop the spread of AIDS. There is no legal requirement to engage only in 'safe' sex, yet if the advice is good and most people follow it then Hare's first reason would apply equally to this case, entirely independently of whether or not there is a law compelling such safeguards.

The first reason, therefore, has little if anything to do specifically with political obligation; and thus the weight of the argument for political obligation must be borne by the other reasons, which Hare himself regards only as 'subsidiary'. The second reason does have some force but it is surely weak: while it is a general reason for obeying all laws it is also a reason against laws generally. The enforcement of a law always has costs, and if this were the principal reason for obeying a law then it would be better for there not to be a law in the first place. Paradoxically, these costs of disobeying a law are entirely parasitic upon the existence of that law and could most easily be eliminated by repealing the law. Furthermore, if policemen are a necessary deterrent to law breaking, which is likely to be part of their utilitarian justification, then it is doubtful whether a single violation of a law does impose any significant extra costs (but see Parfit, 1984, ss 28, 29). Also, the first part of the third reason, as we saw with the first reason, depends upon the particular law actually having the beneficial effects. Further, when the costs to me of observing the law amount to more than the benefits to others of my observing it, then it seems that the law ought to be broken. Evidently, the second part of the third reason is intended to block this kind of calculation, or at the very least significantly to tilt the balance in favour of law-abidingness, yet it seems that even quite high levels of law breaking often do not lead to the complete breakdown of the rule of law. The net effect of one instance of law breaking will almost always be negligible in the context of the preservation and maintenance of a system of law and order.

The force of these utilitarian reasons becomes weaker still when this last objection is further elaborated. It can be argued that it is quite reasonable and seems to be utilitarianly justified to act on the principle that breaking a law is morally right, when more utility will be derived from violating the law and so long as it can reasonably be expected that the conduct of others will not be affected by this violation. In this case, as in many others, the objection of the utilitarian is not to violating the law, but to being found out. Hare does consider this complaint, and he claims that such a view is unsatisfactory because it ignores people's desire not to be taken advantage of. He, therefore, suggests adding a fourth reason for obeying the laws to those listed earlier: 'the fact that, if I break the law, I shall be taking advantage of those who keep it out of law-abidingness although they would like to do what it forbids, and thus harming them by frustrating their desire not to be taken advantage of' (Hare, 1976, p. 11).

Unfortunately for Hare, while this may indeed be a good reason for obeying the law, it is not a reason that is obviously available to the utilitarian. Richard Dagger has argued that the plausibility of Hare's contention must depend upon the plausibility of the assimilation of the frustration of any desire to harm; yet, as he also argues, such an assimilation is unconvincing (Dagger, 1982). For example, if in a fair race my opponent continually beats me, then he frustrates my desire to win, but still he has not harmed me. Dagger's claim has considerable force so far as our ordinary use of the term 'harm' is concerned; however, it is perhaps possible for a utilitarian to claim that the frustration of any desire is a harm to the person whose desire is frustrated (though perhaps only a very small one, and no doubt often outweighed by other harms).

The problem that confronts Hare is, I believe, the less obvious one of how the desire not to be taken advantage of is to be interpreted. The position of people who obey the law is, in the case at hand, not worsened by those who break it; so how then are they harmed? It seems that the desire not to be taken advantage of is really an independent moral principle – basically a requirement of fairness – masquerading as a desire. It is notoriously the case that utilitarianism, with its intrinsic indifference to distributive questions, has considerable difficulties in accommodating such requirements. At the very least, if it is permissible to posit the desire not to be taken advantage of, then it is presumably also legitimate to represent many other non-utilitarian moral commitments as desires; a move that leads to such enormous complications that most utilitarians have sensibly sought to avoid it. On the other hand, where systematic attempts have been made to incorporate a range of diverse values within utilitarianism, one may begin to doubt whether there is very much left of the theory that makes it distinctively utilitarian (e.g. Griffin, 1986).

These reflections show how Hare's attempt to articulate a utilitarian theory of political obligation is fraught with serious difficulties. The most fundamental of these is the persistent tendency, clearly exhibited in Hare's argument, to transform questions about political obligation into more general questions about right conduct that quite simply fail to address the issue of the specific obligations of citizens to their own polity. While this is not strictly a logical implication of rule- or indirect-utilitarianism, it is a tendency to which utilitarians of all hues seem naturally inclined. Taken together with the criticisms made earlier (and of course a whole range of objections to utilitarianism as a moral theory more generally that have not been considered here), they suggest that the prospects for a convincing utilitarian theory of political obligation are at best unpromising. Those few theorists who have sought to incorporate a substantial utilitarian component within their justifications of political obligation have invariably done so in a highly qualified manner (e.g. Flathman, 1972); and there have been few if any attempts to articulate a fully elaborated theory of political obligation in uncompromisingly utilitarian terms. As utilitarianism is a far from new or underdeveloped theory, this is of itself a significant indication of its limitations in this area.

Political obligation and the common good

The second kind of teleological accounts of political obligation to be considered are best described as 'common good' theories. The core of this approach is to argue that political obligation derives from the common good; and the common good may be either that of a particular community or of everybody. This common good, on either interpretation, provides the basis of the obligations of members to their polity. By contrast with utilitarianism, the common good is usually understood as a qualitative conception, including within it moral qualities that are regarded as intrinsically valuable, and does not consist solely of the maximization of desire-satisfaction, pleasure or happiness. Unfortunately, terminological confusion abounds in the area, for not only is the 'common good' on occasion used to mean 'utility-maximization', but the term 'public interest', which is sometimes used as a synonym for 'general utility', may also be used to mean a non-utilitarian conception of the common good (e.g. Milne, 1990). However, the key point is that the common good, as we shall use it, is a more or less specific, qualitative conception of the good life, which is distinct from, and often seen, not least by its proponents, as antithetic to, the idea of maximizing utility.

Political obligation on this view depends entirely upon whether the political arrangements of a community promote what is taken to be the common good. This theory, which in some forms has an affinity with Rousseau's conception of the general will, perhaps receives its fullest elaboration in the work of the nineteenth-century English idealist philosopher, T. H. Green. Interestingly, as noted in Chapter 1, he also appears to have been the first political philosopher explicitly to use the term 'political obligation', by which he meant 'the obligation of the subject towards the sovereign, of the citizen towards the state, and the obligations of individuals to each other as enforced by a political superior' (Green, 1986, s. 1). Green's theory is rich and complex and has deserved better than the rather cursory and dismissive treatment it has mostly received in modern discussions of political obligation (e.g. Simmons, 1979; Green, 1988). Arguably, it offers a more fruitful approach to political obligation than that of the much more fashionable consent theories, and the account of political obligation to be defended in Chapters 6 and 7 certainly owes something to it – and it is encouraging to see it receiving more sympathetic treatment among some recent commentators (e.g. Harris, 1986, 1990; Milne, 1986; Nicholson, 1990; Carter, 2003). However, common good theories of political obligation are not without difficulties of their own, some of which will be considered in evaluating Green's account.

As with utilitarianism, though having a very different content, Green's account of political obligation is part of a comprehensive moral and political theory. Inevitably, this larger context can only be briefly touched upon here. One way of viewing Green's moral and political theory is as an attempt to rescue and reconcile the valid insights of both individualism and collectivism. Green believed that the end of the moral life is self-realization – in this respect there are some close affinities with J. S. Mill's views on self-development – but he also believed that an essential means to self-realization was the framework afforded by life within a state. Self-realization, according to Green, can only be achieved through willing the common good; a good that is common to everyone. Anything that is necessary to the achievement of the common good is necessarily good for everyone. The state, therefore, should be understood as 'an institution for the promotion of a common good' (Green, 1986, s. 124). Green rejects any conceptualization of the problem of political obligation in which the individual and the state are seen as inherently antagonistic, but he is also clear that collectivities have no value apart from their contribution to the self-realization of individual human beings, and is therefore not necessarily open to the familiar charge of illiberalism that is often directed at any form of collectivism.

Green's view of the relationship between individual self-realization and social and political institutions is well encapsulated by Harris and Morrow in the Introduction to their edition of his *Lectures on the Principles of Political Obligation*. They write:

'Green argues that the essential social dimension to individual self-realisation means that the individual must regard social institutions and practices (political organisations, customs, mores, law) as collective efforts after a common good. They are the result of the need to secure and maintain the conditions within which individuals can pursue their self-realisation in their own ways, and of the need to harmonize the ways in which they do so. As such, these institutions and practices need to be acknowledged by the individual as deserving his allegiance and consideration as essential to his own self-realisation – provided they continue to act as means to the common good and not as impediments to it.' (Green, 1986, pp. 6–7)

For Green, therefore, political obligation depends entirely on the polity promoting the end of self-realization. It is important here to be as clear as possible about the precise relationship between self-realization and the political community: individual self-realization is impossible outside of a polity, and the polity is an essential means to self-realization; but not just any polity promotes self-realization. Political arrangements have to be of an appropriate sort if they are to facilitate self-realization: political obligation is owed only if the political arrangements are of a kind which will further individual self-realization. Hence, the so far empty concepts of self-realization and the common good need to be provided with a substantive content, and most of Green's moral and political philosophy is concerned with elucidating and justifying a particular interpretation of self-realization and the common good.

Institutions, including political institutions, can promote self-realization only indirectly, by developing and protecting the conditions within which it becomes a feasible object of endeavour. Self-realization can be achieved only through free action, and neither the state nor any other institution can guarantee its attainment, much less act as a surrogate on behalf of the individual. What the state should secure are the circumstances within which individuals can act so as to realize themselves. The state must have a form that facilitates everyone's attempt at self-realization. The state does this through the maintenance of a structure of rights, a structure that protects everyone's ability to pursue their own self-realization, and mediates and harmonizes the varying aspirations of its citizens. Such rights, therefore, are not merely the creation of the state in the sense that rights are whatever the state happens to say they are: Green is not a legal positivist about rights. However, these moral rights must be incorporated within a legal structure, if they are to be truly effective. Yet, these rights nor are natural – they have no place in some putative state of nature – for self-realization cannot be achieved apart from social relations and life within a polity. As Green expresses the matter:

> 'It is on the relation to a society – to other men recognizing a common good – that the individual's rights depend ... A right is a power claimed and recognized as contributory to a common good. A right against society, in distinction from a right to be treated as a member of society, is a contradiction in terms ... If the common interest requires it, no right can be alleged against it.' (Green, 1986, s. 99)

Rights, moreover, are in a continuing process of historical development, adjusting to people's increasing recognition of the conditions under which their self-realization is possible. Thus, for Green, rights are neither natural nor simply a child of law, and their basis lies in a morality of self-realization rather than in either some prepolitical state of nature or the sovereign power of the state.

Where, then, does this leave Green's account of political obligation? In brief, political obligation is owed to a state by virtue of its supporting and maintaining a structure of rights, which is both an essential component of the common good and a necessary means to any person's self-realization. Such an obligation is dependent upon the state's actually contributing to this end: the sovereign power of the state exists to maintain a structure of rights that contributes to the common good. As Green makes explicit:

> 'If the power, existing for this end, is used on the whole otherwise than in conformity either with a formal constitution or with customs which virtually serve the purpose of a constitution, it is no longer an institution for the maintenance of rights and ceases to be the agent of a state. We only count Russia a state by a sort of courtesy on the supposition that the power of the Czar, though subject to no constitutional control, is so far exercised in accordance with a recognized tradition of what the public good requires as to be on the whole a sustainer of rights.' (Green, 1986, s. 132)

The state is a moral entity that derives its character from its effective incorporation of the essential conditions of the common good. Political obligation is dependent upon a state's being a genuine state in terms of Green's understanding of what this requires. Political obligation derives from the essential role of the state in achieving the common good; facilitating for each and every individual the active pursuit of his or her own self-realization.

Green's moral and political theory has been subjected to comprehensive criticism by commentators such as Pritchard (1968, ch. 4), and his account of political obligation has been criticized in a similar vein by Plamenatz (1968, ch. 3). It is not possible here to assess the merits of all these criticisms, though it is worth noting that Green's work has more recently also attracted some careful and thoughtful defenders (e.g. Nicholson, 1990; Carter, 2003). However, the element of Green's political philosophy that is most crucial to his theory of political obligation is his account of the common good, and this will be the principal focus of attention in the following discussion. The main conclusion of that discussion will be that his account of the common good is fundamentally flawed in a way that crucially damages his theory of political obligation. However, the judgement of Green's severest critics will not be fully endorsed: there are some important positive lessons to be learned from his approach.

Probably the most prevalent and potentially destructive criticism of the idea of the common good is that it is either impossible to determine or non-existent. While this is something of an overstatement of the problem, the problem remains a very serious one for an account such as Green's, which is rich in substantive content. How, for example, are we to decide what is in the common good? How are disputes to be adjudicated? Is there a good that is common to all members of a polity? One, perhaps obvious, source of these questions lies in the fact of disagreement: there is widespread disagreement between people about what is good both for them and more generally. While in general terms, as will be argued later, it is true that people cannot achieve their good apart from being members of a particular political community, yet of itself this does not imply much agreement about the shape or form of that polity. Similarly, for example, both socialists and libertarians could agree with Green at a sufficient level of abstraction that the state should maintain and protect individual rights, though there would be only limited overlap in their accounts of the nature and content of these rights. Green offers his own highly developed account of these rights, but one does not need to be a radical sceptic to be less than optimistic about any such account carrying widespread conviction. Arguments about political values, including arguments about rights, are rarely found entirely compelling. Indeed, one of the most important reasons why political authority is necessary is precisely because people within the same society often have different conceptions of the (common) good, and these differences are frequently incapable of resolution through rational argument. Moreover, there is also disagreement about how far some goods, even if it is agreed that they are goods, can be effectively or legitimately brought about through political means. This does not mean that there are no goods about which there is widespread agreement or that political organization is not sometimes the best, or perhaps only, way in which they can be realized: I shall argue later that peace and security is just such a good, but it is far too limited in its content to supply an adequate basis for the kind of account that Green advances.

There is, though, another, still more serious, problem. This is that Green's use of the idea of a common good is on occasion marked by conceptual confusion. Thus, goods can be said to be 'common' in the sense that people separately hold the same things to be valuable without it being the case that one person's good is the same as that of another. For example, most people value health, and in this sense health is commonly held to be good; but it is not a good held in common in the sense in which we share it. Your health and my health are independent goods; there is no single thing, 'good health', in which we both share. Yet, it seems that Green's argument sometimes requires him to employ the concept of the common good in this illicit sense, for he claims that in promoting the common good each person is promoting something that is also in his or her own individual good. There are, it must be noted, some distinctive goods, so-called 'public goods', which do possess a feature that makes such a claim plausible: this feature is their indivisi- bility. A standard example of such a good is clean air: clean air is a good that, subject to certain qualifications, can be enjoyed by everybody or nobody within a given area. So, in helping to keep the air clean I can be said to be promoting a common good, in the sense of a shared good, because one and the same good – clean air – is simultaneously good both for me and for others. For the most part, though, these do not seem to be the kind of goods that he has in mind. However, because Green's conception of self-realization, of which the common good is an essential component, is as he explicitly acknowledges thoroughly moralized, rather than simply empirical, it might be asked whether his conception can avoid these difficulties.

The answer is that it cannot. This is because Green fails to recognize the possibility of genuine conflict between an individual's personal inter- est or good and the common good. For Green, the common good is also necessarily in each and every individual's personal interest, and to think differently is to misunderstand one's true interests. Certainly, such misunderstandings can and do occur – people may be shortsighted, confused or mistaken about their own interests. However, when it is maintained that *any* apparent conflict between personal interest and the common good *must* be illusory, the claim becomes a metaphysical one, with some potentially sinister implications. It is, for example, a line of thought similar in its logic to that which led Rousseau to conclude that people can be 'forced to be free' (Rousseau, 1973, p. 177). While Green clearly did not intend these more sinister implications, the flaw in the argument remains. The point is well expressed by A. J. Milne, one of Green's most sympathetic critics, when he writes:

'He [Green] ignores the fact that a man's personal self-interest can conflict with the interest of his community . . . According to him, what is morally right is always in a man's personal self-interest because they are the same. Failure to see this betrays an unenlightened conception of personal self-interest. But they are the same only because Green has made them so by definition. This is unacceptable because it obscures the real sacrifice of personal self-interest, which meeting moral demands may involve; for instance, risking one's life on military service.' (Milne, 1986, p. 69)

This denial of the possibility of any conflict between the common good on the one hand, and both competing moral obligations and personal self-interest on the other, is a fundamental failing within Green's account of political obligation. It also marks a clear difference between his theory and the account of political obligation to be defended later: as we shall see, that also attaches deep significance to membership of a political community and what this implies, but it denies that political obligation is always necessarily compatible or in harmony with other moral obligations or our personal self-interest. Nor, indeed, should it be assumed that where such conflict arises primacy must always be granted to political obligation.

Green's political theory is inextricably intertwined with a conception of the common good and an account of its relation to self-realization that is either confused or unconvincing. Inevitably, this must also seriously impact on his theory of political obligation. For the account of political obligation, as we have seen, is in turn too bound up with difficulties surrounding his conception of the common good and the idea of self-realization to be rendered both coherent and convincing. His tendency to conflate within the common good all potentially conflicting values is a consequence of a desire to construct a comprehensive, integrated and harmonious moral system that is shared with many common good theorists. Any such theory, though, must address the problem of identifying and characterizing the common good in a way that can accommodate diverse and conflicting values and interests; a problem that is especially daunting with respect to complex, culturally and ethically plural societies such as those that comprise most modern states. However, although Green's deployment of the common good is unsatisfactory, he is right to see an important connection between political obligation and the shared conditions of life that constitute membership of a polity. It is the interpretation of the relationship between membership and the common good, understood as a shared substantive end, which is misguided. It may be helpful to introduce a comparison to try to illuminate this point. Most people recognize obligations to other members of their family, but it would be a misrepresentation of these obligations to think of them primarily in terms of promoting the common good of the family. While such obligations usually imply a special concern for the well-being of other members of our family, our actions need not be informed by any conception of the common good of our family. This is a line of thought that will be explored more fully in Chapter 6.

Conclusion

I have examined the contours of teleological theories of political obligation in general and two specific examples of such theories in particular. Both the utilitarian and common good theories have been found to be flawed as general accounts of political obligation. However, they are to some extent deficient for different reasons. The very structure of utilitarian theory makes it difficult for it to account for special obligations, like political obligation. Of course, utilitarians will not see this as a failing. For them, if some conventional conception, such as political obligation, does not fit within a utilitarian framework then it is the conventional conception that is at fault; not utilitarianism. And the general merits and weaknesses of utilitarianism is not something that can be explored here. By contrast, common good theories appear to be more congenial to the whole idea of political obligation. However, they were seen to give the wrong kind of account of the relationship between individual members and their polity; one that denied the potential for conflict between them, when both were as they should be.

In this chapter I have not attempted a complete or comprehensive discussion of teleological theories, but enough has been said to reveal their most important limitations. But, like voluntarist theories, they are not entirely wrong: there is also an insight that is central to any adequate account of political obligation that needs to be rescued from them. This is that a polity must in some way serve their interest if it is to have value for its members: there must be some good that a polity secures for its members. Both utilitarianism and common good theories demand too much in this respect; but it is right to expect something from membership of a polity.

In the next chapter, we turn to consider a theoretical approach to political obligation that is neither teleological nor voluntarist. It is an approach that seeks to ground political obligation in a conception of duty. This will then complete our survey of the three principal types of theory of political obligation.

4 Deontological Theories

In the two preceding chapters, I have argued that neither voluntarist nor teleological theories are able to provide convincing accounts of political obligation, although both approaches do seem to latch on to features of it that any adequate account will need to accommodate. Voluntarist theories, though superficially attractive, present a picture of political relations that largely misrepresents the character of a polity and people's experience of their relations to it. Teleological theories are either, as in the case of utilitarianism, unable to tie political obligation to the particular polity of which people are members, or, as with T. H. Green, involve an unconvincing conception of the common good. Overall, therefore, voluntarist and teleological theories both fail to capture distinctive features of political obligation. There is, though, a third type of account of political obligation that aspires to avoid the failings of the other two theories. This approach seeks to explain political obligation in terms of the idea of duty, and therefore the theories may be called, in philosophical terminology, 'deontological'.

It is probably doubtful whether those theories that are grouped here together as deontological really do constitute a single, rigorously distinct type of theory of political obligation. In different forms they seem to have connections with both voluntarist and teleological theories. For example, the entire class of voluntarist accounts could, at a stretch perhaps, be interpreted as a species of deontological theory; that is, in terms of a duty to keep our voluntary undertakings. This is because, as we saw earlier, voluntarist theories are not morally self-sufficient and therefore require some moral underpinning of this kind. But the general lesson to be learnt from such reflections is to beware of the dangers of attaching excessive significance to any classification of moral and political theories, including that employed in this book. The basis of many classifications is primarily pragmatic, in that they are designed to help organize diverse and complex material and to illuminate the logical structure and principal features of different theories. Thus, while I would want to defend the usefulness of the tripartite categorization employed here, these distinctions should not be fetishized or set in stone, and it should be readily acknowledged that the borderline between deontological and one or other of the alternative types of theory is often difficult to draw with any precision. In the case of deontological theories in particular, it is necessary to treat this classification with some caution.

The central idea informing deontological theories is that political obligation must be justified in terms of an account of our duties, which are to be explained neither as the result of our voluntary undertakings, nor simply in terms of the promotion of some good or valuable end. Richard Norman helpfully sets out the basic distinction between teleological and deontological ethical theories as follows:

> 'A teleological theory is one which asserts that an action is right or wrong, in so far as it produces good or bad consequences . . . A deontological theory is one which asserts that at least some actions are right or wrong, and we have a duty or obligation to perform them or refrain from them, quite apart from considerations of consequences. Teleological theories thus treat "good" and "bad" as the basic ethical concepts, and define others such as "right" or "wrong" in terms of these, whereas deontological theories would treat "right", "wrong", "duty" and "obligation" as basic, or at least give them equal status with "good" and "bad".' (Norman, 1983, p. 132)

According to deontological theories, the moral rightness or wrongness of at least some actions is independent of whether or not they maximize utility, promote the common good or contribute to the achievement of any other end. Rather, these actions should be judged morally by whether or not they are required or prohibited by some general moral principle(s), rule(s) or system of duties. In their most extreme form, often associated with Kant, they deny any moral significance to consequences, but in a more moderate form they claim only that there are some actions that we are either required to perform or to refrain from performing, whatever the net balance of beneficial or harmful consequences. An example of such an action might be our duty not to lie. According to this view, telling a lie is usually wrong, even if doing so would promote happiness, minimize suffering or have other beneficial consequences. (Most deontological theorists do not treat lying as always and necessarily unjustified, as Kant did, but they do likewise insist that it is not to be justified simply in terms of its consequences.) Deontological theories, therefore, justify political obligation in terms of a general moral principle or some system of duties. In this chapter I will principally be concerned with two deontological theories in particular: first, the fairness theory and, second, the theory of a natural duty to uphold just institutions. However, we shall begin with a discussion of the idea of 'hypothetical consent', which thus takes up unfinished business from Chapter 2.

Hypothetical consent

The crux of hypothetical consent is that it is *hypothetical*: that is, it does not involve showing that consent is in fact given; only that it would or should be given. Hypothetical consent, therefore, needs to be supported by arguments that establish whether consent is rationally or morally required in the appropriate circumstances. As was argued in Chapter 2, 'hypothetical consent' cannot properly be understood as a genuinely voluntarist theory of political obligation. However, it may be useful to sketch briefly how it can be seen, nevertheless, to emerge from that tradition of thinking. A fundamental problem for voluntarist theories, it will be recalled, is that of identifying some action or undertaking on the part of citizens that could reasonably be identified as a voluntary act giving rise to their political obligations. Tacit consent was one response to this difficulty, but, as has been shown, it does little to solve the fundamental problem. A further worry about voluntarist theories is their susceptibility to the objection that people may in fact sometimes consent to arrangements that are irrational, unreasonable or unfair. While in some circumstances it may be thought proper to hold people to such arrangements on the basis of their consent, in others their consent may be overridden or nullified by the irrational or morally unacceptable nature of the arrangements. Within voluntarist theories this last point is usually taken into account by characterizing the circumstances of voluntary agreement in such a way that indisputably irrational, unreasonable or unfair agreements will not meet the conditions for voluntary consent. But this attempt to circumscribe the conditions under which consent should be understood as genuine, can be taken in either of two very different directions. The first is that favoured by voluntarist theories, which is to look for specific actions that meet the appropriately described conditions; but this search, as has been argued earlier, has not met with much success. The alternative direction is to dispense with actual acts of consent entirely, and instead focus upon what it would be rational, reasonable or fair to agree to under the appropriately described circumstances. These considerations would then have force, regardless of whether or not people, in fact, consented.

From this perspective, actual consent drops out of the picture alto-gether. The important question becomes not whether people do or did actually consent to some particular government or political system, but what would be fair, reasonable or rational for people to consent to within appropriately characterized circumstances. It is this move that marks the transition from actual consent theories (explicit or tacit) to hypothetical consent theories – 'hypothetical' because there is no actual consent, only 'hypothesized' consent; a consent hypothesized on the basis of what would be fair, reasonable or rational in the relevant circumstances. The question for hypothetical consent theorists is not whether a person does consent but whether he or she ought to consent. Indeed, it is important to appreciate just how far 'hypothetical consent' departs from actual consent, for it is not merely that actual consent is not a necessary condi-tion of hypothetical consent, it is not a sufficient condition either. Actual consent, on this view, is at most only a piece of unreliable evidence about what it might be reasonable or rational to consent to. Within the theory of hypothetical consent, however, it is essentially redundant; hence the earlier argument to the effect that the logic of hypothetical consent is categorically distinct from that of voluntarist theories.

A further feature of this transition that should be noted is the enhanced role of the *theorist* of political obligation. Within genuinely voluntarist theories, there is an irreducible role for actual agents in the real world: ultimately it is *they* who do or do not consent. Although within volun-tarist theories there is a recurrent tendency to qualify and circumscribe this role, it cannot be eliminated entirely if such theories are to remain genuinely voluntarist. And it is this element of voluntariness that is the prime attraction of such theories. However, within hypothetical consent theories there is no such role for actual agents in the real world: their 'choices' are hypothesized and modelled by the political philosopher. It is philosophical argument that establishes whether the conditions of 'consent' have been met, and it has nothing to do with the decisions of the people who are supposedly obligated. Hence, there is no need to look to the histories and actions of actual people; instead, it is the validity of the theoretical arguments that is crucial.

Probably the best known account of hypothetical consent is that provided by Hanna Pitkin (1972). Although she develops her account in the process of interpreting the arguments of Locke and Tussman, our interest is not in the adequacy of these interpretations, but in the merits of her account of hypothetical consent. According to Pitkin, what is important is not whether consent is actually given but the basis upon which one ought to consent. The fundamental issue then is about the grounds upon which such 'consent' is based. In short, on this view, there is a decisive shift within hypothetical consent theory away from the actions of the people consenting to the qualities or attributes of the government or political system that would justify consent. Thus, according to Pitkin, the relationship between consent and obligation in hypothetical consent theory is the reverse of that within voluntarist theories:

> 'It is not so much your consent . . . that obligates you. You do not consent to be obligated, but rather are obligated to consent . . . you are obligated neither by your own consent nor by that of the majority but by the consent rational men in a "hypothetical state of nature" would have to give.' (Pitkin, 1972, p. 61)

It is the *reasons* for consent and not the *fact* of consent that explains political obligation. The argument shifts entirely to what it would be rational or obligatory to consent to in appropriately specified circumstances. As Pitkin expresses it:

> 'your obligation to obey depends not on any special relationship (consent) between you and your government, but on the nature of the government itself . . . In one sense this "nature of government" theory is thus a substitute for the doctrine of consent. But it may also be regarded as a new interpretation of consent theory, what we may call the doctrine of *hypothetical* consent. For a legitimate government, a true authority, one whose subjects are obligated to obey it, emerges as being one to which they *ought to consent*, quite apart from whether they have done so. Legitimate government acts within the limits of authority rational men would, abstractly and hypothetically, have to give a government they are founding. Legitimate government is government which *deserves* consent.' (Pitkin, 1972, pp. 61–2)

While it is unfortunate that Pitkin persists with the idea that hypothetical consent should be regarded as a 'reinterpretation' of consent theory, confusion between the logic of voluntarist theories and hypothetical consent is deeply enshrined within the social contract tradition.

What Pitkin demonstrates is that hypothetical consent offers a very different kind of theory from voluntarist accounts of political obligation. For it is clear that consent seems to have ceased to do any useful or distinctive work in the theory and has become no more than honorific: its role almost seems to be to provide us with reassurance that our obligation results from our voluntary choice even when it does not. This recourse to what is essentially only a comforting subterfuge is no doubt a tribute to the tenacity and continuing attractiveness of voluntarism in much of the thinking in this area. However, granted that hypothetical consent is not a form of voluntarism, it still remains to be asked how persuasive an account it is of political obligation.

The status of hypothetical agreements or choices is an issue that has been much discussed in recent political philosophy. A good deal of this discussion has been generated by the arguments of John Rawls's *A Theory of Justice*, although it should be noted that he does not present a hypothetical consent account of political obligation (Rawls, 1999). His account of political obligation, at least in that book, is couched in terms of a 'natural duty' to support just institutions, which will be considered later in this chapter. However, as is well known, the idea of a hypothetical contract is central to his account of how we are to arrive at principles of justice. For Rawls, principles of justice are those that would be agreed upon by rational and reasonable people in circumstances that are accepted as fair. This requires us to think ourselves into what Rawls calls 'the original position'; a situation in which we are shorn of the kind of knowledge that would enable us to bias principles of justice in favour of our own interests, values or conceptions of the good: this is essentially what makes the original position a fair situation in which to decide on principles of justice. However, as Rawls makes abundantly clear, this is to be understood only as a thought experiment. It is not a state of affairs that either has or could exist in 'real life', and there is also no literal sense in which a social contract results.

One influential line of criticism to which this argument has given rise, and which can equally be levelled against hypothetical consent theories of political obligation, concerns how people can be morally obligated by an agreement they have not entered into or a contract that they have not in fact made. As Ronald Dworkin has trenchantly remarked: 'a hypothetical contract is not simply a pale form of an actual contract; it is no contract at all' (Dworkin, 1975, p. 18). Or, as Jean Hampton puts it, 'if someone tells me a story in which hypothetical people make hypothetical contracts, how does that story have any effect on what I am *bound to* do?' (Hampton, 1986, p. 268). But matters are not quite as straightforward as this kind of objection might be taken to imply.

Such objections are indeed decisive against hypothetical consent where genuine consent is claimed to be the basis of the obligation. However, they have little force if it is recognized, as it is by Pitkin (and Rawls), that actual consent is essentially irrelevant to the argument. Certainly, it is mysterious how consent that was not given, or an agreement that was not entered into, can *of itself* be morally binding. (What, it might be asked, does 'of itself' refer to here since *ex hypothesi* there was no consent or agreement?) But, in fact, there are cases where hypothetical consent of this sort does appear to have some moral force. For instance, it is surely reasonable to claim that, in some circumstances, to show that we would have agreed to something, even though in fact we did not agree, may provide us with a strong moral reason for acting *as if* we had agreed. At least in normal circumstances, for example, if someone saves my life by knocking me out of the way of a falling rock, it would be perverse to then accuse them of assault because I did not actually consent to the person pushing me. Similarly, if reasonable efforts were made to seek my agreement to some course of action, but for non-culpable reasons I could not be contacted, and if the action was undertaken in good faith, then I may accept that the fact that I would have agreed does bind me to support that course of action. It may be reasonable to claim that this places me under some moral obligation even though if I were asked now I would not in fact agree to the action. Take the following situation: a business opportunity presents itself and a couple of friends need to make an urgent decision and correctly believe that I would have agreed to join with them, but that it was impossible at the time to contact me. They therefore expect me to bear my share of the costs and demonstrably show that they have taken steps to ensure that I would receive my share of the anticipated rewards. However, by the time I am asked I can see that the decision is not going to work out at all well, and that therefore it would be to my advantage not to be a party to it. Nevertheless, the fact that I would have agreed could reasonably be thought to bind me to the decision, too: I would be treating my friends unfairly by exploiting the benefit of hindsight, if I were to refuse to accept any responsibility for the decision with which I would enthusiastically have concurred (and they had good reason to believe that I would have concurred) at the time it was made.

It may appear, then, that this kind of example at least provides a toehold for hypothetical consent as a basis for political obligation. Unfortunately for proponents of hypothetical consent, however, it does not offer the support for their position that is needed. The reason is that this is a rather special kind of example, an instance of what might be called hypothetical *actual* consent. This, though, is not the kind of consent that is characteristically involved in hypothetical consent theories of political obligation. A modification of the example should make clear why not. Suppose now that I would not in fact have agreed to the decision that my friends made, even when they made it. I might have thought that their decision was the best one that could have been made, but I would not have agreed to go along with it because it was suggested by a friend whom I felt rather competitive towards. How do I react now if my friends tell me that, though they accept I would not in fact have agreed, nonetheless we all believe that the decision they made was at the time the best one? It seems far from clear in this example that I am under any obligation to be bound by their decision. What, though, if I am told that had I been thinking rationally I would have agreed (and I may accept that acting on the basis of disliking my partner would have been irrational)?

One cannot be so cavalier as to maintain that what is rational provides no reason for acting: indeed, it clearly does provide *a* reason. But it is also true that the reason is not one based on the person's consent. The reason is in fact a reason only if it is true that the decision was the rational decision to make. Thus, what this example brings out is that this reason is entirely independent of my consent or agreement; in fact it directly conflicts with the fact that I neither did nor would have consented to the decision. This kind of hypothetical consent, therefore, can be asserted not only in face of the fact that I did not consent, but also even if I would not have consented had I had the opportunity to do so; that is, with my hypothetical actual consent. Again, the conclusion to which this leads is that hypothetical consent has little to do with consent but is really a theory about what constitutes good reasons for action. Although there is a sense of hypothetical consent that does genuinely connect with voluntarism and that could in some circumstances provide a reason for binding an agent on the basis of an action (the giving of consent) which is only counterfactually true, this is not the sense of hypothetical consent typically employed in hypothetical consent theories of political obligation.

There are at least two good reasons why such theories do not employ the idea of hypothetical actual consent. First, and most obviously, because, as with more straightforward versions of consent theory, it is impossible to show that many people have in this sense hypothetically consented to their government or political system. Second, while in some circumstances hypothetical actual consent may generate obligations, there are others where it clearly does not. The fact that I would have placed a bet on a particular horse in a race had I not been unavoidably detained on the way to place the bet does not entail that I am subsequently obligated to pay the stake to the bookmaker when the horse loses (any more than he would be obliged to pay me if the horse wins!). It is no doubt a difficult and complicated matter systematically to distinguish those circumstances in which hypothetical actual consent does generate obligations from those in which it does not. But, any theory of political obligation employing such a notion of consent would need to be able to do so: it would have to show, not merely that people would have hypothetically actually consented, but also that the appropriate circumstances obtained for the consent to warrant the attribution of an obligation. Unsurprisingly, it turns out that in this regard hypothetical actual consent faces similar difficulties to those that confront actual consent theories of political obligation, as discussed in Chapter 2.

The remaining type of hypothetical consent, perhaps best called 'hypothetical rational consent', is not a genuine consent theory at all, or at least, in the terminology employed earlier, it is not a voluntarist theory. Rather, it is best understood as a theory of good reasons, and as applied to political obligation it is a theory of good reasons for obeying the government or respecting the political system. Such a theory explains political obligation in terms of a duty owed to the state or government. However, having distinguished a type of hypothetical consent theory that is distinct from voluntarist theories, the question now becomes whether this theory can be adequately distinguished from teleological accounts of political obligation. In short, is hypothetical consent a logically distinct kind of duty-based account of political obligation different from teleological theories? In order to answer this question we need to focus more directly on the nature of the duty that explains political obligation. If the duty derives entirely from the promotion of a particular goal, such as maximizing utility, then hypothetical consent is simply a disguised teleological theory. However, if, as is more usual, the duty is not entirely explicable in these terms, then hypothetical consent implies some underlying deontological theory. Here, I shall principally examine two attempts to provide a deontological basis for political obligation; both of which as it happens have been advanced at different times by John Rawls. These two accounts are the fairness or 'fair-play' theory and the 'natural duty to uphold just institutions', although I shall also mention other possibilities. We begin by considering the fairness theory.

Fairness and political obligation

The fairness theory of political obligation appears to have been first formulated by the legal philosopher, H. L. A. Hart (1967), and has been developed by John Rawls (1964) and others, especially George Klosko (1992). Interestingly, Hart specifically relates the fairness theory to the social contract tradition. He argues that social contract theorists were right to recognize that political obligation is 'something which arises between members of a particular political society out of their mutual relationship' but were wrong to identify this 'situation of mutual restrictions with the paradigm case of promising' (Hart, 1967, p. 63). The fairness theory, therefore, shares with social contract theories the idea that political obligation involves an essentially reciprocal relationship, but dispenses with any residual voluntarist component of such theories. The key elements of the fairness theory (although that is not his term for it) are characterized by Hart as follows:

> 'when any number of persons conduct any joint enterprise according to rules and thus restrict their liberty, those who have submitted to these restrictions when required have a right to a similar submission from those who have benefitted by their submission. The rules may provide that officials should have the authority to enforce obedience and make further rules, and this will create a structure of legal rights and duties, but the moral obligation to obey the rules in such circumstances is *due to* the co-operating members of the society, and they have the correlative moral right to obedience. In social situations of this sort (of which political society is the most complex example) the obligation to obey the rules is something distinct from whatever other moral reasons there may be for obedience in terms of good consequences (e.g. the prevention of suffering); the obligation is due to the co-operating members of the society as such and not because they are human beings on whom it would be wrong to inflict suffering.' (Hart, 1967, pp. 61–2)

In this way, Hart distinguishes the fairness theory from consequentialist theories, particularly utilitarianism, in addition to distinguishing it from social contract theories. The core idea informing the principle of fairness is an underlying conception of reciprocity – that the distribution of the benefits and burdens of membership of some association or group should be fairly shared. This draws on a powerful and widely shared moral intuition: although people may have different views about exactly what constitutes a fair distribution of burdens and benefits, that the distribution should be fair, or at least not unfair, seems to be a pretty basic idea within moral thinking. Fairness, therefore, would seem to offer a potentially compelling basis for political obligation, if of course the argument can be sustained. Unfortunately, Hart's own statement of the principle is tantalizingly brief, and he ignores the question of whether benefits have to be voluntarily accepted, without it being clear that this is because he does not think it matters. Because Hart's concern with political obligation is only subsidiary to his attempt to provide a justification for natural rights, it is better to consider the fairness theory initially through Rawls's more extended elaboration of it.

There are some differences of detail between Hart and Rawls in their exposition of the fairness theory – 'fair play' in Rawls's terminology, and I shall henceforth use the terms interchangeably – but the substance of their accounts are very similar. This similarity is readily apparent from the following passage:

> 'Suppose there is a mutually beneficial and just scheme of social cooperation, and that the advantages it yields can only be obtained if everyone, or nearly everyone, cooperates. Suppose further that cooperation requires a certain sacrifice from each person, or at least involves a certain restriction of his liberty. Suppose finally that the benefits produced by cooperation are, up to a certain point, free: that is the scheme of cooperation is unstable in the sense that if any one person knows that all (or nearly all) of the others will continue to do their part, he will still be able to share a gain from the scheme even if he does not do his part. Under these conditions a person who has accepted the benefits of the scheme is bound by a duty of fair play to do his part and not to take advantage of the free benefits by not cooperating.' (Rawls, 1964, pp. 9–10)

Rawls proceeds to develop his account in more detail but there are already at least three components of the principle of fair play as he presents it that can be seen to give rise to questions, especially in the context of a theory of political obligation. These concern, first, what is to count as a cooperative scheme; second, the requirement that the terms of cooperation be just or fair; and, third, determining what is involved in accepting a benefit. There are other aspects of Rawls's account about which questions could also be raised; for example, his claim that the benefits of a cooperative scheme must depend upon everyone or nearly everyone cooperating. Both Simmons and Greenawalt argue that the obligations of fair play could obtain even where the acquisition of the benefit is consistent with a substantial proportion of the beneficiaries not contributing – that is, where there is a large number of free riders (Simmons, 1979; Greenawalt, 1987). For example, one may be obliged not to walk across a lawn by a cooperative scheme requiring everyone to use the paths, even though the grass may be protected from undue wear, the object of the scheme, if only 40 per cent of people observe the requirement. This criticism of Rawls is surely convincing; after all, most societies are able to maintain reasonable levels of personal security in the face of numerous crimes of violence. However, it is more of a technical problem in its formulation than a serious blow to the fair-play theory. Nothing of importance would be lost if the offending condition were reformulated in a way so as to avoid this criticism.

As was noted earlier in the context of Hart's statement of it, the principle of fairness is distinct from both voluntarist and teleological theories of political obligation. A brief elaboration of these comparisons may help to illuminate the merits of the fair-play theory, before considering the more serious objections. Daniel McDermott identifies the principal advantage of the fair-play theory as compared to voluntarist (or consent) theories when he writes:

'The great strength of the fair-play theory is that it rests on an uncontroversial empirical claim: people in many existing societies really do benefit from the provision of goods by their political communities. Unlike consent theory, which begins with an ideal of a consensual rights-transfer that would, in a perfect world, result in legitimate state authority, but which then collapses when confronted with the facts of the real world, the fair-play theory begins with a claim about the real world that only the most hardened anarchist would be likely to disagree with.' (McDermott, 2004, p. 217)

The persistent problem that, as we have seen, plagues voluntarist theories of political obligation is that of plausibly explaining the voluntary undertaking by which the obligation is supposedly acquired. The fair-play account would appear to circumvent this problem because its underlying model of political relations is subtly but importantly different from that informing voluntarist accounts, including consent theory. Whereas the latter basically interprets the polity as a voluntary association, the fair-play theory is premised upon a conception of the polity as an essentially cooperative enterprise. The justification of political obligation on this view has to do with sharing the burdens of cooperation as the price to be paid for a share of the benefits, rather than with the decision to join the cooperative enterprise in the first place. And, while the basic idea of consent is simple and easily understood, the underlying intuition of the principle of fair play, when unpacked – that it is wrong to free-ride – is, as mentioned earlier, also one that is widely shared.

However, the fair-play theory, while clearly dependent upon the existence of the benefits as part of its rationale, is also not simply reducible to a teleological account of political obligation. Crucially, it is not only the benefits deriving from cooperation that justify the obligation, but also the fact that one is a participant in a cooperative arrangement that is fair. Thus, though a necessary condition of the obligation according to the fair-play theory, such benefits are not a sufficient condition. We must also look to how the benefits are distributed. And this may be seen as a further attraction of the fair-play theory: it is not only concerned with benefits and burdens but with how they are apportioned If the distribution of benefits and burdens is fair, we have no good reason not to do our bit in supporting and maintaining the cooperative enterprise.

Having noted some of its merits, we should now return to the first of our three questions identified earlier: what is meant by a scheme of social cooperation? On the face of it, this may seem unproblematic: a scheme of social cooperation could be characterized as a group of people working together for mutual benefit. There are, however, two issues that arise in relation to this apparently straightforward conception. First, it is far from clear what 'working together' or 'cooperation' actually involves. There are obvious examples of such cooperation: a group of people engaged in a clearly defined, common endeavour, such as sailing a ship, playing football for the same team, building a house together or forming a club, and so on. However, are two teams playing football against each other engaged in a scheme of social cooperation? Or, are two firms in a competitive market, both trading legally, but each trying to drive the other out of business, engaged in a scheme of social cooperation? Their mutual respect for the law hardly seems sufficient to answer the question affirmatively, for one might equally say that two states at war, if they are scrupulous in observing the various conventions and rules of war, are also engaged in a cooperative scheme. War is not mutually beneficial to the two states, and nor, necessarily, is a competitive market to the two firms. But, even if it could be said that the competitive market is in some sense mutually beneficial, and if both firms agree that the market provides fair terms for the conflict between them, would it still be right to think of them as engaged in a scheme of social cooperation?

It could, perhaps, be argued that the legal structure regulating a competitive market is a means of cooperatively managing conflict; yet, while there is something to the thought that, for example, conventions governing duelling involve social cooperation, it is distinctly odd to describe the opponents as engaged in a scheme of social cooperation. And although we can, indeed, characterize a market or a duel as fair or unfair – we can have a very clear idea in both contexts as to what would be unfair – the relationship between firms in a market or duellists is clearly not really about providing a fair distribution of mutual benefits. In short, there is a distinction between participating in a socially constructed practice, which may be said to involve cooperation only in a rather technical and attenuated form, and engaging collaboratively in a common endeavour for mutual benefit. While both may involve obligations, it is surely the latter that Rawls and other proponents of the fair-play theory have in mind. One problem for proponents of the fair-play theory of political obligation is that while there are many microsituations within a society that provide clear examples of schemes of social cooperation in the stronger sense required by the fair-play theory, it is less clear that a society or state can plausibly be so conceived. Clearly, there can be benefits from being a member of a polity; not least, as I shall argue later, the goods of peace and security, but at least some of those benefits are more like conditions for managing conflict than the result of a cooperative enterprise. The model of political relations as a scheme of social cooperation seems partial and incomplete: so much of politics is about coercion and the threat of coercion, about managing fundamental conflicts of value and interest, that it sits uneasily with what appears to be an overly comfortable and optimistic conception of political relations as a scheme of social cooperation. It would be equally one-sided to deny any place to social cooperation in an account of political life; but the overall role of social cooperation within fair-play theories shows some similarities to that of the role of the common good within some teleological theories; and they seem to face some similar difficulties.

It is insufficient, according to the fair-play theory, that a scheme of social cooperation be mutually beneficial: if it is to generate the appropriate obligation, it must also be fair. The reason for this is that people should not be expected to accept that they are under an obligation to support a cooperative scheme, including those from which they benefit, if the distribution of the benefits and burdens arising from it is unfair. Suppose, for example, that two people acting cooperatively produce an extra ten units of value, the input of each person is of equal worth (however that is measured), and there are no other factors that differentiate them. It is true that both parties benefit from this arrangement even if one of them receives only a single extra unit of value and the other receives the remaining nine extra units. But why is the person who only receives the one extra unit obligated to support the arrangement, even though, relative to a situation of non-cooperation, it is clearly mutually beneficial? In short, without a requirement of fairness or justice in distribution, a scheme of social cooperation can be both advantageous to all and yet exploitative (a claim, for example, that many Marxists would make about states with capitalist economic systems); hence the claim that cooperative arrangements must be fair as well as being mutually advantageous, if they are to give rise to justified obligations.

However, this example, because of the simplification introduced for purposes of illustration, obscures a potentially rather large problem: this is that what is fair is itself highly controversial and contestable. Suppose we complicate the example by adding that the person receiving an extra nine units also has a large number of dependants, whereas the person receiving one extra unit has no dependants: how will these changed circumstances affect our judgement of the fairness of the distribution? Or, suppose that one of them is more talented or industrious than the other? Or, that one has a physical disability? Once these complications are introduced, although fairness will still be important, people's understanding of what is fair is likely to differ. In short, at the level of moral intuitions there is unlikely to be agreement about what constitutes fairness in a whole variety of different circumstances; as soon as the simplifying and highly unrealistic *ceteris paribus* assumptions of the initial example are replaced by a more complex and realistic picture, we are confronted by a morass of diverse and conflicting judgements.

It was, in large part, in recognition of these conflicting ordinary judgements about what the right principles of distribution are that Rawls developed his enormously influential and highly sophisticated theory of justice. The principal aim of that theory is to transcend, or at least significantly reduce, the scope of these conflicting judgements by finding a point of view at a higher level of abstraction that would embody our agreed moral judgements, and yet also provide a generally acceptable method for adjudicating or mediating serious disagreement about the fair terms for social cooperation. The purpose of his idea of the 'original position' is precisely to characterize a viewpoint from which we can agree on the principles that should determine a just distribution of the benefits and burdens of social cooperation (Rawls, 1999). It is not feasible here to go into the details of Rawls's rich and complex theory of justice; but three general points of relevance to the fair-play account of political obligation are, in particular, worth noting. First, some substantial theory of justice or fairness, whether or not it is that of Rawls, will be necessary to fill out the fair-play account. Otherwise, the theory is purely formal and empty of content. Second, the precise content of that theory will be crucial to a full explanation and characterization of the obligation deriving from a principle of fair play. Third, neither Rawls's theory of justice nor any other theory has won widespread acceptance, either among philosophers or ordinary people; and hence, even among those who are committed to a fair-play theory of political obligation, there are likely to be significant differences about the substance of the principle and what can be inferred from it about political obligation. Taken together, while not constituting a conclusive argument against the fair-play theory, these observations indicate the very real difficulties that such a theory must overcome.

The final question concerning the fair-play theory relates to the claim that participants in a scheme of social cooperation must 'accept the benefits' of such a scheme. When a person voluntarily and with full knowledge of what is involved enters a scheme of social cooperation, what is meant by 'accepting' the benefits of the cooperative scheme is unlikely to be a problem. However, such clear cases cannot be straight-forwardly invoked by proponents of the fair-play theory of political obli-gation: a crucial feature distinguishing fair-play from consent theories is that, according to fairness theories, no voluntary undertaking is neces-sary for an obligation to be incurred. It is sufficient, according to the fair-play theory, that a person accepts the benefits of a mutually benefi-cial and fair scheme of social cooperation. The question that arises, therefore, concerns the conditions that have to be met for it to be appro-priate to talk of *accepting* a benefit. For example, is the mere receipt of a benefit sufficient? That it is not can be seen if we consider the problem of imposed benefits, most forcefully articulated by Robert Nozick (1974, pp. 90–3).

To explain this problem, let us return for the moment to the simple example of a scheme of cooperation to protect the grass from excessive wear. A woman might agree that unspoiled grass is a benefit, and she might also agree that the general rule that nobody should walk across the grass involves a fair distribution of the benefits and burdens within such a cooperative scheme, but does it follow that she is therefore obliged to refrain from walking across the grass if others similarly refrain from doing so? It is difficult to see how such an obligation must necessarily follow, for the woman might still prefer to walk across the grass while allowing that if everyone else acts similarly then the benefit of an unsul-lied lawn will be lost. It is not possible to infer from the facts that she regards the unsullied lawn as a benefit and that other people are prepared not to walk across the lawn to ensure that this benefit obtains, that she values the benefit sufficiently highly to obligate her not to walk across the lawn. After all, she might prefer not to be inconvenienced by the detour, accepting that everyone else, too, has the right to walk across the grass, and that if they do it is certain that the grass will be spoiled. Such a view may simply be a manifestation of her, perfectly reasonable, prior-ities: she values a nice lawn but she values not having to make an irritating detour even more. In short, she agrees that a cooperative scheme prohibiting everyone walking across the grass would be fair and beneficial but it is not a scheme in which she wishes to participate, because it does not reflect her priorities. It is far from clear, therefore, how the woman acquires an obligation to share the burdens simply because others agree not to walk across the grass, which will be sufficient to produce the benefit of an unsullied lawn.

The example of the lawn is a very simple one, and matters are still more difficult when richer and more complex political examples are considered. One need only think of problems such as the control of pollution, national defence and welfare policy to see how complicated and contentious the issues are likely to become. In particular, matters become extremely thorny when the benefits from any scheme of cooperation are costly and difficult to avoid. The more a benefit is 'imposed' upon a person, and the higher the cost of producing the benefit, the more the claim – that it is simply through receiving the benefit that a person incurs an obligation to comply with the terms of even a fair scheme of cooperation, giving rise to what is agreed to be a benefit – seems to be implausible. Thus, it is reasonable to believe that 'accepting a benefit' must involve being more than a mere recipient of a benefit.

There are two principal lines of argument that have been advanced in response to this problem. First, emphasis has been given to the idea that the beneficiaries have to be parties to, or participants in, the scheme of social cooperation, and not merely beneficiaries of it: that is, what is envisaged is a genuinely cooperative structure and not the arbitrary or random imposition of benefits. The second line of thought stresses rather that the acceptance of benefits must be voluntary: acceptance is a voluntary action, hence is not something that can be imposed upon a person against his or her will. Unfortunately for defenders of fairness theories, both these strategies lead back to voluntarist accounts of political obligation, and thus to the difficulties associated with them. The first has to confront the problem that being a member of a polity is not for the most part something over which people have much choice. It might be possible to try to distinguish membership from participation, perhaps in terms of the resident/voter dichotomy, but again this seems to encounter similar problems to those faced by consent theory. The second line of argument must address the problem that many of the benefits of living in a polity cannot be rejected. The difficulty in this case is once more that of identifying reasonable and realistic means of rejecting the benefits.

In short, therefore, the problem for proponents of the fairness theory of political obligation is that, although the idea of 'the acceptance of benefits' can be understood in either of two ways, neither has much plausibility as a general justification of the supposed obligation. On the one hand, acceptance of benefits is equivalent to the mere receipt of benefits; while on the other, acceptance of benefits entails some voluntary act of acceptance. The first interpretation provides a plausible account of the realities of political life – we do receive benefits about many of which we have no real choice – but this does not necessarily justify a corresponding obligation. The second interpretation, by contrast, provides a potentially plausible justification of how an obligation is generated by accepting benefits, but one that has little application to the realities of political life.

One response to this problem is to bite the bullet and simply deny that acceptance is a crucial condition. This is the route taken by George Klosko through his idea of 'presumptive benefits'. These are public goods that 'it is supposed that all members of the community want, whatever else they want' because they are indispensible to any decent or worthwhile life (Klosko, 1992, p. 39). Because they are goods that everyone can be assumed to want, we do not need to worry about their 'acceptance'. And if, when asked, some people claimed not to want these goods, they would be mistaken. Moreover, because they are public goods they are unavoidable and non-excludable. These conditions have the effect of eliminating trivial goods – which we could not reasonably suppose that everyone wanted – and non-public goods that could be provided in some other way. I think that there is something to this idea, but, like arguments in terms of the common good, it will only justify a very limited range of goods. More importantly, as A. J. Simmons has argued, it is not clear that this is really a view that fits comfortably with the fairness theory (Simmons, 2001, p. 35). For what matters about presumptive goods is simply that, because of their importance and their public character, we should do what is necessary to ensure that everyone has them, not that they should necessarily be provided *fairly*. So, while I shall later suggest something quite similar to Klosko in arguing for the fundamental importance of peace and security, I do not claim that the provision of such a good has anything particular to do with fairness.

Thus, overall, it is difficult to see how a genuine fairness theory can successfully circumvent all the difficulties just raised: the fairness theory appears to be either unconvincing or largely irrelevant as a general theory of political obligation. However, that conclusion is not inconsistent with acknowledging that in so far as people believe themselves, or are justifiably believed by others, to be participants in polity, which does supply them with benefits that they genuinely accept on a broadly fair basis, this gives them a good reason to help maintain their polity. The argument here does not deny this last claim; but that claim is not sufficient to support a general theory of political obligation.

Natural duty, gratitude and Samaritanism

Before turning to Rawls's later theory of political obligation – the natural duty to support just institutions – it should be noted that this is but one of several possible accounts of political obligation in terms of a natural duty. Kent Greenawalt, for example, has distinguished five such theories; though he concedes that 'these theories rest on diverse foundations, and a plausible challenge to my whole enterprise is that I am treating similarly theories whose underlying bases are radically different' (Greenawalt, 1987, p. 160). One such class of natural duty theories that he considers are traditional natural law arguments. Natural law can be taken as a paradigm example of a deontological theory. Traditional natural law theories, which have some kind of religious or theist under-pinning, however, will not be discussed in any detail here. In so far as they are distinct from theories that are discussed, their particular features depend in a fundamental way on whatever set of theological or deist beliefs inform them. Whatever their merits, therefore, they cannot be expected to offer a general theory of political obligation that is persua-sive to non-believers; and it is obviously impossible to consider the larger questions about religious belief and the existence of God as an aside to the main concerns of this book. Historically, of course, such theories have been immensely important, and a classic Christian expres-sion of the idea can be found in the famous opening verse from St Paul, *Romans* ,13: 'Let every soul be subject unto the higher powers. For there is no power but of God: the powers that be are ordained of God.' It was this kind of Biblical passage that underpinned the divine right of kings, one theoretically quite sophisticated example of such a view that was long dominant in medieval Europe. However, it should not be thought that theological justifications of political obligation are entirely a thing of the past, as the resurgence of near theocratic states such as Iran shows. Moreover, generally, for those who adhere to a religious doctrine that does have what they regard as a convincing justification for political obligation, this will provide a good reason for supporting their polity when the conditions of that justification are met. But, although various religions provide their own justifications, for those of a different religion or of no religion at all, in so far as that justification depends upon premises about the nature of God's will or such like that are not shared, any particular religiously based account of natural law will lack general persuasiveness.

There are two other natural duty explanations of political obligation that are briefly worth noting before moving on to Rawls: these are those expressed in terms of principles of gratitude and Samaritanism, respectively. I begin with the principle of gratitude. This idea can be found lucidly and forcefully expressed as early as Socrates's claim that we owe a debt of gratitude to our political community similar to that which we owe our parents. In both cases, he contended, gratitude is appropriate because of the succour and support that they have provided (Plato, 1969, pp. 90–1). The analogy between the duty we owe our parents and the duty that we owe the polity rests on a comparison between the family and the polity that has been a recurrent theme in discussions of political obligation, about which more will be said later; but not all accounts of political obligation in terms of a duty of gratitude rely upon it. Sir David Ross, for example, identifies a prima facie duty of gratitude owed generally to those who benefit us. In the context of political obligation he claims that 'the duty of obeying the laws of one's country arises partly (as Socrates contends in the *Crito*) from the duty of gratitude for the benefits one has received from it' (Ross, 1930, p. 27). The kernel of this conception is briefly stated by one of its critics, A. J. Simmons:

> 'The gratitude account of political obligation maintains that our receipt of the benefits of government binds us to repay the government because of considerations of gratitude. It maintains further that this repayment consists in supporting the government, part of which support consists in obeying the law.' (Simmons, 1979, p. 183)

Unfortunately, most references to gratitude as an explanation of political obligation are extremely brief and underdeveloped; and though it has been the subject of some interest this has been mostly of a critical sort (e.g. Smith, 1973a; Simmons, 1979, ch. 7).

Much of this criticism has centred on questions about whether the government or polity is an appropriate object of gratitude; whether it has done anything that merits gratitude; whether, even if gratitude is appropriate and merited, it need take the form of political obligation; or indeed whether gratitude is properly understood as a duty or obligation at all. The gratitude account also seems potentially open to the objection to claims about duties arising from unsolicited benefits discussed in relation to the fairness theory: must we be grateful for benefits that have been imposed upon us? It has, however, also been defended in a sophisticated and developed form by A. D. Walker, who argues that most critics misrepresent the argument from gratitude as resting on a principle of requital or reciprocity: that receipt of a benefit places a person under an obligation to requite the benefactor (Walker, 1988, 1989). Walker, however, reformulates the argument from gratitude in a manner that he claims avoids the objections to this principle. He argues as follows:

'1. The person who benefits from X has an obligation not to act contrary to X's interests.
2. Every citizen has received benefits from the state.
3. Every citizen has an obligation of gratitude not to act in ways that are contrary to the state's interest.
4. Non-compliance with the law is contrary to the state's interests.
5. Every citizen has an obligation of gratitude to comply with the law.' (Walker, 1988, p. 205)

As he explains, this reformulation of the argument from gratitude does do something to meet the standard objections, but it still leaves many problems unresolved. (It may also be thought to be worryingly open to exploitation by unscrupulous political powers, but that would not be a conclusive objection.) However, the principal difficulty with the argument from gratitude, including Walker's account of it, is that nothing he says convincingly suggests that the kind of obligation he characterizes is best understood as one of gratitude.

Walker himself writes that his argument 'suggests a view of political communities as communities whose members are, or should be, bound to one another by ties of goodwill and respect' (Walker, 1988., pp. 210–11). This is fair enough, but it is not a sufficient basis for a duty of gratitude. Relationships of respect, and even in many cases of goodwill, need not imply a duty of gratitude. Indeed, there would be something rather distasteful in suggesting that gratitude is the appropriate response to being shown respect, as if it were something that had been generously bestowed on one rather than something to which one was properly entitled. Gratitude may be a more appropriate response to goodwill, at least in some contexts, but it is far from clear that relationships such as citizenship are suitable contexts, and in any case goodwill seems too nebulous and attenuated a basis for political obligation. At best, we might accept that gratitude is in some circumstances an appropriate response to some benefit that the polity bestows on us, but in so far as, for example, it merely treats us fairly then it only treats us as we should be treated. Of course, we may in some rather unspecific way be grateful that we live in a polity that treats us fairly, but we do not have reason to be grateful to *it*, whatever exactly that means.

Let us, then, turn to the principle of Samaritanism to see whether that fares any better. Christopher Wellman has developed this in an original and often ingenious way, drawing on fairness theories but also going beyond them. His central claim is that political obligation (in his account, specifically, the duty to obey the law) can be justified in terms of its being 'a fair share of the communal Samaritan chore of rescuing all of us from the perils of the state of nature' (Wellman, quoted in Wellman and Simmons, 2005, p. 89). The argument essentially rests on an analogy between our natural duty of rescue (Samaritanism) – the duty we have to rescue those in serious danger when we can do so at no great cost to ourselves – and to our political obligation (duty to obey the law). Very simply, the argument runs as follows. The state is necessary, or at least provides the most effective way, to save us from the dangers we would face in a state of nature (a condition without an effective polity). Because securing us against these dangers involves extensive and complex issues of coordination and control, a state must be able to exercise legitimate coercion if it is to be able to fulfil that role. In so far as the state seeks to perform this role, we are under a general duty to do our fair share to support it. The only realistic and suitable form for this support to take is obedience to the law. However, political obligation extends only so far as the benefits the state brings really are essential and justified by the Samaritan argument; cannot be delivered more effectively in any other, less coercive way; and do not make unreasonably costly demands on citizens. Thus, the general duty to obey the law does not extend to an illegitimate regime or an unjust law. Nor does it extend to a great many things that actual polities routinely do, 'even things that they can do well. For each potential state function we should ask whether the goods secured are important enough to justify the non-consensual coercion that inevitably accompanies political coordination' (Wellman and Simmons, 2005, p. 73).

Wellman's account of political obligation is not without its attractions. In particular, his emphasis on the polity's provision of the collective goods of peace and security is a point that will be taken up later. However, it also suffers from some serious weaknesses and limitations. The principal weakness is that the foundational analogy between political obligation and the duty to rescue appears far-fetched, lacking much intuitive plausibility. For example, as A. J. Simmons remarks, it is far from clear, unlike in the standard Samaritan examples, that 'legal obedience constitutes an appropriately easy or low-cost sort of rescue of our fellow citizens' (Simmons, quoted in Wellman and Simmons, 2005, p. 181). Furthermore, the structure of Samaritan examples is very different from that of political obligation, in that the former are infrequent and occasional – not at all like a continuous obligation to obey the law – but also quite general, unlike political obligation, which is owed to a particular polity. Paying one's taxes simply does not seem to have much in common with rescuing a drowning child. Among the limitations of the theory is that it does not cover much of what we might want an account of political obligation to incorporate: it justifies the obligation only to obey a very restricted class of laws. (In fairness, however, those who want very much to limit the role of government might see this as an advantage.) In short, while the Samaritan argument may have something to teach us, it is pretty unconvincing as an attempt to provide a general account of political obligation.

Although the arguments from natural law, gratitude and Samaritanism may each provide some limited support in specific contexts for the idea of political obligation, all of them lack the scope that is needed for a general account of it. It is now time, then, to consider Rawls's second attempt to present a theory of political obligation: his idea of a natural duty to support just institutions.

Rawls's duty to uphold just institutions

In *A Theory of Justice* Rawls does not develop the fairness theory as his favoured account of political obligation, and in one of the more significant departures from his earlier work he advances instead an explanation in terms of 'a natural duty to promote and support just institutions'. (To be precise, Rawls distinguishes obligations – which all arise from a principle of fairness – from natural duties; and hence in his use of the term most people do not have any *political obligations*, only natural duties to a just polity. However, I shall ignore this point: the natural duty to promote and support just institutions clearly plays the role within Rawls's theory of what would generally be regarded as an account of political obligation.) His exact statement of the relevant natural duty, which has two parts, is as follows:

'First, we are to comply with and to do our share in just institutions when they exist and apply to us; and second, we are to assist in the establishment of just arrangements when they do not exist, at least when this can be done with little cost to ourselves.' (Rawls, 1999, pp. 293–4)

While it is possible to see residual elements of the fairness theory in his talk about 'doing our share' in just institutions, this account is in key respects significantly different from his earlier theory. In fact, Rawls does retain the fairness theory as a specific partial justification for the political obligation of people 'who have assumed favoured offices or positions, or who have taken advantage of certain opportunities to further their interests' (Rawls, 1999, p. 308); but the details of this special class of persons need not concern us here. He explicitly rejects the fairness principle as a satisfactory account of political obligation for most people for similar reasons to those that we have already examined. He writes that according to the fairness theory:

> 'citizens would not be bound to even a just constitution unless they have accepted and intend to continue to accept its benefits. Moreover, this acceptance must be in some appropriate sense voluntary. But what is this sense? It is difficult to find a plausible account in the case of the political system into which we are born and begin our lives.' (Rawls, 1999, p. 296)

On this basis, Rawls concludes that a satisfactory account of political obligation, if it is to have general application, cannot depend upon the voluntary acceptance of benefits; and he is clear that his revised theory obligates each member of the polity, 'irrespective of his voluntary acts, performative or otherwise' (Rawls, 1999, p. 294). Nor in this revised account does political obligation directly derive from a fair distribution of the benefits and burdens of social cooperation; such considerations remain important for Rawls, but they are encompassed within the theory of justice rather than the account of political obligation. Instead, our political obligation arises from a natural duty to support and to promote just institutions.

It is only proper to point out that Rawls is not principally concerned with the issue of political obligation in *A Theory of Justice*, and his arguments in support of his claim that there is a natural duty to support and to further just institutions are not especially clear or well-developed. Basically, though, they appear to be of two sorts. First, there are the arguments from the inadequacy of other accounts of political obligation, such as his reasons for discarding the fairness theory. Certainly, the arguments of this book are consistent with Rawls's rejection of fairness, consent and utilitarian theories of political obligation, the three other accounts he mentions. However, arguments against other theories can at best provide only indirect support for his particular theory – the weaknesses of other accounts do not furnish any positive reasons in its favour.

Second, there is the argument that the natural duty would be chosen by people in the original position (Rawls, 1999, ss. 3, 4). As explained earlier, the original position is a theoretical construct devised by Rawls to justify basic principles of justice: the central idea is that it is justified because 'chosen' (although it is not a real choice) in a situation that is accepted as fair. It would take us too far from our present purposes to explore this construct in more detail, but in any case Rawls's arguments in this context amount to little more than the claim that we need some principle of political obligation, and that the natural duty to support and to further just institutions seems preferable to any alternative. However, although Rawls's arguments in favour of the choice of the natural duty principle in the original position are not very strong (Rawls, 1999, s. 51), I do not think this means that we should simply reject it; for it could still offer a convincing account of political obligation, independent of Rawls's idea of the original position. In fact, it will not be possible entirely to ignore his theory of justice, as we shall see shortly, but at least initially we will focus on more general concerns.

One objection that has been advanced against the natural duty theory concerns whether it can convincingly encompass the 'particularity requirement', which I have argued is a necessary feature of any adequate account of political obligation. How, that is, does a general duty to support and promote just institutions bind members to a particular polity? After all, such a duty would seem to apply to them as persons or moral agents and not specifically as members of this or that particular polity. There are some obvious and compelling circumstantial reasons why it is likely in practice to be far easier to support or promote just institutions in the polity of which someone is a member and in which he or she resides. For example, we are normally called upon to observe the laws of our own polity much more often than those of other polities; we can campaign more effectively locally than in a different part of the world; our knowledge and understanding of our own community is likely to be much greater; and we are simply more likely to be involved on a day-to-day level with the institutions and practices of our political community than with those of any other. But, such practical considerations do not establish any distinctive duty attaching to membership of our polity: they merely explain why we are likely to have call to exercise this duty more frequently in relation to our own polity. The general duty would still apply equally to supporting or promoting just institutions in other polities as in our own.

Rawls may appear to have anticipated this objection and successfully circumvented it by writing of just institutions that 'apply to us'. The point here seems to be explicitly to distinguish the just institutions of the polity of which one is a member from other just polities of which one is not: that is one very plausible interpretation of what 'applies to us' means. However, it is precisely the apparently *ad hoc* character of this requirement – the sense that it is introduced only to rebut this potential criticism without having any other justification – that has aroused the suspicions of some of Rawls's critics (Simmons, 1979, pp. 147–52). Is it not more consistent and plausible, they ask, to hold that if there is a duty to support and promote just institutions, this duty is generally applicable: that wherever and whenever one has the opportunity, perhaps subject to the qualification about personal costs, one should support and promote just institutions? However, although this criticism has some force, it is not clear that it is entirely fair to Rawls. His theory of justice is a theory for a particular society. It is not only that his principles of justice apply within a particular society, but that the method by which they are arrived at or justified is also limited to the members of that society. Rawls does, therefore, have a reason, internal to his theory, for restricting the scope of this natural duty to the institutions of the society of which one is a member. Such a reply is at least consistent with his theory, and suggests that his limitation of the requirement of the natural duty to support just institutions to those that 'apply to us' may not be as arbitrary as his critics claim. How convincing one finds that response is likely to be determined in part by how sympathetic one is to Rawls's theory of justice, which is not a question it is possible to settle here.

Whatever the merits of this response to this first objection, there is also a second area of difficulty in his account of the natural duty to support and promote just institutions that needs to be considered. This relates to the importance of the *justice* of institutions to which we are bound. The worry here is about more than the endemic disputes about justice mentioned earlier, although the seriousness of such persistent contestation should not be underestimated. Although Rawls's theory of justice is supposed to go some considerable way towards eliminating that worry, there is an extensive literature that calls into doubt his success (e.g. Daniels, 1975). However, leaving aside these doubts, there is also the problem of how people stand in relation to institutions that do not meet the criteria of justice. Rawls claims that the natural duty obtains where institutions are 'just or nearly just', and it is not my intention here to exploit any possible difficulties in defining what is 'nearly just'. What, however, of institutions or polities that are not 'nearly just'? Do we have any natural duties (political obligations) in those cases? While the requirement that one should try to promote just institutions is of some

help, it does not take us very far in answering this question, which
concerns our response to institutions that are not nearly just or to institutions that are substantially unjust. And although it may seem self-
evident that people are under no obligation to support or comply with
unjust institutions, there are reasons for questioning this conclusion, as I
shall go on to explain.

Undeniably, there are some institutions so seriously unjust that there
is no decent alternative to a thoroughgoing opposition to them (although
interestingly the personal cost qualification that Rawls inserts might
suggest the reverse, because seriously unjust institutions or polities are
likely to be those that it is most risky and dangerous to oppose).
However, there is injustice and yet worse injustice. As the best is the
enemy of the good, so the worst is the enemy of the bad. Something like
this seems to underlie Hobbes's conception of political obligation; that
short of a direct threat to one's life one is better off under any political
authority than in the state of nature, which is the only alternative. But it
is not necessary to accept Hobbes's general theory to see that there is
some truth in the thought that sometimes at least it is better to support
bad or unjust institutions because the only realistic alternatives are
worse. This is a view that needs to be expressed with appropriate
caution for it can be, and often has been, exploited as a specious justification for complacency in the face of remediable injustice, but there
cannot be any convincing *a priori* argument to show that such a view is
never justified, and human history would suggest that there is a reasonable amount of evidence to support it. Compromise, pragmatism and
above all prudence are a necessary part of political morality in a world
that does not conform to the moral ideals of philosophers. Inevitably, in
practice, it may sometimes be difficult to distinguish these qualities
from opportunism, timidity or cowardice, but political life, more than
most areas of human activity, is not a realm in which it is sensible to
expect too much.

An account of political obligation must address itself realistically to
circumstances that are not ideal or nearly ideal, and even to situations
that are distinctly morally unappealing. A theory of civil disobedience
might do something to fill such a lacuna, but the problem runs much
deeper, as civil disobedience, too, may not always be appropriate either.
In some circumstances we may have an obligation to support institutions
considerably less than nearly just, yet Rawls's account of political obligation in terms of a natural duty to support just institutions is at best
silent, and at worst misleading, on this matter. The force of this point is
further enhanced when we consider that on Rawls's account of justice

(or, indeed, according to most theories of justice) few if any states, either present or past, meet or have met the conditions for being even nearly just. There is, perhaps, here a point of more general significance. Political philosophy necessarily involves some measure of idealization and simplification; it cannot accommodate all the rich complexity and nuance of political life. However, this tendency towards idealization has real dangers to which we need to be alert. What may begin as a seemingly laudable attempt to focus on essentials by abstracting from the incidental contingencies of political life can easily degenerate into a largely politically irrelevant idealized abstraction, bearing at best a very remote relationship to the world as we experience it. It is our world, not the idealizations of the theorist, which we have to try to understand and in which we have to decide how to act. And, correspondingly, any account of political obligation should seek to make sense of people's relationship to the polity of which they are actually members, rather than to a polity so idealized that it never has existed and likely never will.

Conclusion

Leaving aside the specific criticisms of Rawls, however, the conception of political obligation as a natural duty does, I believe, move us closer to a more adequate understanding of political obligation. It needs to be detached from Rawls's theory of justice, and to be significantly revised in other particulars, as I shall indicate in Chapter 6. Before proceeding to that argument, though, it is necessary to consider one response to the failure so far to come up with any very convincing general theory of political obligation: this is to draw the seemingly obvious conclusion that people do not generally have any political obligations. It may be granted that there are particular instances and circumstances where one or other of the theories is able to provide a more or less convincing justification of a few specific cases of political obligation, but none provides a convincing general account. Perhaps, therefore, for most people political obligation is a chimera. This kind of conclusion has become increasingly commonplace in recent years in the literature discussing political obligation: it is also a central strand in anarchist thought. It is appropriate, therefore, as a preliminary to the positive account of political obligation defended later, to examine the claims of those who deny that (most) people have any such obligations; and, in particular, to assess the merits of the various forms of anarchism.

5 Anarchism: Political and Philosophical

Taken together, the three preceding chapters have considered a wide variety of theories of political obligation, and all those that could be counted as standard theories. The upshot of the discussion so far is that, notwithstanding several of the approaches having distinctive merits, all are ultimately unconvincing: none of the theories provides a satisfactory general account of political obligation. Perhaps inevitably, the failure of these theories has given rise to real doubts about there being a convincing general account of political obligation, and it is therefore not surprising that a number of philosophers have come to more or less sceptical conclusions about the possibility of any philosophically cogent account of political obligation (e.g. Smith, 1973a; Wolff, 1976; Simmons, 1979, 2001). The perceived failure of attempts to justify political obligation has led in turn to the claim that there are few, if any, such obligations. In short, on this view, there is no special moral relationship between people and the polity of which they are members. Typically, this sceptical conclusion about political obligation is the basis for some kind of anarchism; and is the subject of this chapter. In particular, we shall be concerned with the question of the viability of the anarchist vision of political relations and whether the wholesale rejection of political obligation really offers a convincing alternative to the theories that have so far been rejected. If, as will be argued, this turns out not to be the case, then we shall need to return once more to our search for a more satisfactory account of political obligation.

Anarchism and political obligation

For the purposes of our discussion, anarchism will be considered principally as a theory or doctrine that rejects the possibility of any persuasive general theory of political obligation, although of course there is much more to anarchist thought than that. So, anarchism should not be understood as seeking to offer an *alternative* theory of political obligation, but rather as rejecting all such theories. It can be seen as a kind of limiting case in the discussion of political obligation. However, since matters are rarely clear cut, it should be noted immediately that anarchism broadly interpreted does not *necessarily* imply that people do not have any particular political duties, although many anarchists would in fact subscribe to such a view. This is because some anarchists do seem to embrace, perhaps without being fully aware of it, a residual and minimal, but non-statist, conception of political authority. Rather, what anarchists consistently reject is any robust *general* theory or account of political obligation; that is, an account which would explain, for example, why most people in modern states have political obligations. However, it is one of the main contentions of this chapter that anarchists do require something very like an account of political obligation if they are to be able to respond at all convincingly to some of the most common objections to anarchism. Inevitably, there remains some obscurity both about exactly what is or is not to count as a general theory of political obligation and what is a genuinely anarchist view. Although anarchism often provokes strongly proprietorial or sectarian responses among its adherents, the approach adopted here will be catholic rather than exclusionary: the principal task is not to try to define anarchism, but to assess the cogency of a broad range of positions that deny that any satisfactory general account of political obligation is possible.

Anarchism, like most moral and political theories, constitutes a rich and internally variegated tradition of thought and ideas rather than a single view or position, and there is perhaps some truth in the claim that 'one of the attractions of anarchism has been the extent to which it has offered something for everybody' (Joll, 1971, p. 213). It is not a simple doctrine, the tenets of which can be straightforwardly listed, and there are a number of more or less fundamental divisions and schisms within it. While something of a general nature will be said about anarchism to begin with, four reasonably distinct forms will be the focus of more detailed examination. In the subsequent discussion, therefore, anarchism is classified into two broad types that I label 'political' and 'philosophical'. Political anarchism is further divided into 'individualist' and 'communal' strands, while philosophical anarchism is divided into what I call 'positive' and 'negative' versions. This last distinction is broadly similar to that of A. J. Simmons between '*a priori*' and '*a posteriori*' philosophical anarchism (Simmons, 2001, pp. 104–5). To recap, the purpose of these discussions is to consider the merits and limitations of the various forms of anarchism as they bear on the problem of political obligation. No attempt, therefore, is made to provide a comprehensive assessment of anarchism as a political theory, although it is fair to say that the question of political obligation tends to lie at the heart of anarchism in all its forms. Indeed, the denial of political obligation has been one of the principal motivating forces of anarchist thought quite generally.

If there is one feature that unites anarchists, it is opposition to and rejection of the state (although, as will be explained later, negative philosophical anarchists are something of a partial exception to this and other generalizations about anarchism). As one commentator baldly states, 'opposition to the State is central to anarchism' (Carter, 1971, p. 28). And even negative philosophical anarchists will concur with this view of any actual states. Thus, A. J. Simmons asserts: 'commitment to one central claim unites all forms of anarchist political philosophy: all existing states are illegitimate' (Simmons, 2001, p. 103). Anarchists conceive the 'state' as a specific form of political organization with distinctive properties. David Miller summarizes these well as follows:

> 'First, the state is a *sovereign* body, in the sense that it claims complete authority to define the rights of its subjects – it does not, for instance allow subjects to maintain customary rights which it has neither created nor endorsed. Second, the state is a *compulsory* body, in the sense that everyone born into a given society is forced to recognize obligations to the state that governs that society – one cannot opt out of these obligations except by leaving the society itself. Third, the state is a *monopolistic* body: it claims a monopoly of force in its territorial area, allowing no competitor to exist alongside it. Fourth, the state is a *distinct* body, in the sense that the roles and functions which compose it are separate from social roles and functions generally, and also that the people who compose the state for the most part form a distinct class – the politicians, bureaucrats, armed forces and police.' (Miller, 1984, p. 5)

There is some disagreement among anarchists about the extent to which forms of political organization other than the state are open to similar objections to those they make against states; but, as a rough rule of thumb, the more state-like a political entity the greater the hostility towards it likely to be shown by anarchists. Yet, it is important to appreciate that few anarchists reject all forms of government or political organization. The common use of the term 'anarchy' or 'anarchic' to mean chaotic, disorganized or the absence of order would be a pejorative parody if taken as some kind of representation of anarchist political thinking (which is not to deny that some anarchists have advocated anarchy in this colloquial sense as a political tactic). Generally, though, anarchists favour a non-coercive social order and not the absence of order *per se*; typically, that is a social order without soldiers, policemen, bureaucrats and other functionaries of the coercive apparatus of the state. What, though, is it that anarchists characteristically object to about the state (or state-like entities), and how does this bear on political obligation?

One objection to the state that is common among anarchists is that it is a harmful and destructive institution. The state is divisive, inegalitarian, punitive, restrictive and antisocial. By 'antisocial' what is meant is that the state is destructive of those natural social bonds that arise uncoercively through cooperation, mutual respect or affection. For many anarchists it is these bonds that genuinely hold society together and not the laws, threats and institutionalized violence of the state. Most anarchists probably subscribe to one or other version of what has been called the 'theory of spontaneous order':

> 'the theory that, given a common need, a collection of people will, by trial and error, by improvisation and experiment, evolve order out of the situation – this order being more durable and more closely related to their needs than any kind of externally imposed authority could be.' (Ward, 1973, p. 28)

Sometimes this theory is supported by references to seminal historical events, such as the early years of the French Revolution and the Paris Commune, and sometimes by invoking the experience of local cooperatives or self-help groups. While these are essentially empirical claims about the relative effects of states and voluntary associations, for most anarchists they have the status of almost self-evident or axiomatic truths.

Thus, it is not the reform of bad states to which anarchists aspire; for most, this would be a self-defeating exercise. Rather, what anarchists seek is the end of states: their abolition and not their improvement. Bakunin provides a typically colourful and uncompromising statement of this view:

> 'It is obvious that freedom will not be restored to humanity, and that the true interests of society – whether of groups, of local organizations or of all the individuals who compose society – will find true satisfaction only when there are no more States. It is obvious that all the

so-called general interests which the State is reputed to represent, and which in reality are nothing else than the general and continuing nega-tion of the positive interests of regions, communes, associations and the vast majority of individuals subjected to the State, are in fact an abstraction, a fiction, a lie.' (Quoted in Woodcock, 1977, p. 81)

Inevitably, the plausibility of many of the anarchist claims will be contested. If, for the sake of argument, the empirical accuracy of their characterization of states is accepted – itself of course highly contestable – much will depend upon the extent to which the failings of states are open to ameliorative action and, equally importantly, one's view of the likely consequences of their preferred alternatives. Even if states are pretty bad, the familiar reply is that we would be even worse off without them, an issue that will be pursued later. Often at the root of arguments between anarchists and their critics, as with many such disagreements, are differing conceptions of human nature and differing views about what constitutes the necessary conditions of a tolerable or worthwhile social life. These are not issues that can be explored in full here, and in any case most of them are not issues that it seems possible to resolve with any finality (Berry, 1986). There is, however, one point that is worth making in defence of anarchism at this stage: this is that anarchists need not, and mostly do not, subscribe to the absurdly perfectionist account of human nature with which they are sometimes saddled by their critics. It is true that anarchists generally will be inclined towards the more optimistic end of the continuum of views about human nature, though for many this applies only to a suitably socialized conception of human nature; but they need not be committed to the view that life in an anarchic condition will be entirely harmonious and without conflict, or be free from disappointments and frustrations. Arguably, all that the anarchist needs to show is that human life will be better without the state than with it: certainly, there need be no accompanying image of an idyllic and tranquil utopia in which all significant disagreement is absent and human life is perpetually untroubled and serene. However, granting this point, whether or not anarchist views of human nature remain unre-alistically optimistic is an important and unavoidable issue in assessing its merits.

A second objection that anarchists make to the state and its institu-tions, and one that is of particular interest in the context of political obli-gation, is that the state has no authority over, or no right to compel, coerce and otherwise control, its citizens. With the decline of beliefs about the divine right of kings and natural hierarchy as bases for political authority, the question arises about what entitles the state or government to command, and ultimately to coerce, its citizens. Anarchists maintain that the state has no such authority and that the various attempts, such as social contract theory, to show that it does are at heart a sham and a fraud. And the discussion of the various theories of political obligation so far in this book tends to support the anarchist view in this respect. According to most anarchists the state basically consists of one group of people dominating and coercing another, invariably much larger, group of people. There are, as will be seen later, two versions of this claim. The strongest and most ambitious, associated particularly with positive philosophical anarchism, asserts that the very idea of legitimate political authority is conceptually incoherent. The second, more modest, claim is that although legitimate authority is in principle possible, states and state-like institutions do not in fact possess it, and cannot in reality do so; principally because the nature of the modern state is incompatible with the requirements of such authority. In either version, the anarchist challenge to the authority of the state, if successful, is deeply subversive of any general conception of political obligation.

Before proceeding to a consideration of the four different forms of anarchism identified earlier, it is first helpful to articulate the broad lines of the distinction between political and philosophical anarchism. This distinction turns on the basis of the rejection of the authority of the state, and is most clearly manifest in what follows from it. Political anarchists are almost by definition inclined to view the state as an evil institution that must be destroyed as a precondition of human liberation and flourishing. In their view, not merely do people have no political obligations to their state, they should actively oppose its existence. Philosophical anarchists on the other hand, while denying that states have any legitimate political authority, do not *necessarily* conclude from this that the state must be abolished or even that it should be actively resisted. For philosophical anarchists, the question of whether one should support a state depends largely upon what a state does. In so far as the state performs a valuable role it may be appropriate to support it; but not because it has any particular authority either to do what it does or to command allegiance.

The political implications of philosophical anarchism are, therefore, much more open-ended and indeterminate than for political anarchism. In short, political anarchists are principally exercised by the practical effects of the state, especially its allegedly socially destructive consequences, while philosophical anarchists are more narrowly identified by their denying the state any claim to political authority, but leaving open questions about how one should respond to actual states, notwithstanding their illegitimacy. Inevitably, this distinction is somewhat rough and ready, yet it marks a real divide: indeed, many political anarchists would reject the claims of philosophical anarchists to be genuine anarchists at all. However, as observed earlier, because our concern is not to distinguish the 'authentic' voice of anarchism or to identify true believers, this particular question will not be pursued further here. Rather, our concern will be to consider political obligation in the context of these four strands of thought, and for this purpose nothing of significance really depends on whether or not they are labelled as 'anarchist'. Anarchism in this context is perhaps best understood as an analytic construct and only incidentally, if at all, as an indication of a specific political commitment.

In any case, it would be wrong to exaggerate the affinities even between the different strands of political anarchism. At the extremes, individualist and communal anarchism share very little other than their antipathy to the state and a superficially similar commitment to the value of freedom. The positive visions informing them and their underlying assumptions are often radically divergent, and their rival advocates and supporters are often intensely hostile to each other. Individualist anarchism is firmly rooted in a belief in the sovereignty of the independent, atomistic individual, subject to no moral claims other than that of respecting a system of rights that involves no more than the recognition of the similar independence of other sovereign individuals. By contrast, communal anarchism is much concerned with social solidarity and mutual interdependence. One basic aspect of this difference is well brought out by David Miller, and explains why I referred to their common commitment to the value of freedom as superficial:

> 'Individualists and communists [communal anarchists] would no doubt agree that their fundamental aim was personal freedom: but whereas individualists would define this negatively, as the absence of interference or coercion, communists would define it positively, as the opportunity to satisfy needs and wants, and claim that, far from one person's freedom being limited by the freedom of others, no one could be really free except in a solidaristic community where each person worked to promote the well-being of the rest.' (Miller, 1984, p. 45)

It is principally these differences and the theoretical disagreements that underlie them that necessitate the separate consideration of individualist and communal strands in anarchist thought. I begin by considering individualist political anarchism.

Individualist political anarchism

Individualist political anarchism is marked by its attachment to the independence of the individual. It is a doctrine that was mostly developed in the nineteenth century, largely as an extreme version of classical liberalism. Classical liberals, though always suspicious of the role of the state, had felt it necessary, at least to some extent, to embrace it as a guarantor of personal liberty, but individualist anarchists followed through liberal suspicion of the state to its furthest point. Whereas for classical liberals the state is at least a necessary evil, for individualist anarchists it is simply an evil. In their view, each person possesses a right to his or her own life, liberty and property; each may act without inhibition or restriction, provided only that they do not violate the similar rights of others. Again, it is helpful to quote Miller:

> 'Each person was seen as having an inviolable sphere of action within which he reigned supreme, encompassing both his body and the property he had rightfully acquired. Within the privileged sphere he could act just as he pleased, and moreover he was entitled to give away or exchange anything that fell within it. Thus people met as sovereign in their own territories. The legitimate relations between them were those of exchange, contract and gift.' (Miller, 1984, p. 30)

Everybody has a right to defend him or herself against unjustified attack, and the only obligations that people have is not to infringe the rights of others. Social relations are basically contractual and are understood as essentially similar to economic relations within a free market. Each person may pursue his or her own ends unobstructed by others; altruism is permissible but there is no requirement to show any positive concern for others, including providing material support for those who would otherwise be destitute. As can be seen, this form of anarchism is typically rooted in a doctrine of natural rights that take the form of rights of non-interference. These rights require us only to refrain from interfering with others' actions; they establish merely negative duties and impose no positive duties upon us to protect, succour, support or in any way assist other people. It is an outlook often associated with extreme laissez-faire economics, thoroughgoing moral permissiveness, vehement opposition to all welfare legislation and a belief that any form of compulsory economic redistribution is wicked. Such a view has been especially prominent in the United States where it was developed in the nineteenth century by thinkers such as Lysander Spooner (1966) and Benjamin

Tucker (1893), and its modern exponents include David Friedman (1973) and Murray Rothbard (1978).

Individualist anarchism is deeply antithetic to political obligation. In principle such anarchism is compatible with a voluntary contract to form a state but individualist anarchists believe that in fact no states have been based upon a contract. Lysander Spooner, for instance, ridiculed the claims of the US government to authority based on a contract embedded in the Constitution (Spooner, 1966). Furthermore, individual anarchists also maintain that no sane adult would ever voluntarily enter into such a contract. To agree to such a contract would be tantamount to voluntarily becoming a slave, and this is not an option that would be chosen by an even minimally rational person. For the individualist anarchist, a contract (or any similar voluntary agreement) is the only possible source of political authority and the only legitimate basis for political obligation; but since there is no such contract, there is correspondingly no authority and no obligation. Political obligation is a fraud or delusion perpetrated by governments: there are only individuals with their rights and the relationships that they voluntarily choose to enter into with each other. The state, and indeed all non-voluntary forms of government, is simply a means by which some people exploit and coerce other people.

The vision of the individualist anarchist is austere and uncompromising, but it is also impoverished and neglectful of some basic truths about the human condition and the circumstances of human development. All human beings begin life as vulnerable and entirely dependent, not merely briefly or inadvertently but unavoidably and for many years. Before any human being can become the independent bearer of the right to non-interference of individualist anarchism, he or she must be fed, clothed, tended when sick, educated and more generally cared for and nurtured. While much of this will spring from love or goodwill on the part of parents and those with a sympathetic interest, such goodwill cannot always be relied upon, either because it may not be present or because it may not have access to the material resources necessary for it to be effective. Furthermore, although such dependence is most extensive and clearly apparent in infancy and childhood, it does not disappear with maturity. None of us can effectively insure ourselves against all of life's contingencies; some adversities and misfortunes can only be reliably overcome, or at least their worst aspects mitigated, by recognizing a shared human predicament and creating common institutions that imply general obligations of aid to each other. Thus, although individualist anarchism rightly recognizes as a basic fact that there is a straightforward sense in which we are each separate individuals, it ignores the complementary truth that we are not self-sufficient beings. Society and social relations are as much a reality as individuality: we experience life through our living with others in circumstances that are not, and never can be, entirely of our own choosing. We are all unavoidably the product, in major part, of the culture, practices and social relations within which we are nurtured and develop. The myth of the 'self-made man' (and it usually is a man), in the sense of someone who has achieved success unaided by others, is one of the more pernicious delusions of capitalism. Further, it is implausible to believe that society could ever be intelligible, simply and without remainder, in terms of voluntary contractual relations between separate individuals: language, culture and a whole range of social institutions cannot be so understood. Rather, each of us is born into a complex web of social relations, institutions, practices and culture that contribute to making us what we are; and which, crucially, carry with them normative dimensions. These cannot all be conceived of as wholly external to a self-sufficient individual with a core or essence substantially independent of such formative experiences, and nor can they be fully understood entirely without reference to any normative concepts and attachments.

It may be asked of the individualist anarchist, therefore, why only duties of non-interference should be recognized as morally compelling. One difficulty here is that it is notoriously difficult to provide a very plausible derivation of natural rights. There is little agreement among those who have attempted this task, and the problems that confront any such undertaking are very considerable. Second, why should we believe that we owe others nothing? Why should we not think that, by way of reciprocity at least, we owe others for our succour and support? Implicitly, but fundamentally, individualist anarchists tend to rely on institutions such as the family to provide an essential substratum of social life. Yet, even, for example, where parental support for children is entirely voluntary and uncoerced, does it follow that the children acquire no obligations to their parents? Why should it be assumed that some rights of non-interference are 'natural' but not, for example, obligations of gratitude? Individualist anarchism suffers from a peculiarly myopic social vision in this as in other respects. Further, are parents who are not inclined to care voluntarily for their children under any obligation to do so? If the parents cannot be made to do so, or are unable or incapable of doing so, does the obligation fall on the community? While there could be an attempt to answer the former question in terms of the voluntary act of procreation – although I do not think that this would be sufficient – no such answer is possible to the second question. So, unless we are prepared to accept there is no obligation at all to care for children without parental support, then there are at least some obligations other than those arising from natural rights to non-interference. In short, leaving aside the very considerable problems involved in interpreting and justifying natural rights, especially property rights, the moral perspective informing individualist anarchism seems unjustifiably truncated and arbitrary: it neither embraces a consistent amoralism nor a morality rich enough to encompass even the minimal standards of moral concern essential for social life.

These criticisms are not sufficient to show that individualist anarchists are necessarily wrong to reject the state or that their denial of political obligation must be mistaken. Rather, they are intended to cast doubt in a more general way on the coherence and attractiveness of the ontological assumptions and moral implications of individualist anarchism. They suggest that it is not merely political obligation but, ultimately, the viability of any sustainable set of social arrangements that is undermined by individualist anarchism. Individualist anarchism inclines towards a picture of human relations that is neither metaphysically nor morally persuasive, implying as it does an essentially atomistic conception of the person. Persons, however, are necessarily social; and as such are partly constituted through a social context that cannot be understood simply as a consequence of their prior choices (Taylor, 1985, ch. 7). In this way, though individualist anarchists could still be right to reject the whole idea of political obligation, their own case for doing so is deeply flawed. However, the same objections cannot be levelled against the other form of political anarchism. Communal anarchism is acutely sensitive to the social character of human life, and it does not rest on assumptions about the sovereignty of the atomistic individual; reciprocity and mutual obligation are an essential part of the communal anarchist's vision, and it is to that embodiment of anarchism that we now turn.

Communal anarchism

What I call 'communal anarchism' is a view associated with the classical anarchists such as Bakunin, Kropotkin and Proudhon. It is a view that shares much with the socialist tradition of political thought; and, indeed, its proponents are often inclined to see it as the authentic voice of socialist aspirations. Whatever the merits of such a claim, there is one respect in which communal anarchism is clearly distinct from many varieties of socialism. Communal anarchists reject the state and other forms of politically centralized or professionalized control that have been mainstream to much of socialist theory and practice. This centralizing strand in socialism is something that anarchists are keen to resist. Historically, the division between anarchists and other socialists was initiated by Marx's critique of Proudhon and emerged most clearly in the split between Marx and Bakunin around 1870 and the bitter disputes within the First International, which marked both a theoretical and political bifurcation within socialism – a division which continued well into the twentieth century (Woodcock, 1963, ch. 9). It is a dispute that is also reflected in debates today within political groups that have some affinities with anarchism, such as parts of the Green movement. Of course, many non-anarchist socialists have also favoured a significant measure of devolution of power, and the division is not always a clear or sharp one. Conversely, anarchists have been able to appeal to Marx's vision of communist society in *The German Ideology* as one of their inspirations. Initially, the dispute was more about means than ends, though increasingly in the twentieth century, beginning perhaps in very different ways with Leninist notions of 'democratic centralism' and Fabian elitism, a socialist tradition has developed in which some form of political centralization is seen as unavoidable, if not always desirable. Thus, what began largely as a dispute about the most effective means of instituting a particular form of society on which there was at least notional agreement developed into a disagreement about the form of society that best represents a desirable and realistic aspiration. The reason many socialists have come to reject the communal anarchist vision of society is that it has increasingly appeared to many of them as utopian, in the pejorative sense of not merely being unrealized but of being unrealizable in the technological conditions necessary for the material abundance on which the achievement of socialism depends. This is a point to which we shall return later.

While the spirit informing communal anarchism is very different from that of individualist anarchism, both share a general rejection of coercion (except under very specific and limited circumstances) and a desire to base social organization upon a principle of free association and some notion of equality. Communal anarchists are inclined to a more benign and cooperative conception of human nature – they believe that people will naturally join together to form groups to coordinate economic activities and provide mutual aid and support for each other. People are not the atomistic bearers of natural rights so much as mutually concerned and interrelated, but independent-minded, individuals. In particular, communal anarchists reject individualistic anarchists' views about the sanctity of private property. Nor is communal anarchism neglectful of, or at all embarrassed by, the fact that individuals grow up within societies and are socialized accordingly. This has two aspects for communal anarchists. On the one hand, it is the principal source of nationalism and the 'false consciousness' that explains people's attachment to their state and their failure to appreciate the real situation in which they find themselves in the modern state. On the other hand, it also offers hope for the future, for if people are brought up in accordance with their true nature, then this will make an anarchist community a genuine possibility. For communal anarchists, an authentic society is seen as a shifting series of common practices and cooperative arrangements to which people voluntarily subscribe and which are subject to continuous reaffirmation and re-creation: relations are basically harmonious; although, as mentioned earlier, this does not preclude either diversity or non class-based disagreement and conflict.

Communal anarchist conceptions of social obligation or responsibility, however, are rather obscure: it is not a subject that receives much emphasis within communal anarchism. There is a tendency for its proponents to subscribe implicitly to a benign form of ethical naturalism, believing that once the oppressive and corrupting influence of the organized coercion of the state is removed, the more naturally cooperative and beneficent aspects of human nature will naturally rise to the surface. Communal anarchists are certainly not unaware of the problems of social coordination and antisocial behaviour but they rely on education, custom and emergent voluntary associations to solve these problems. They believe that once private property has been eliminated people will be motivated to work without material incentives and that social problems, particularly crime, will significantly diminish. The Russian anarchist, Peter Kropotkin, provides a good example of a communal anarchist's approach to the problem of antisocial behaviour:

'Man is a result of those conditions in which he has grown up. Let him grow in habits of useful work; let him be brought by his earlier life to consider humanity as one great family, no member of which can be injured without the injury being felt by a wide circle of his fellows, and ultimately by the whole of society; let him acquire a taste for the highest enjoyments of science and art – much more lofty and durable than those given by the satisfaction of lower passions – and we may be sure that we shall not have many breaches of those laws of morality which are an unconscious affirmation of the best conditions for life in society.' (Quoted in Woodcock, 1977, pp. 362–3)

Elsewhere, Kropotkin sharply distinguishes custom from law and accepts the need for political organization, allowing even that it might properly be called 'government', so long as it emerges naturally from social life (Kropotkin, 1970). For Kropotkin, law is an essentially arbitrary and coercive imposition of the will of a minority, whereas custom is the coagulation of the spontaneous cooperation among people in response to their common needs. The state is institutionalized coercion, 'government' is a natural process of social coordination. Proudhon, who was rather less optimistic about human nature, seems to allow even greater scope for institutions of coordination within his idea of 'mutualism', which to some degree sought to reconcile property with communism, and through his conception of 'federation' (Proudhon, 1979). The problem is that this recognition of the need for institutional forms of social regulation and control starts to undermine the non-coercive character of communal anarchism: much seems to depend on the contention that custom and other forms of cooperative arrangements are non-coercive. The key question is: how plausible is this claim?

Coercion and constraint are matters of degree, and notions of complete and absolute freedom or pure liberty are incoherent, as anarchists such as Proudhon explicitly acknowledged (Proudhon, 1979). However, communal anarchists are more inclined to recognize this in their writings on different forms of social arrangements than in the rhetoric of their uncompromising condemnation of the state. Thus, communal anarchists are somewhat ambivalent about the extent to which custom and the institutions of social coordination must be constraining or coercive (Ritter, 1980). In response to the common criticism of anarchism that it is utopian and unrealistic, anarchists are inclined to stress, in addition to the positive power of education, the serious consequences of social ostracism, refusal to cooperate and expulsion from the community. Unfortunately, while these features of anarchist forms of social control may rebut the charge of ineffectiveness, they do so at the cost of undermining their claim to embody an absence of coercive constraint. If people have little real choice but to observe prevailing customs and to engage in social cooperation on whatever terms happen to exist, lest they suffer serious economic and social disadvantage, then the element of voluntary choice would appear to be significantly reduced, and the supposed contrast, for example with the coercion exercised by capitalist employers and the state, seriously weakened.

Furthermore, much of what we know of small-scale self-regulating communities does not suggest that they are characteristically marked by freedom and diversity, and the anarchist emphasis upon 'education' can easily be thought to be sinister in the light of the twentieth century experience of totalitarianism. Nor, in the absence of institutions ensuring fairness and impartiality in the treatment of both complainants and offenders, is one likely to have much confidence in purely informal systems for the investigation, adjudication and arbitration of disputes. It must also be something of an embarrassment to anarchists that most of the many experimental anarchist communities have ended in failure and discord. An inhospitable external environment may do something to excuse some of these failures, but it is palpably unsatisfactory as an all-purpose explanation of them: historical studies of anarchist communities have clearly demonstrated the importance of internal conflicts and disputes in generating fragmentation and dissolution (Woodcock, 1963, pt 2; Miller, 1984, ch. 11).

There is, therefore, a deep tension at the heart of communal anarchist thinking between a hostility to coercion, the importance of independent judgement and the value of self-determination on the one hand, and on the other the recognition that if society is to hold together there will need to be both a widespread moral consensus and very high levels of virtue among the citizenry. Political obligation in such a context is deeply problematic. The idea of a compulsory association, such as the state making demands of its members, is antithetic to the most fundamental convictions of communal anarchists, yet some well developed and fairly demanding conception of 'social' obligation is implied by the positive vision of how an anarchic community might survive and flourish. It is in large part because of this problem that communal anarchists are rarely able, in their positive vision of an anarchist society, to redeem fully the ringing rhetoric that informs their denunciations of political authority when criticizing existing practices and institutions.

It is important to recognize that the issue here is not whether some other set of institutions might be preferable to those that currently exist – one would have to be remarkably complacent to believe that no improvements at all are possible – but whether anarchists can coherently, consistently and realistically do without institutions that exercise coercive authority. The burden of the argument in this section has been that they cannot, and that this is shown in the work of the classical communal anarchists such as Proudhon and Kropotkin. There is a more or less implicit recognition that social life is impossible without a significant element of coercion: the questions which then arise are not about the need for coercion but about who is to exercise it, for what purposes and subject to what limits. These are the unavoidable issues of political life and are equally the concern of political philosophers of whatever persuasion – of Plato and Hobbes as much as of anarchists. Hence, communal anarchists, notwithstanding their apparently explicit repudiation of political obligation, seem surreptitiously to reintroduce coercion, or to rely on suspiciously similar surrogates that are open to more or less the same objections as those that anarchists make against the coercive authority of the state. The approach to political obligation that is likely to be most consistent with the assumptions and values of communal anarchism is some form of voluntarism. Only a voluntarist account is likely to minimize the coercive aspects of political authority that are so objectionable to anarchists. However, this is an approach the limitations of which have been considered already, in Chapter 2, and thus it is unnecessary to pursue the issue further here. Instead, we now need to see whether philosophical anarchism fares any better than political anarchism.

Philosophical anarchism

Whereas political anarchists are almost inevitably strongly motivated to seek the destruction of the state, as A. J. Simmons notes:

> 'What is distinctive about philosophical anarchism . . . is its stance with respect to the moral content (or practical force) of judgments about state illegitimacy. Philosophical anarchists do not take the illegitimacy of states to entail a strong moral imperative to oppose or eliminate states; rather, they typically take state illegitimacy simply to remove any strong moral presumption in favour of obedience to, compliance with, or support for our own or other existing states.' (Simmons, 2001, p. 104)

Philosophical anarchists typically arrive at their conclusions about political obligation by one (or both) of two broad routes. The first, which might be called justification by default, simply concludes from the failure of all positive attempts to justify political obligation that there is no such obligation. The claim that people are under some form of political obligation needs to be justified; and none of any of the supposed justifications is successful; hence, by default, there is no reason to think that there are any (or many, excluding some special circumstances) political obligations. Simmons objects to this characterization of negative philosophical anarchism because:

> '"The failure of all positive attempts" is only a reason (let alone a good reason) to reject political obligation if one also believes that these posi-

tive attempts add up to a complete or comprehensive attempt (refuting a handful of miserable, silly, half-hearted, or obviously incomplete positive efforts to show that X clearly gives one no reason to believe not-X). "Negative" anarchist arguments thus need to be based either in an ideal of legitimacy (which existing states can be shown not to exemplify) or in some account of what an acceptably complete positive account would look like.' (Simmons, 2001, pp. 105–6, n. 8)

I do not think that this criticism is quite right. Naturally, it is assumed (and is surely obvious) that philosophical anarchism must engage seriously with the best arguments in favour of political obligation that are offered, as Simmons himself does. However, we could never know that we have considered every possible argument, and while many negative philosophical anarchists, like Simmons, do have their own ideal of legitimacy, this need not be the case. The negative philosophical anarchist can simply hold that none of the positive arguments for political obligation succeed by their own standards, and nor can they unless and until someone proposes some satisfactory alternative standards that are more convincing. Thus, philosophical anarchism can reasonably be understood as what remains when all the available arguments in favour of political obligation have been shown to fail. This form of philosophical anarchism will be considered more fully shortly.

The second broad route by which some philosophical anarchists arrive at their view, however, is bolder; relying not only on the failure of attempts to justify political obligation, but offering positive arguments of their own as to why there are not, and could not be, any political obligations. The potential power of positive philosophical anarchism is obvious. Negative philosophical anarchism is necessarily open to the emergence of new arguments to justify political obligation, whereas positive philosophical anarchism, if successful, closes off this possibility. Correspondingly, the greater ambition of positive philosophical anarchism leaves more scope for a critical response: its defenders have to provide a convincing argument and not merely rely on the argumentative failures of their adversaries. Thus, it may be appropriate to think of positive philosophical anarchism as the strong or more ambitious version of philosophical anarchism and the negative approach as the weak or more modest version of this position. Of course, these terms say nothing about the plausibility of either of them.

One of the earliest statements of a view that can be plausibly thought of as embracing positive philosophical anarchism can be found in the work of the eighteenth-century utilitarian and anarchist, William

Godwin. Godwin held a unique combination of views, for he believed that the rigorous utilitarianism that he espoused also issued in broadly anarchist political conclusions. This apparently unlikely conjuncttion of ideas resulted from a highly distinctive feature of Godwin's thought: his claim that although we are each obligated to promote the general happiness, we are all both entitled to decide for ourselves whether or not to adopt such an obligation and also free to determine how best to implement it. This is what Godwin calls 'the principle of private judgement' (Godwin, 1976, bk 2, ch. 6). As has been seen already, some such principle is central to most anarchists' thinking, but it is fundamental to positive philosophical anarchism. However, having noted Godwin's contribution, this will not be explored further here. Instead, the focus will be on the most recent, explicit and sophisticated formulation of positive philosophical anarchism: this is to be found in the work of R. P. Wolff.

In his *In Defense of Anarchism* Wolff argues that any recognition of political authority is inconsistent with the over-riding obligation that each person has to act as an autonomous moral agent. As Wolff expresses it:

'The defining mark of the state is authority, the right to rule. The primary obligation of man is autonomy, the refusal to be ruled. It would seem then that there can be no resolution of the conflict between the autonomy of the individual and the putative authority of the state . . . If all men have a continuing obligation to achieve the highest degree of autonomy possible, then there would appear to be no state whose subjects have a moral obligation to obey its commands. Hence, the concept of a *de jure* legitimate state would appear to be vacuous, and philosophical anarchism would seem to be the only reasonable political belief for an enlightened man.' (Wolff, 1976, pp. 18–19)

He therefore claims that moral autonomy and political authority cannot be reconciled, and he concludes from this that:

'if autonomy and authority are genuinely incompatible, only two courses are open to us. Either we must embrace philosophical anarchism and treat *all* governments as non-legitimate bodies whose commands must be judged and evaluated in each instance before they are obeyed; or else, we must give up as quixotic the pursuit of autonomy in the political realm and submit ourselves (by an implicit promise) to whatever form of government appears most just and beneficent at the moment.' (Wolff, 1976, p. 71)

As 'the fundamental assumption of moral philosophy is that men are responsible for their actions' and because 'moral autonomy is simply the condition of taking full responsibility for one's actions, it follows that men cannot forfeit their autonomy at will' (Wolff, 1976, pp. 12–14) and 'it is out of the question to give up the commitment to moral autonomy' (Wolff, 1876, pp. 71–2). Thus, any claim to political authority must be jettisoned. It is important to note here that Wolff is not denying that it may be morally right in some circumstances to do what a state commands, for there may be many morally convincing reasons for so doing that have nothing to do with a state's commanding the action. However, he is denying the claim that the state's commanding something is, as such, ever a reason for doing what it commands; the philosophical anarchist will not regard laws and edicts as having any authoritative claim on a person merely because they issue from a state or government, whatever its form or constitution. For the philosophical anarchist, as Wolff bluntly expresses it: 'all authority is equally illegitimate' (Wolff, 1976, p. 19).

Wolff's conception of autonomy is clearly central to his argument and we therefore need to examine it a little more closely. His approach is broadly Kantian in claiming that:

> 'moral autonomy is a combination of freedom and responsibility; it is a submission to laws which one has made for oneself. The autonomous man, insofar as he is autonomous, is not subject to the will of another. He may do what another tells him, but not *because* he has been told to do it . . . That is to say, a man cannot decide to obey the commands of another without making any attempt to determine for himself whether what is commanded is good or wise.' (Wolff, 1976, p. 14)

If this amounted only to the contention that no person can entirely escape responsibility for his or her actions, then there would be little with which to argue. Further, if he were simply warning against an uncritical acceptance of the claims of authority, then his exhortation might be regarded as laudable. Wolff, however, is arguing for something much more robust than either of these rather innocuous claims. The particular force of his argument from autonomy comes from combining the claim that we have a duty to preserve and enhance our autonomy with the claim that others commanding or requiring us to act in certain ways cannot function as moral reasons for action at all for the autonomous person. For Wolff, being the author of one's actions is not simply a fairly weak postulate or presupposition of moral agency but is itself a value or ideal that agents should aspire to realize to the maximum extent possible:

'There are great, perhaps insurmountable, obstacles to the achievement of a complete and rational autonomy in the modern world.
Nevertheless, so long as we recognize our responsibility for our
actions, and acknowledge the power of reason within us, we must
acknowledge as well the continuing obligation to make ourselves the
authors of such commands as we may obey.' (Wolff, 1976, p. 17)

It is clear that autonomy in this sense is for Wolff the over-riding moral
obligation of every person. The implication is that we must deny any and
all claims to be in a position of authority, not least those of the agents of
the state. Claims to such authority, therefore, cannot give anyone good
reasons for acting as the self-proclaimed authorities command.

Wolff proceeds to consider and reject various attempts to reconcile
moral autonomy and political authority. These will not be discussed
here, for if his argument about the nature of authority and autonomy is
correct such attempts are necessarily doomed to failure. Although Wolff
is not always as clear as he might be about the status of his argument, I
take it to be primarily an argument about the *logical* inconsistency of
autonomy and authority. It is true that this is confused by Wolff's
puzzling admission that a state based on universal direct democracy
would be legitimate, while also believing it would involve an unjustified
surrender of moral autonomy. This admission has led some commentators to assert that his argument is not really about logical impossibility at
all, but more simply and familiarly about the moral undesirability of
political authority (e.g. Frankfurt, 1973). While this is one possible
reading of Wolff's argument, it is not the most plausible, and would
anyway make it much less interesting and distinctive. Thus, I shall
continue to assume that the argument does attempt to demonstrate the
logical impossibility of morally justified political authority. Moreover,
this reading seems to accord best with Wolff's apparent intentions for, as
he puts it, 'the arguments of this essay suggest that the just state must be
consigned [to] the category of the round square, the married bachelor,
and the unsensed sense-datum' (Wolff, 1976, p. 71). He could hardly be
clearer that reconciling political authority and moral autonomy is not a
practical difficulty but a logical impossibility. Clearly, if he is right then
there cannot be a satisfactory theory or justification of political obligation. Furthermore, he is equally candid in drawing attention to the way
in which his position is deeply subversive of there being any morally
significant sense in which people are members of their polity: he denies
that there is any special moral relationship between persons and the
political community of which they are members:

'In a sense, we might characterize the anarchist as a man without a country, for despite the ties which bind him to the land of his child-hood, he stands in precisely the same moral relationship to "his" government as he does to the government of any other country in which he might happen to be staying for a time. When I [Wolff is a US citizen] take a vacation in Great Britain, I obey its laws, both because of prudential self-interest and because of the obvious moral consider-ations concerning the value of order, the general good consequences of preserving a system of property, and so forth. On my return to the United States, I have a sense of re-entering my country, and if I think about the matter at all, I imagine myself to stand in a different and more intimate relation to American laws. They have been promulgated by my government, and I therefore have a special obligation to obey them. But the anarchist tells me that my feeling is purely sentimental and has no objective moral basis . . . My obedience to American laws, if I am to be morally autonomous, must proceed from the same considerations which determine me abroad.' (Wolff, 1976, pp. 18–19)

This raises important issues, some of which will be touched upon later, but it is the alleged logical inconsistency of authority and moral auton-omy that needs to be examined first, for this is the linchpin of Wolff's argument. It is on the validity of this claim that the persuasiveness of his argument ultimately depends.

There are, or so I shall suggest, two features of Wolff's argument that are especially open to challenge. First, there is the claim that moral autonomy has the status of an over-riding moral obligation. He does not really argue for this conclusion but simply asserts that it cannot reason-ably be denied. However, this claim seems to exploit an element of ambiguity in the idea of moral autonomy. The view that we should take responsibility for our own actions is perhaps unexceptionable, or at least can be accepted for the sake of argument here. This is not, however, obviously incompatible with acting on the authority of others, as Wolff at times appears to concede. In this sense, autonomy is a presupposition of agency and implies only that agents take some responsibility for their own actions, even when acting on someone else's authority. This is because in acting on someone else's authority one is still choosing so to act, and one remains responsible for that decision. The command of an authority 'determines' the action of the agent only because an agent decides to follow the command; the agent chooses to act as the author-ity requires. As has been frequently pointed out, acting under someone's authority involves both judgement, accepting that this or that person has authority, and a decision to act in accordance with what the authority commands (see Winch, 1972). Neither the faculties of judgement, nor those of choice or decision, are short circuited when an agent acts in accordance with the instructions of an authority. So, in this respect, while Wolff is correct to claim that autonomy is a presupposition of moral action and therefore *qua* moral agent cannot be repudiated, there is nothing in this interpretation of autonomy that is *necessarily* inconsistent with recognizing others as having authority over one, which is not of course to deny that in specific cases autonomy and the actions of an authority can conflict.

There is also a second, much richer, interpretation of moral autonomy that Wolff employs in his argument. In this sense, moral autonomy is an ideal, a good to be sought in acting, and not simply a presupposition of moral agency as such. On this view, we are required to 'achieve autonomy wherever and whenever possible' (Wolff, 1976, p. 17). It seems to be an ideal rather closer to that advanced by J. S. Mill in his *On Liberty* than to Kant's conception of moral autonomy. Here, the concern is very much with living a certain kind of life: one informed by a desire to cultivate one's rational and decision-making capacities to their fullest possible extent and involving the acquisition of a wide range of knowledge about the options that could be chosen (Raz, 1986). However, while there might be much to commend this way of life, there appears to be nothing obligatory about such an ideal. It is, for instance, quite possible to live a good life without aspiring to this ideal of autonomy. Furthermore, even if for many of us moral autonomy is a positive ideal, one element of a good life, it is rarely the only component and much of the time is not the dominant one either. It takes its place along with other moral ideals, for example those having to do with concern for other people, as one of many action-guiding principles that have to be weighed against each other in deciding how to act in the particular circumstances in which we find ourselves. It is, in fact, highly implausible to think that autonomy should invariably override all other values.

It may also be asked whether all kinds of authority are necessarily inconsistent with moral autonomy, even in this stronger sense. It does not appear that they must be. A person committed to moral autonomy as an ideal is likely to be generally sceptical of claims to authority, but it is not *necessarily* inconsistent with the ideal of moral autonomy to act on another's authority. For example, one way in which one person can acquire authority is by being granted it by another. Suppose Mr X contracts with Ms Y that he will do whatever housework she requires on Tuesday if she will mend his automobile on Monday. If Ms Y repairs the automobile then she has the authority to determine a whole range of Mr X's conduct on the Tuesday. Mr X is required to do the washing, cleaning, dusting and so on as Ms Y commands. Is this a violation of Mr X's autonomy? Surely not – unless one wishes to argue, as Godwin apparently did, but Wolff, more sensibly, does not, that we should never enter into contracts or make any promises. In fact it is hard to see how social life could be carried on if we did not make such undertakings and enter into voluntary agreements with each other that often effectively give one party some authority over the other. There need be nothing sinister about such relationships and they need not impair an agent's autonomy; indeed, in many instances they should rather be seen as expressions of it. (It is quite possible for authority to be exercised over someone in order to promote that person's autonomy.) It is, as Wolff notes, true that such authority is limited, and I have argued in Chapter 3 that *political* authority cannot be satisfactorily understood as being based upon a contract or promise. However, Wolff's argument, it will be remembered, was that there was a *logical* inconsistency between all authority and our moral autonomy, and it is enough to refute this claim to show that there are *any* instances of authority that are compatible with moral autonomy.

What of the more specific claim that there is a fundamental incompatibility between *political* authority (understood non-voluntaristically) and an overriding commitment to the ideal of moral autonomy? Even in this case, which is the most favourable to Wolff's argument, matters are not as straightforward as they might appear. As we have seen earlier, Wolff himself concedes that 'there are great, perhaps insurmountable, obstacles to the achievement of a complete and rational autonomy', but he simply assumes rather than shows that political authority is both an obstacle to the achievement of autonomy and also one that could be surmounted. This begs the question against those who take the view that the state, or anyway some structure of political authority, is at least a necessary or unavoidable evil, and therefore to an extent insurmountable, let alone those who argue that it is an essential condition for living any worthwhile life, and therefore need not even be an obstacle to autonomy. There is nothing intrinsic to the view that moral autonomy is an overriding obligation that dictates the state or political authority in general must be seen as an eliminable obstacle to the achievement of that ideal. It could be argued that the state, notwithstanding some element of coercion, provides an essential part of the context within which such an ideal has to be pursued. Political anarchists are unlikely to endorse such an argument, but that is because they have additional moral and empirical objections to the state. At the very least, it can be plausibly maintained that even an over-riding commitment to the ideal of moral autonomy does not, of itself, dictate that political authority must be rejected. Finally, as has been shown earlier, such an over-riding commitment to the ideal of moral autonomy is in any case far from morally compelling. Indeed, because it is so implausible to think that it should always be regarded as our overriding moral obligation, there is no convincing reason to believe that political authority is inconsistent with responsible moral agency. Wolff does not succeed, therefore, in mounting a convincing case for philosophical anarchism on the basis of a contradiction between political authority and moral autonomy.

Finally, though, even if philosophical anarchism cannot convincingly demonstrate its own validity, there remains the negative case for it – the justification by default, as I have called it. If none of the arguments purporting to justify political obligation are successful, then are we not left with philosophical anarchism as the only available alternative: philosophical anarchism triumphs *faute de mieux*? One preliminary point, though, which should be noted about negative philosophical anarchism, is how distant it is in many respects from the concerns of political anarchism. A. J. Simmons, for example, a leading proponent of negative philosophical anarchism writes:

'We must conclude that citizens generally have no special political bonds which require that they obey and support the governments of their countries of residence. Most citizens have neither political *obligations* nor "particularized" political *duties*, and they will continue to be free of such bonds barring changes in political structures and conventions . . . It is likely that many would find our conclusion (that citizens generally do not have political obligations) objectionable because they believe it to have the following consequence: if citizens do not have political obligations, then they are free to disobey the law whenever they choose . . . But, from a conclusion that no one in a state has political obligations, *nothing* follows immediately concerning a justification of disobedience. For, political obligations are only one factor, among many that would enter into a calculation about disobedience. There are, even in the absence of political obligations, still strong reasons for supporting at least certain types of government and for obeying the law.' (Simmons, 1979, pp. 192–3)

This form of philosophical anarchism need share none of the political anarchist's hostility and suspicion towards the state, nor need it endorse a positive commitment to moral autonomy, especially in the highly demanding sense employed by Wolff. From the point of view of most political anarchists, it is probably true to say that philosophical anarchism does not deserve to be described as anarchism at all. The kind of scepticism towards political obligation shown by the philosophical anarchist, especially the negative philosophical anarchist, is in fact compatible with many very different political commitments (Pateman, 1985, pp. 137–42). While it is in principle entirely consistent with political anarchism, negative philosophical anarchism does not necessarily favour it over a wide range of alternative political outlooks. The denial of political obligation need not be especially favourable to scepticism about the value of institutions such as law, government or the state.

The distinctive feature of philosophical anarchism, in either of its two forms, is the denial that there exists any special moral relationship or particular ethical bond between members or citizens and their polity. The core of this view is:

> 'the conclusion that most of us have no political obligations . . . we are not *specially* bound to obey *our* laws or to support *our* government, simply because they are ours (or because of what their being ours entails). Insofar as we believe ourselves to be tied in some special way to our country of residence, most of us are mistaken.' (Simmons, 1979, p. 194)

This is a 'mistake' that needs to be explained, however, for as both Wolff and Simmons recognize it is a conclusion that runs counter to what is widely believed: they both accept that many, probably most, people are inclined to think that there *is* some kind of special relationship between them and their polity, which distinguishes it, for example, from their relationship to other polities. By contrast, Wolff and Simmons contend that, in the absence of any convincing moral justification of political obligation, such a belief is simply mistaken. It is in the interests of government and those in power to foster such a belief, but it is not a belief that has any justified basis.

One response to philosophical anarchism therefore is to attempt to show that better sense can be made of the idea of political obligation than that afforded by the traditional accounts that have been subject to such extensive and damaging criticism. Effectively, negative philosophical anarchism offers an invitation to any putative defender of political obligation to provide a more convincing account of it, for the best arguments against negative philosophical anarchism are likely to be arguments in favour of some positive account of political obligation. Negative philosophical anarchism does not show, even if it is successful, that political obligations do not or cannot exist, but only that the various arguments in favour of them are unsuccessful in showing that most people have such obligations. Perhaps it is particularly worthy of note in this context, that the conclusions of philosophical anarchism largely concur with those advanced earlier in Chapter 2 concerning the implausibility of genuinely voluntarist accounts of political obligation. In the next chapter I shall start to sketch what I believe is a more satisfactory account of political obligation, which avoids voluntarism and responds to the challenge of philosophical anarchism. However, there is one general consideration about negative philosophical anarchism that should be examined more closely and which will help to prepare the ground for the positive account of political obligation that follows.

Philosophical anarchism and the polity

Both Wolff and Simmons deny that we have any special ethical bonds, including any political obligations, towards *our* government, state or polity. Whatever obligations we may have towards the law or government apply quite generally, and are justified, if they are justified, simply because a particular law or command requires us to do what is anyway the right thing; they do not tie us in any specific way to the law or government of the polity of which we are members. However, there is perhaps at least a degree of oddness in this claim, to which neither Wolff nor Simmons is sufficiently attentive. This concerns what sense can be made of the claim that a government or polity is *ours* in the absence of some special relationship between it and us. What would it mean to say, for example, that the British government is *my* government? There is something here that needs to be explained but which philosophical anarchism, far from explaining, renders mysterious. It may be that some philosophical anarchists would wish to dispense entirely with this way of speaking and thinking. It might be suggested, following a hint from Wolff, that such a way of speaking manifests only a sentimental illusion. However, it is important to appreciate that it is not *merely* a way of speaking, not an empty form of words, which is at issue. Such expressions also embody complex patterns of thought and feeling that are far from insignificant or marginal to our understanding of our circumstances and of ourselves. They are integral to a way of thinking that may not be obviously or readily dispensable; or, at least, so I shall go on to argue. Of course, simply to show that most people share these beliefs and emotions does not, of itself, demonstrate that they are not illusory: political philosophy cannot be reduced to mere opinion polling. However, it should make us reluctant to embrace too readily philosophical anarchism: negative philosophical anarchism is inclined to assume that the 'burden of proof' lies with defenders of political obligation, but where a belief is widely shared and deeply implicated in a web of thoughts, feelings and practices, which have not been shown to be incoherent or morally pernicious, there is at least some reason for shifting that burden towards the sceptic. Thus, the question might be asked: what is wrong with such a way of thinking?

At least as important, though, as where the burden of proof is taken to lie, is the issue of what kind of 'proof' or justification is appropriate. This, inevitably, is a question that underlies all discussions of political obligation, and is central to moral and political philosophy more generally. While it is not a question that can be explored at all fully here, it is worth noting that Simmons employs particularly rigorous and demanding standards of moral justification. I have little doubt that very few, if any, moral and political principles are capable of meeting the kind of standards to which Simmons, and some other philosophers, aspire. Do we have rigorous, logically impeccable and entirely convincing justifications of equality, human rights, personal liberty, the rule of law, circumstances when war is permitted, and so on? It is true that some moral and political philosophers have believed themselves to have effectively settled such questions, but what distinguishes virtually all such claims is that they remain subject to widespread and persistent controversy. It would be nugatory to invoke once again the point that the number of its adherents does not determine the validity or truth of an argument. This must be granted; but such an observation only helps to *define* the problem, not to resolve it. Even allowing for high levels of irrationality, ignorance, self-interest and such like, all of which it would be reasonable to discount, the situation does not seem so very different if we focus only on competent and similarly trained and educated political philosophers, among whom philosophical agreement is also remarkably low (Rorty, 1989).

Another possible response to the question of what sense can be made of the claim that a government or state is *ours*, would be to offer an explanation that dispenses entirely with any notion of political obligation. This may be possible, but it is not easy to see what such an account would look like, and especially to see how its normative dimension would be accommodated; nor have negative philosophical anarchists attempted such an explanation. At the very least, this would require some creative philosophical work on the part of negative philosophical anarchists. In the absence of such accounts it is difficult to offer a prognosis about their likely success, but it does not seem that such a task will be easy or straightforward.

What these considerations suggest is that the fundamental challenge of negative philosophical anarchism lies in its subversion of political relationships through undermining the shared understandings that are constitutive of them. In short, it is mistaken to think, as critics and defenders alike have sometimes been inclined to assume, that political life can be left more or less unchanged by dispensing with any conception of political obligation and adopting the perspective of the philosophical anarchist. Unless it can be shown that we can continue to talk intelligibly and credibly of *our* government or *our* state, then a root and branch reimagining of our political relations would appear to be a necessary consequence. That, of course, is not a knockdown argument against philosophical anarchism; perhaps some such radical reimagining is practically possible. Nor, as has already been indicated, does such a conclusion show philosophical anarchism to be false. But, it does support what most political anarchists have always proclaimed: that we can reject political obligation and still carry on pretty much as before. Perhaps a more rigorous thinking through of the consequences of embracing philosophical anarchism will lead back towards some form of political anarchism, though that is not the only possibility. If we accept that 'all political authority is equally illegitimate' then it could, somewhat paradoxically, in practice encourage a more acquiescent and uncritical attitude to state power.

Conclusion

All forms of anarchism are a challenge to political obligation and, as such, a challenge to fundamental aspects of our understanding of political life. This challenge may be uncomfortable but it cannot be refused simply for that reason. In this chapter I have tried to examine the nature of that challenge and to explore some of its more significant implications. Only occasionally have I claimed to refute anarchist claims: as I have indicated, arguments in political philosophy rarely permit such certainty. However, I have sought to show that the anarchist challenge to political obligation is not without serious difficulties of its own. Inevitably, any full response to that challenge must also include a more positive account of political obligation, and it is to that I turn in Chapters 6 and 7. In the next chapter, though, I also continue the critique of Simmons's arguments, focusing in more detail on his criticisms of the view that I eventually want to defend: the associative account of political obligation.

6 Associative Political Obligation and its Critics

Thus far we have examined several general theories of political obligation, which have all been found wanting to varying degrees. None of them, it has been argued, provides a very plausible basis for attributing political obligations to most members of any existing polity, or to any polities that have existed or are likely to exist. As this rather cumbersome way of expressing our interim conclusion perhaps suggests, this does not mean that none of the theories have anything to be said for them or that they cannot or could not explain how some people in some circumstances may come to have political obligations. The point is that they do not provide what they purport to offer, which is a convincing *general* justification of political obligation. A general theory, as set out in Chapter 1, does not need to explain how *everyone* has political obligations, but it should cover at least the standard case of people who acquire membership through being born into the polity. None of them, I want to suggest, effectively captures the intuitive idea of political obligation: the idea that we are ethically bound to our particular polity, although we never chose to join it and although it may be flawed in a variety of significant ways.

In the last chapter we considered one kind of radical response to this failure: the various forms of anarchism. What unites these views, notwithstanding important differences, is the general rejection of the idea of political obligation. While weaker forms of philosophical anarchism do not strictly preclude the possibility of political obligation, the conditions that its defenders believe to be necessary for political obligation to be justified are so demanding that there seems little realistic prospect of them ever being met for the vast majority of people. Political anarchists deny even this possibility. However, the anarchist position, in any of its forms, is also less than compelling. The price of embracing anarchism is, on some very plausible assumptions about the normal conditions of human life, potentially unacceptably high, and anarchism also simply denies the common view that we do have political obliga-tions, without offering a satisfactory explanation of why this common view is mistaken. This might appear to leave us with nowhere to go: we cannot justify political obligation for most people in terms of any of the standard theories, but nor are we persuaded that we can or should dispense with the idea. But, as I will try to show in this chapter, we have not yet exhausted all the options. In particular, I shall seek to set out and defend what has become known as an 'associative' account of political obligation.

Pluralist theories

Before undertaking that task, there are still other options that should be mentioned. First, although it can be considered only briefly here, is an approach that arises from the thought that perhaps it is a mistake, as we have done so far, to treat each of the theories separately. Instead, we should aim to combine all or, more likely, some of the principles that the various standard theories articulate within a multi-principle or pluralist account of political obligation (e.g. Gans, 1992; Wolff, 2000; Klosko, 2005). In one version of this position, it is argued that we should reject the assumption that 'all citizens should have the same type or level of political obligations' (Wolff, 2000, p. 182). There is certainly something to this line of approach, and it is highly probable that different accounts of political obligation are appropriate for unusual and non-standard cases. Moreover, it is also reasonable to hold that some people, like government officials, may have additional reasons for their political obligations that are not shared by other members of their polity, and which place on them additional responsibilities. It may, too, simply be the best that we can do, if there is no more convincing approach to explaining political obligation: it could even be viewed as a potential, alternative, default option to weak philosophical anarchism.

However, there are also some good reasons for doubting whether this kind of pluralist theory is entirely convincing. One issue is that it has to be shown that different reasons can be made to hang together in a coher-ent overall account: it is not enough to collect together a miscellany of principles and arguments that are merely *ad hoc*, and perhaps rest on conflicting ethical or metaphysical assumptions. It may, though, be possible to overcome that problem, and more important, perhaps, with respects to this kind of pluralist theory is what is lost if we give up the assumption that, for the most part at least, people share a broadly similar set of political obligations – something that Wolff is at least willing seriously to contemplate. For the idea of trying to work out for each and every individual his or her level or type of political obligation seems impossibly daunting, and perhaps open to the danger of sliding back into a position in some respects similar to a weaker form of philosophical anarchism. Even if it is argued that this is an exaggeration of the complexity involved, as most people will fall into a limited range of groups, it is still highly unlikely that, if there is a plurality of different principles of varying weights and applying to people differentially, the picture will be at all clear or easily understood. And there remains the task of identifying which reasons justify exactly what sort of political obligation. But it is not only a matter of the difficulty of working all this out, it is also that what might be called the deep messiness that results fails to do justice to the thought that membership of a polity, and the corresponding obligation, is fundamentally a single status shared by pretty much all members of a polity, unless they are acknowledged to be a 'special case'. The idea that we are all differently related to our polity, and for different reasons, might be thought to be another way of admitting defeat in the quest for an adequate general account of political obligation. While acknowledging that many theories of political obligation are too simple, it is hard to see this as quite the virtue of a pluralist theory that Wolff takes it to be.

It is, no doubt, at least partly for these kinds of reason that George Klosko rejects any idea that people generally have different levels or degrees of obligation to their polity. Rather, he presents his theory not as justifying different obligations for different people, but as a combination of principles that justify the same obligations for all citizens; a multiple principle theory, which 'combines the principle of fairness, a natural duty theory, and . . . the "common good" principle in a theory that is able to overcome problems with theories based on single principles' (Klosko, 2005, p. 3). The thought here is that a plurality of principles explains how citizens (for the most part) all have the same obligations Of course, he too still has to find a way of satisfactorily combining these principles into a coherent overall structure, and he does in fact make a sophisticated attempt to explain how they are interrelated; an attempt that cannot be explored in detail here. However, in arguing that precisely the same combination of principles applies to each citizen within a polity, Klosko would appear to lose one of the principal advantages of the variable obligation view defended by Wolff, and in consequence lays himself open to a different challenge: this is the task of showing how all three of his principles apply equally and in the same way to all citizens. In fact, it does not seem to me that he is successful in this regard, which is not surprising because showing this was, as we saw earlier, one of the major problems faced by proponents of the theories based on these principles separately. And it is hard to see how this problem can be overcome simply by combining the principles.

I do not, though, wish to claim that these arguments against either Wolff or Klosko are sufficient to show that the very idea of a pluralist theory must be misconceived. It is also only fair to note that the serious attempt to formulate such theories is a recent endeavour; but the problems that have been identified are fairly fundamental and surely do much to undermine the apparent attractiveness of pluralist theories. However, it must be conceded, none of the counter-arguments above addresses what is perhaps the strongest card in the hand of the pluralist theorist: that we cannot seem to do any better. Later in this chapter and in the next, the case will be made for saying that we can do better. So the principal argument against a pluralist theory of obligation – that there is a better account of political obligation without the problems attendant on a pluralist theory – remains to be stated. Both because that account in some respects draws on aspects of other theories and because it allows for 'special cases', there may still be a residual role for an element of pluralism.

Before embarking on that account, we will look at another option; one that involves a very different kind of response to the perceived failure of justifications of political obligation. This has been advanced by proponents of what I shall call, following Carole Pateman, 'the conceptual argument' (Pateman, 1973). These theorists infer from this failure that there is something philosophically misconceived about the very enterprise of trying to offer a general justification of political obligation (MacDonald, 1951; Rees, 1954; McPherson, 1967; Pitkin, 1972).

The conceptual argument

It could be said that whereas anarchists try to resolve the problem of political obligation by explaining away the *obligation*, proponents of the conceptual argument seek to resolve it by explaining away the *problem*. For, under the influence of certain tendencies associated with the later philosophy of Wittgenstein, and sometimes perhaps a degree of complacency about the merits of liberal democratic forms of government, it has been denied that there is any general problem of political obligation. The essential claim of the proponents of the conceptual argument is that the problem of political obligation, understood as the search for a general justification of it, is a pseudoproblem, the result of conceptual confusion. Thus, the 'failure' of traditional theories does not mean that political obligation is unjustified, but that it does not stand in need of justification. Although there are some significant differences in the way that this argument has been developed, the defining element of this view is that any attempt to provide grounds for, or supply a justification of, political obligation in general is fundamentally misconceived.

This view maintains that the concepts of state, government or political authority on the one hand, and the concept of political obligation on the other, are logically or conceptually connected. Thus, it is argued, there is a conceptual confusion in supposing that the former could obtain without the latter, and, as this is just what those who seek a general justification of political obligation do suppose, their project is fatally undermined. The justificatory project assumes that state, government or political authority could exist without there being any corresponding obligations, and that therefore some further general account of the source or moral justification of political obligation is needed. However, according to the conceptual argument, the existence of an internal or logical relationship between state, government or political authority and political obligation means that some kind of independent justification of the latter is neither necessary nor possible. Some care, though, is needed in presenting the conceptual argument. its proponents do not wish, for example, to deny the possibility of justifying obedience (or disobedience) to this or that particular law or government. Such a judgement, though, will always be contextual and specific. What *is* denied is that there can be any *general* justification of political obligation and, in trying to understand this claim, it is necessary to look in more detail at some of the arguments that have been adduced in its support.

Probably the earliest statement of the conceptual argument is to be found in a once influential article by Margaret MacDonald in which she writes:

'A general proof of the existence of material objects seems impossible, and to ask for it absurd. No general criterion of all right actions can be supplied. Similarly the answer to "Why should I obey *any* law, acknowledge the authority of *any* State, or support *any* Government?" is that this is a senseless question. Therefore any attempted reply to it is bound to be senseless, though it may perform other useful or harmful functions. It makes sense to ask "Why should I obey the

Conscription Act?" or "Why should I oppose the present German Government?" because by considering the particular circumstances and characteristics of all concerned, it is possible to decide for or against obedience and support. We all know the kind of criteria according to which we should decide these issues. But although it looks harmless and even very philosophical to generalise from these instances to "Why should I obey *any* law or support *any* government?" the significance of the question then evaporates. For the general question suggests an equally general answer, and this is what every political philosopher has tried to give. But no general criteria apply to every instance. To ask why I should obey *any* laws is to ask whether there might be a political society without political obligation, which is absurd. For we mean by political society, groups of people organised according to rules enforced by some of their number.' (MacDonald, 1951, pp. 183–4)

This passage, and indeed her whole argument, which is very briskly presented, is not easy to interpret or assess and my discussion of it is both selective and, to a degree, speculative. A crucial part of the argument is the comparison of the demand for a general justification of political obligation with that for a general proof of the existence of material objects. In brief, the argument with regard to the latter appears to be that a demonstration of the existence of any particular material object necessarily presupposes a background within which the existence of some material objects is taken for granted. What might be called 'comprehensive scepticism' about material objects is unintelligible because we have no idea how to demonstrate their existence in general; and so to think that, lacking such a general proof, the existence of all material objects is doubtful or in some way problematic is absurd.

Whatever the merits of this view, and there is an extensive and sophisticated philosophical literature concerning scepticism, it is difficult to see how the argument can be analogously developed in the case of political obligation. In part, at least, this is because the analogy does not hold, in that what is typically sought by someone wanting a general justification of political obligation is a particular moral argument and not a general justification of morality as such. It is the latter that might more plausibly be thought to be comparable to the demand of the sceptical epistemologist for a general proof of the existence of material objects. MacDonald claims that, in dealing with the problem of political obligation, 'political theorists want an answer which is always and infallibly right, just as the epistemologists want a guarantee that there are material objects', and that both are 'equally senseless requests for they result from stretching language beyond the bounds of significance' (MacDonald, 1951, p. 184). Whether or not this is so, the basis of this analogy remains unconvincing, and as it stands does not therefore offer any real support for MacDonald's claim.

At its clearest, MacDonald's objection to general theories of political obligation seems, much more straightforwardly, to be that no such theory can do justice to the complex considerations involved in deciding, on any particular occasion, whether or not obedience to a law is justified. Whereas general theories 'seek to reduce all political obligation to the application of an almost magic formula', it is simply impossible to provide comprehensive and precisely formulated criteria for when a law should obligate (MacDonald, 1951, p. 185). But this is a less than sensitive description of what most theories of political obligation have been about; and in any case it is a very different kind of objection from attempts to provide a general proof of the existence of material objects. There the impossibility, if there is one, lies not in the complexity of the considerations but in the unintelligibility of generalized doubt. What the conceptual argument requires is an equivalent to the latter in the case of political obligation. Nevertheless, although MacDonald's argument cannot be judged a success, the questions that she raises about what can be expected of a theory of political obligation are legitimate and to the point. In particular, her emphasis upon the variety and complexity of considerations affecting practical political judgements might be thought to point back to the pluralist accounts of political obligation discussed in the preceding section. However, this point can be accepted without endorsing the conceptual argument. It may, indeed, be argued to provide diamerically opposed reasons for scepticism about the possibility of a general theory of political obligation. As John Dunn has written:

> 'the prospects for a theory of rational political obligation as this has generally been conceived are beyond hope, not because (as has sometimes been supposed) there is nothing for such a theory to be about, but there is so much that such a theory *has* to be about (so much to which it *has* to do justice), if it is to stand a chance of proving valid.' (Dunn, 1980, p. 299)

While his conclusion may be similar to MacDonald's – that 'as rational and responsible citizens, we can never hope to know once and for all what our political duties are' (MacDonald, 1951, p. 86) – Dunn's rejection of the claim that 'there is nothing for such a theory to be about' is clearly intended to distance his view from the conceptual argument. At best, though, this kind of point alerts us to what not to expect from a general account of political obligation: it cannot be expected to provide a determinate, detailed and context-independent account of what exactly our political duties require of us.

Thomas McPherson has developed a much fuller version of the conceptual argument. In a crucial passage summarizing his position, he writes:

> 'That social man has obligations is therefore not an empirical fact (which might have been otherwise) that calls for an explanation or "justification". That social man has obligations is an analytic, not a synthetic proposition. Thus any general question of the form "Why should we accept obligations?" is misconceived. "Why should I (a member) accept the rules of the club?" is an absurd question. Accepting the rules is part of what it *means* to be a member. Similarly, "Why should I obey the government?" is an absurd question. We have not understood what it *means* to be a member of a political society if we suppose that political obligation is something we might not have had and that therefore needs to be justified.' (McPherson, 1967, p. 64)

McPherson, therefore, does not deny that particular obligations may stand in need of justification or that on occasion they may not turn out to be justified. Rather, his claim is that:

> 'What it does not make sense to ask for justification of is the existence of *obligations in general*, for that we are involved in obligations is analytically implied by membership of society or societies . . . We may wonder whether the government is right to require this or that of us, but we cannot (logically cannot) dispute that membership of political society involves obligations to government.' (McPherson, 1967, pp. 64–5)

Unfortunately, however, McPherson occasionally equivocates between this view – that it does not make sense to ask for a general justification of political obligation – and the clearly incompatible view that such a general theory is possible but that 'it would have to be (against the protests of theorists of the past) an eclectic one. Although no theory provides the whole answer, each of them might provide perhaps some part of the answer' (McPherson, 1967, p. 52). (Once again, this pushes in the direction of a pluralist theory.) However, it might reasonably be asked how even an eclectic theory could possibly provide a satisfactory answer to an 'absurd question'. But, notwithstanding this and other ambiguities in the formulation of his argument, it is tolerably clear that McPherson's intended claim is that the enterprise of seeking a general justification of political obligation rests on a conceptual confusion and is as a result radically misconceived.

Taking that to be his view, a more deeply rooted difficulty, and one that has been latched on to by McPherson's critics, is that he appears to claim that the argument is supposed to apply only to modern liberal democracies (even just to modern Britain). He writes in his 'Introduction' that 'most of what I say in this book is intended to apply to modern liberal democracies – more particularly to modern Britain. Some of what is said is, of course, capable of a much wider application' (McPherson, 1967, pp. 2–3). However, because he does not distinguish what applies only to 'modern liberal democracies' from what is 'capable of a much wider application', critics such as Carole Pateman have rightly taken him to task. For, if the conceptual argument is intended to apply only to liberal democratic polities, without further explanation of why it is limited in this way, the claim that it is purely a conceptual argument becomes problematic. As Pateman puts it:

> 'Any argument that moves straight from the conceptual connection between "being a member of political society" and "political obliga-tion" to conclusions about our obligations to specific institutions is stretching purely conceptual analysis beyond its proper limits. To argue from "being a member of a political society" directly to "having a political obligation to the (liberal democratic) state" is to make the implicit assumption that "political society", "government" and "the state" all imply each other and that there is a logical, not just an empir-ical connection, between the notions of political society and the state.' (Pateman, 1973, pp. 223–4)

The substance of Pateman's argument is surely correct. If the conceptual argument is limited to liberal democracies (let alone only to modern Britain!), this must be through an unargued identification of the polity or 'political society' with liberal democracy. Although it might in principle be possible to argue such a case, McPherson does not do so, and the prospects for such a case being argued at all persuasively are surely quite poor. (Perhaps a *moral* case could be argued more convincingly, but again this would not then be a conceptual argument.) As it stands, limit-ing the conceptual argument to liberal democracies appears arbitrary and unjustified.

A second aspect of McPherson's argument that has given rise to serious objection, and which distinguishes his view from most accounts of political obligation – Margaret Gilbert's theory is a significant exception, as will be seen later – is his denial that political obligation is moral in character. Rather, he maintains, political and moral obligations are distinct species of the genus *obligation*. However, it is much easier to see what political obligation is not, on this account, than what it is. Political obligation is not a legal obligation, for McPherson explicitly distinguishes the two; nor is it a straightforwardly prudential obligation (McPherson, 1967, pp. 26–7, 77–8). More particularly, political obligation is neither moral in character nor subordinate to moral obligation. And McPherson is particularly concerned to point out that 'the kind of moralising politics that I am objecting to is the kind engaged in by philosophers who attempt to subordinate political principles to moral' (McPherson, 1967, p. 82). Although I am sympathetic to this last point, it remains unclear exactly what political obligation means, and the force of its being an 'obligation' is stubbornly mysterious. This is, nevertheless, an issue worth pursuing a little further because McPherson's reasons for denying that it is moral shed some light on wider questions about political obligation.

His first reason for denying that political obligation is moral raises an issue that has already been extensively discussed in connection with voluntarist theories. He writes:

> 'We should, I think, generally be reluctant to use the expression "moral obligation" for a duty not voluntarily assumed. Some cases covered by the expression "political obligation" by contrast are certainly cases where we have obligations that we have not voluntarily assumed.' (McPherson, 1967, p. 70)

Thus, his first argument has a familiar ring to it, and rests on the assumption that because all moral obligations are voluntarily assumed and at least some political obligations are not, it follows that political obligation cannot be moral. His second argument also has to do with an alleged difference between the moral and the political. For, while the former is 'concerned with personal relations', the latter concerns 'our relations to the state and it to us' (McPherson, 1967, p. 74); and what is appropriate for personal relations is different from what is appropriate in our relations with the state. He claims that 'certain kinds of behaviour are looked upon as not falling within the sphere of morality at all. The question as people see it is whether they are politically right or wrong . . . and this seems to them just a different question to the moral one' (McPherson, 1967, p. 78). This second point suggests that people simply do not judge political actions in moral terms. However, while it is highly plausible to hold that political morality may have some distinctive features that distinguish it from personal morality, the contention that political actions are not (or cannot be?) subject to moral appraisal seems so obviously at variance with the kind of discussion of politics that is near universal that I shall ignore it. In general terms, therefore, McPherson's thought seems to be that the sphere of moral obligation is that of voluntary, personal relations, while political obligations are concerned with relations between individuals and particular kinds of non-voluntary institutions (McPherson, 1967, p. 81).

McPherson is, I think, wrong in construing either of these arguments as reasons for denying that political obligation should be understood in broadly moral terms. However, although the use he makes of these arguments is mistaken, they do reveal important features of any adequate account of political obligation. First, as was argued in Chapter 2, he is right to claim that political obligations are not usually voluntarily assumed. But, he is wrong in thinking that this means that such obligations cannot be moral. There is no reason to limit morality in this way, and even if one wants for some reason to use the term 'obligation' more restrictively, then one could just as well talk of political duties, which are no less moral than obligations. Second, McPherson is right to recognize that a satisfactory account of political obligation may differ significantly from any that could be given exclusively in terms of obligations deriving from personal relations without reference to their institutional setting. However, he is mistaken in believing that this is sufficient to distinguish political from moral obligations, for many moral obligations, too, are incomprehensible without reference to social institutions. For example, obligations to the office of the vice chancellor within a university are distinct from any obligations to the particular person who happens to occupy that position, but both are undeniably moral qualities, although the former necessarily depends upon social institutions. Overall, therefore, neither argument provides a convincing reason for denying what has usually been thought uncontroversial: that political obligation is a broadly moral relationship.

These criticisms of McPherson's argument are more than sufficient to undermine its validity. However, some of the spirit, if not much of the substance, of the conceptual argument can, I believe, be captured within the associative account of political obligation that is defended in what follows. The core of this argument, as I shall interpret it, is that having political obligations is part of how we understand what it is to be a member of a polity. In this limited but important respect there is a conceptual dimension to the argument. But, McPherson's misleading references to clubs, which immediately bring to mind the picture of the polity as a voluntary association, confuses matters; membership of a polity, as he elsewhere recognizes, is not generally the result of a voluntary undertaking to join. Political association is for most people in an important sense non-voluntary, and political obligation does not derive from a voluntary decision to form or join a polity. Political obligation instead needs to be understood as constitutive of a certain sort of relationship. These are features of at least some versions of the conceptual argument that will be incorporated and elaborated in the associative account of political obligation. However, it also needs to be acknowledged that it is insufficient merely to assert without any further explanation that being a member of a polity means having political obligations. Critics of political obligation are owed more than this; and indeed this is what the associative account seeks to supply.

Introducing associative obligations

Most of the rest of the book will be taken up with articulating and defending what has become known in the literature as an 'associative' account of political obligation, a term that seems to have been coined by Ronald Dworkin. By this he means 'the special responsibilities social practice attaches to membership in some biological or social group, like the responsibilities of family or friends or neighbours', and he goes on to observe 'that political obligation might be counted among them' (Dworkin, 1986, p. 196). Although the position has improved somewhat in the last twenty or so years, it also remains true that associative obligations have been 'much less studied by philosophers than the kinds of personal obligations we incur through discrete promises and other deliberate acts' (Dworkin, 1986, p. 196). In the remainder of this chapter, I shall first set out no more than the bare bones of associativism. Thereafter various criticisms of the associative approach will be assessed, along with a brief consideration of one, especially impressive, alternative associative account of political obligation. This latter is Margaret Gilbert's plural subject theory, which sets out a highly original and philosophically sophisticated account of political obligation (Gilbert, 2006). In Chapter 7 a fuller version of the associative account will then be elaborated.

It may seem rather odd to begin by responding to criticisms of the associative account before properly elaborating it. One reason for doing so is in order to lay the ground for the fuller account by seeking to rebut some initial sources of scepticism about the whole idea of associative obligations. It is important to make the idea of associative obligations at least plausible. Another reason is that it facilitates the introduction of the principal generic features of an associative account before articulating the specific version of the theory that is defended in the next chapter. For, although the specific account set out in Chapter 7 is as good as I am able make it at present, it is the general idea of an associative account of political obligation that I most want to defend. There are very likely to be aspects of the more detailed story that could be improved upon or need correction, but which would remain within the parameters of an associative account. It is important, therefore, to distinguish the general conception of an associative account of political obligation from the specific details of any particular version of it. Thus, I begin by saying something quite generally about associative obligations, with the fuller account of associative political obligations deferred until the next chapter.

In a particularly eloquent passage, Samuel Scheffler gets to the heart of the idea of associative obligations when he writes that:

> 'Ordinary moral opinion . . . continues to see associative duties as central components of moral experience. In so doing, it recognizes some claims upon us whose source lies neither in our own choices nor in the needs of others, but rather in the complex and constantly evolving constellation of social and historical relations into which we enter the moment we are born. For we are, after all, born to parents we did not choose at a time we did not choose; and we land in some region we did not choose of a social world we did not choose. And, from the moment of our birth and sometimes sooner, claims are made on us and for us and to us . . . And if, in due course, we inject our own wills into this mix – straining against some ties and enhancing others, sometimes severing old bonds and acquiring new ones – the verdict of common moral opinion seems to be that we can never wipe the slate entirely clean. Our specific historical and social identities, as they develop and evolve over time, continue to call forth claims with which we must reckon, claims that cannot without distortion be construed as contractual in character, and which are not reduced to silence by general considerations of need.'
> (Scheffler, 2001, p. 64)

It is this ordinary idea of obligations, arising from social practices rather than voluntary choices or from our common humanity, which the conception of associative duties or obligations seeks to capture. They are the obligations of family, collegiality and political community. Such obligations are not owed to everyone: they are special obligations owed to other members of a particular group or association to which we belong. But, unlike special obligations that are created through voluntary choices or decisions, such as those that arise from promises or a decision to join a club, associative obligations cannot be explained in terms of individual voluntary acts or decisions. It is this combination of not being owed to everyone and not arising from a voluntary choice that makes associative obligations different and distinctive; and also, it should be noted, what makes them for many philosophers especially controversial.

In many respects, probably the clearest examples of associative obligations are familial obligations: the duties that we owe to other members of our family. The family is a context in which we commonly acknowledge moral bonds to particular people by virtue of them standing in a particular relationship to us, which are not self-assumed and cannot be explained in terms of individual choices or voluntary undertakings. While it could at least be argued that the obligations of spouses to each other are the result of voluntary commitments, it is clear, for instance, that the obligations of siblings and of sons or daughters to their parents cannot be similarly explained. The relationships in which we find ourselves with our parents and siblings are not ones that we have chosen, and not having chosen our family is not generally thought to be an adequate reason for denying that we have obligations to them. The difference between these obligations and those arising from promises or consent are worth making a little more explicit. If an obligation is claimed to arise from a promise or from consent, it is a decisive objection to such a claim that no promise was made or no consent given. This is, in another context, the familiar objection to contract and consent theories of political obligation. However, there is nothing equivalent to a promise or consent in the case of people's obligations to their parents and siblings; yet, at least on a widespread and strongly held view, there *are* obligations. And, while fairness, mutual benefits, gratitude and other considerations are no doubt relevant to what might be called 'the moral economy' of the family, none of these principles seem to be truly adequate to explain familial obligations. We have obligations to other members of our family because they are our family, and often we would be puzzled as to what to say if someone asked us why that made a difference – we would be inclined to think that they had simply failed to understand what being part of a family means.

On a similar basis to the obligations that people have to their families, notwithstanding the many and undeniably significant differences between families and polities, it can be argued that people have obligations to their polity. Individuals most often become members of a polity by being born in a particular place or of particular parents, just as they are born into a family; and the obligations that they acquire vary according to how the nature of the relationship is understood and are also often somewhat indeterminate and subject to a measure of dispute. Membership of a polity is normally acquired simply by virtue of having been born into a particular political community and is most often sustained through continued residence within its territory. These are the conditions that characterize membership of a polity for most people. Of course, there are many relevant phenomena that cannot be accounted for in quite this way, such as resident aliens, stateless persons, naturalization and so on, just as the familial case is complicated by facts of abandonment, divorce, adoption and so on. However, though these are significant complications, and some account of them would need to be given in a more comprehensive discussion, they are comparatively marginal and need not seriously impinge upon the argument here. This argument is concerned with what is best thought of as the standard, or paradigmatic, case of membership of a polity, which is as just set out; and it would be as mistaken to base any general account of that on, for example, naturalization, as it would be to base any general account of the family on adoption. For most people, their political obligations, as we might say, come with the territory.

As the example of the family already shows, associative obligations are 'an important part of the moral landscape: for most people responsibilities to family and lovers and friends and union or office colleagues are the most important, the most consequential obligation of all' (Dworkin, 1986, p. 196). Some of the obligations that Dworkin lists can perhaps be at least partially explained in terms of a voluntary choice but others, including some of the most important, such as those of family and, I would add, political obligations, for the most part cannot. For, while political obligation may not always figure in people's explicit thoughts in the direct and pervasive manner that familial obligations do for most people, brief reflection will nonetheless show that they have an important place in our lives in even the most mundane of circumstances: we take account of the law, pay our taxes, utilize the resources that the polity makes available to us, and most, although not all, of us vote in (some) elections and in other ways participate in the institutions and processes of our political community. Furthermore, when circumstances are difficult and troublesome, for instance in times of war or crisis more generally, our political obligations can confront us in the most vivid and dramatic of ways. The idea of dying for one's country may be rather unfashionable in some quarters, but it remains meaningful for most people.

However, for all their apparent centrality in our lives, the idea of associative obligations generally, and of associative political obligations in particular, have come in for much criticism, and I shall say a little more about what an associative account involves in the context of responding to some of the more challenging criticisms that have been levelled against it. In particular, I shall focus on the arguments of probably their most incisive and tenacious critic, A. J. Simmons (1996). According to Simmons, five interrelated features characterize the idea of associative political obligations. These he characterizes as antivoluntarism, the authority of shared moral experience, particularity, the analogy with the family and the normative power of local practice. 'Antivoluntarism' is the explicit rejection of the claim that political obligations must be explained in terms of a voluntary choice on the part of the person obligated. The commitment to the 'authority of shared moral experience' amounts to the idea that any adequate account of political obligation 'must be true to moral phenomenology, must be realistic' (Simmons, 1996, p. 249). 'Particularity' is the requirement that political obligations relate to 'obligations of obedience or support owed to one particular government or community (our own), above all others' (Simmons, 1996, p. 250). The fourth feature suggests that political obligations can be illuminated in some important respects through an analogy with familial obligations. Finally, the 'normative power of local practice' involves the claim 'that local associative obligations, including political obligations, are internally justified or self-justified, that local practice can independently generate moral obligations' (Simmons, 1996, p. 252). He argues that, taken together, these features 'jointly define a definite argumentative space within which the theses' proponents must locate their arguments for (justifications of) political obligation' (Simmons, 1996, p. 252). And within this general approach he further identifies two broad strategies for arguing for associative political obligations that he regards as having at least some prima facie plausibility, although in the end he firmly rejects both. The first is a form of nonvoluntarist contract theory, and the second he dubs the 'communitarian theory' (Simmons, 1996, p. 261). The account of associative political obligations defended in the next chapter broadly adopts the second strategy, but a brief excursion into Margaret Gilbert's theory will enable us to begin by considering Simmons's criticisms of the first approach.

Gilbert's plural subject theory

In *A Theory of Political Obligation* Margaret Gilbert develops a rich, complex and original theory of political obligation (Gilbert, 2006). Gilbert's theory aims to explain why the widespread belief that people are normally under political obligations to their polity is well-founded, but it is also part of a broader social ontology in which she explains how social groups and the obligations they give rise to are constituted. In brief, she contends that 'social groups are plural subjects; plural subjects are constituted by joint commitments which immediately generate obligations' (Gilbert, 1993, p. 126). For obvious reasons, it is not possible here to go into the details of the arguments for her social ontology (Gilbert, 1989), but at least a brief indication of her account of how social groups are constituted is necessary in order to understand her views about political obligation.

Gilbert uses a very simple example to develop her theory of social groups or, as she calls them, 'plural subjects' (Gilbert, 2006, ch. 5). Suppose two people knowingly and intentionally start walking together. Whether or not they have discussed the matter, whether they have explicitly decided to walk together or 'just fall into it', it is common knowledge between the two of them that they are walking together. On her account, this amounts to a 'joint commitment' to walk together, as both would acknowledge that this is what they are doing. In giving expression to this joint commitment they constitute themselves as a 'plural subject'; that is as a 'we', who are walking together. And through becoming a plural subject each of the walkers acquires obligations to the other. For example, in the case of the two walkers, each is under an obligation, absent of any special circumstances, to walk at a pace consistent with the other being able to keep up, not to veer off in an unexpected direction without any explanation, and so on. Obligations are implicit in what it is to be a plural subject, and 'each participant has obligations to the other participants to behave in a way appropriate to the activity in question' (Gilbert, 2006, p. 114). And, once a plural subject has been created, it cannot be arbitrarily dissolved by one of the parties to it without violating the obligations that have been incurred. In this way, through a joint commitment that creates a plural subject, the parties acquire obligations to each other that they did not have before. However, it is crucial to appreciate that for Gilbert these obligations are not necessarily *moral* obligations, a point of considerable importance that I shall return to at the end of this section.

Gilbert believes that this argument can be generalized from the kind of small-scale example of two people walking together to less transient and much larger and impersonal social groups, including a polity. These too are plural subjects and 'membership in a social group in the plural subject sense carries obligations with it' (Gilbert, 2006, p. 91). Thus, she argues that 'members of a political society are obligated to uphold its political institutions by virtue of their membership in that society, and membership is a matter of participation in a joint commitment to accept together with the other members the political institutions in question' (Gilbert, 2006, p. 289). Participation here is primarily a matter of social convention and not of personal attitude; very roughly, if one behaves as a member of a society and one is understood to be a member by others, then one is a member, whatever mental reservations one may inwardly hold. Controversially, Gilbert further maintains that because a joint commitment always brings obligations into being, one is obligated by membership of a polity whatever the nature of that polity, although of course it may be that other considerations outweigh one's political obligations: 'membership in a society always obligates, but members are not always required to support its institutions, all things considered' (Gilbert, 2006, p. 290) – although, once again, it is important to remind ourselves that for her political obligations need not be understood as moral obligations. Gilbert insists that her theory is concerned only to explain them, not to praise or denigrate them: whether they are good or bad is a distinct question from whether or not they exist (Gilbert, 2006, pp. 285–6).

This very brief account inevitably does scant justice to Gilbert's rich and ambitious theory. Moreover, it is not an easy theory to classify, and there may be some doubts as to whether it should be treated as an associative account at all. She has, for example, been willing to present her account as a reinterpretation of 'actual contract' theory (Gilbert, 1996, ch. 6). However, I agree with Richard Dagger, when he writes that 'Gilbert's account of political obligation seems to rely more on the idea of membership than on individual commitments' (Dagger, 2000, p. 106). As Gilbert explains:

> 'According to the theory, an understanding of joint commitment and a readiness to be jointly committed are necessary if one is to accrue political obligations, as is common knowledge of these in the population in question. One can, however, fulfil these conditions without prior deliberation or decision, and if one has deliberated one may have had little choice but to incur them.' (Gilbert, 2006, p. 290)

Furthermore, Gilbert also claims 'that actual contract theory is a special case of plural subject theory' (Gilbert, 2006, p. 215). This seems to indicate fairly clearly that any actual contract or its equivalent does not have a foundational status within her theory, but is merely one of many ways in which people can make a joint commitment, something that no sensible defender of associative obligations need deny. Thus, even if I do not agree with much else in his discussion of her work, I concur with Simmons that it is appropriate to treat Gilbert's theory as an associative account of political obligations.

Simmons's first point against Gilbert is his claim that she confuses *felt* obligations with *real* (or genuine) obligations. The fact that people often talk of 'our' government and feel that they have obligations to it does not, it is claimed, show that those people really do have such obligations. And it must be accepted that it is certainly possible for people to be mistaken about what they think or feel their obligations to be, and this is an important feature of their 'grammar'. For instance, a person may believe something that is factually untrue. Thus, Y may believe that X has done something to help her and that therefore she is under an obligation of gratitude to X, whereas in fact it was Z who helped her. Here, the premise of the obligation is straightforwardly empirically false. Or, a person may be conceptually confused about his or her obligations. For instance, one cannot have specifically familial obligations to anyone who is not a member of one's family, and any claim to the contrary is necessarily confused. However, these are not the kind of mistakes that Simmons has in mind. He advances the altogether more ambitious contention that there might be some kind of mass delusion, and that people who think that they do have political obligations are generally confused, oppressed or unthinking. So they might, but then again they might not. In so far as Simmons does not dispute that many intelligent, reflective and independent-minded people have thought of themselves as having political obligations, it is not unreasonable to expect some weighty arguments in support of the claim that such people are suffering from a mass delusion. But, in the absence of any compelling arguments or evidence that they are mistaken, the bare possibility that they *could* be mistaken does not of itself establish very much. Of course, Simmons thinks that there are good reasons for believing such people to be deluded, and we shall look at some of those reasons shortly, but the point here is that this claim about the bare possibility of error has no independent weight. Defenders of associative political obligations are not committed to denying the mere possibility of error. 'Ordinary moral opinion' is the starting point, but the argument for associative obligations does not simply *assume* that, just because people believe something, it *must* therefore be true.

Simmons's second objection is that Gilbert confuses 'political acqui-
escence with positive, obligation-generating acts or relationships'
(Simmons, 1996, p. 257). This, however, begs the question in that
Simmons's argument simply presupposes that obligations could only
result from what he calls 'positive obligation-generating acts or relationships'. Although it is not quite clear what this expression is supposed to
cover, it clearly cannot be intended to include the kind of 'joint commitments' with which Gilbert is concerned. If it were, of course, it would
not be an objection to her view. But, if not, Simmons would seem to do
no more than assume what is a matter of dispute (Scheffler, 2001, pp.
71–2). In fact, though, it is not clear that he really does subscribe to this
assumption, for he also accepts that there are 'general, non-voluntary
duties that bind us simply because we are persons' (Simmons, 2001, p.
95). True, these are not associative obligations, but once we grant that
legitimate moral claims do not arise only through 'positive obligation-
generating acts or relationships', we need more than mere assertion that
Gilbert's elaborate and sophisticated account of how some obligations
can be acquired *must* fail.

Simmons's third objection is that Gilbert confuses reasonable expectations with entitlements. Simmons claims that 'simple reasonable
expectation in no way implies obligation or entitlement' unless people
are directly and personally involved with each other. He cites a hypothetical example of some housewives in Königsberg setting their clocks
by Kant's consistent punctuality in always taking his daily walks at the
same time. As he rightly says, the mere fact that the housewives have in
this respect come to rely on Kant does not place him under an obligation
to keep taking his walks at the same time every day. In Simmons's view,
the kind of relationships that hold between fellow citizens are more like
those between Kant and the Königsberg housewives in his example than
the kind of direct, personal relationships that could generate obligations
based on reasonable expectations. In short, citizens have not 'committed
themselves to one another – they have not tacitly agreed together on
anything – in a way that would ground for them political obligations'
(Simmons, 1996, p. 258).

Again, this seems less than the 'conclusive point' that Simmons takes
it to be. He is no doubt right, *if* we require commitment to be the kind of
voluntary undertaking that we find in some versions of consent theory.
However, this is just what Gilbert's account of 'joint commitments'
denies. Nor does this denial appear to be unreasonable. While mere regu-
larity is not necessarily sufficient to generate an obligation, as the Kant
example illustrates, it seems hard to imagine how social life could

proceed in complex societies like our own unless there were some obligations explicable in terms of reasonable expectations arising from broad and impersonal patterns of behaviour, rather than just close interpersonal relationships. (And, we might reasonably ask, why *are* they justified only in the latter class of case, and not in others?) Social conventions and institutions, and even mere custom and practice, *may* generate obligations under appropriate circumstances. In English law, for instance, if a farmer allows people to walk across his land for long enough and they make plans based on this expectation, then they may come to have a *right* of pedestrian access through his land. He then has an *obligation* to respect that right. The obligations and rights here are legal, but there is no obvious reason to think that moral obligations could *never* be similarly generated (although, as we have seen, Gilbert does not regard political obligations as necessarily moral). Thus, being law-abiding (or in some cases, perhaps, pretending to be) can itself be taken as a rather good example of how people come to acquire obligations through generating reasonable expectations in others. It is entirely plausible, for instance, to think that people are, at least to some extent, reciprocally bound by their regular practice of obeying the law, whether or not their conformity to the law is entirely voluntary.

In summary, so far as this first argumentative strategy is concerned, Simmons has not succeeded in showing that accounts of political obligation in terms of nonvoluntary commitments, such as Gilbert's, must fail. He too readily *assumes* that only a voluntary act could justify such obligations, rather than showing how or why this must be so. This is not to imply that Gilbert's account is without any problems. For instance, the move from the kind of transient, dyadic relationship of two people walking together to a complex, persisting entity like a polity is not as straightforward as Gilbert suggests. There seems to be a kind of clarity about both what is and is not involved in the former case that is rather less evident with regard to a polity. Nor is it altogether quite clear what Gilbert takes to be the behaviour that counts as constituting the joint commitment involved in membership of a polity. I also suspect that Gilbert needs to say something more about the purpose of the political institutions that, on her account, members commit themselves to uphold. However, none of these points is conclusive, and Gilbert may well be able to respond to them within the parameters of her theory. By far the most controversial aspect of her argument, though, is her denial that political obligation need be moral in character.

The problem is that if political obligations are denuded of any ethical dimension then at least two troubling questions seem to arise. First, what kind of demand is it that political obligations make on us? It is hard to avoid the answer that this is worryingly opaque and that the force of such obligations is left altogether obscure. Moreover, if one starts, as Gilbert does, from the observation that most people believe themselves to have some special bond or relationship with their polity, then it is highly doubtful that their belief can be adequately explicated without incorporating any ethical dimension. The second question concerns the nature of the debate about political obligation. For, if all moral content were evacuated from the idea, then the dispute between defenders and critics of associative obligations would become largely nugatory. However exactly one wants to characterize Gilbert's conception of political obligations, critics may be fairly relaxed about them if they have no ethical import, for it is *that* claim to which they typically object (Higgins, 2004, pp. 173–8). That we have merely 'institutional' obligations, which as such have no moral claims on us, is not a claim that most critics feel they need to deny. Whether her theory could be suitably reconstructed to accommodate this point is an interesting question to which the answer is not self-evident, although there are reasons for thinking that such a reconstruction would also raise other problems; for example, her claim that all joint commitments, no matter how evil their purpose, give rise to obligations becomes much harder to swallow if these are taken to be *moral* obligations. Indeed, this may be the most powerful reason for her reluctance to embrace an ethical interpretation of her theory of joint commitments. Without such a reconstruction, though, I believe that Gilbert's theory must ultimately fail, notwithstanding its many attractions, as political obligation has to be understood as having an essentially ethical component.

While the issues discussed in the two preceding paragraphs, especially that of the status of the obligation, raise important questions for Gilbert's theory, I have also argued that Simmons's objections to her approach are less powerful than he claims. It is now necessary to turn to the second argumentative strategy and to ask whether it is also possible to mount a defence of the communitarian argument for associative obligations. I shall try to show that it is.

Simmons's critique of communitarian associativism

Simmons distinguishes two theses as central to the communitarian version of the associative approach. He terms these the 'identity argument' and the claim for 'the normative independence of local practice'.

In the end, though, he thinks that the first thesis – the identity argument – only has any real force if the claim for the normative independence of local practices is viable. We will follow Simmons, however, in examining each in turn, beginning with the identity argument. The key contention of this thesis is 'the fact that my identity is partly constituted by my role as a member of some political community means that my identity includes being under political obligations' (Simmons, 1996, p. 261). Against this view, Simmons argues, first, that from the mere fact that some social role partly constitutes my identity, nothing follows about the justification for ascribing moral obligations. After all, my identity may be partly constituted by evil or pernicious practices. This is why he thinks that the identity argument needs to be supplemented by the thesis of the normative independence of local practices. However, this does not mean that the identity thesis does no independently useful work, and this observation connects with his second objection to it. In this he responds to the idea that what is important about identity is identification; the claim that the argument is not so much about what our socially constituted identities *are*, as what *we understand them to be*. But, Simmons argues, self-identification does not fare any better, and for similar reasons – identification may itself be with something immoral or pernicious. His general point is that the fact that we identify with our polity or government is of itself of no ethical significance. He thinks it is best explained, as we saw earlier, as 'a kind of false consciousness' that we have been socialized into accepting (Simmons, 1996, p. 264).

This repeats, if in a different context, Simmons's first objection to Margaret Gilbert's nonvoluntary contract theory. However, it is no more compelling here than it was there. Obviously, the *possibility* of something like false consciousness cannot be ruled out *a priori*, but it does not seem to have much to commend it in this case. The general fact of socialization is just that, a fact, which has no particular implications for the validity of the beliefs into which we are socialized. Initially, at least, we are pretty much socialized into all of our beliefs, including those that are true. We can, moreover, reverse the logic of Simmons's position. Unless there is a powerful reason to reject such beliefs, especially if they are widespread across a diverse range of people, within and between cultures, then it does not seem unreasonable to operate at least on a presumption of their validity: it is Simmons who needs to advance an argument against such beliefs. It is not enough to point to the fact that we *could* identify with immoral roles or positions. For we *could* also join evil associations voluntarily or promise to perform evil acts. Whether voluntary or nonvoluntary, associations can be good, bad or indifferent, a point that is widely neglected in unfavourably comparing associative obligations with voluntarily assumed obligations, and one to which we will shortly return.

In sum, Simmons's objections to locating political obligation in a sense of identity are less than compelling. He is probably right that the identity argument, if shorn of *all* ethical content, would not be *sufficient* to explain political obligation. However, while for analytical purposes he distinguishes this strategy from the normative independence thesis, both arguments can be, and typically are, deployed in a mutually supportive relationship. If, then, the normative independence thesis can also be defended against Simmons's criticisms, understanding political obligations in terms of associative obligations may turn out to be markedly more resilient than he allows. It is the normative independence thesis that, for Simmons, is the crux of the defence of associative obligations. He presents this thesis as the general claim 'that local social practices (and our roles and places in them) independently determine (some or all) moral requirements' (Simmons, 1996, p. 262). The additional, specific claim is that political obligations are an example of such normative independence. Although conceding that he cannot 'deal decisively' with the general claim about normative independence, he maintains that there are powerful considerations against the general thesis, and still weightier ones against locally generated associative *political* obligations.

Simmons's arguments against the normative independence thesis involve deeper and more philosophically far-reaching issues than most of the objections against associative obligations examined so far. He says that 'the pressure to deny the normative independence of local practice derives primarily from one obvious fact and from one broad theoretical disposition' (Simmons, 1996, p. 266). The obvious fact is that local practices can be unjust, oppressive or pointless. The theoretical disposition is the belief that universality, or at least a very high degree of generality, is an essential feature of moral judgements. However, he concedes, there is also a fact and a theoretical disposition that makes the normative independence thesis attractive. The fact is that we often do ascribe obligations to people on the basis of their occupying a particular social role, without reference to general moral principles. The theoretical disposition 'is the belief that universalism in moral theory is a failed moral tradition' (Simmons, 1996, p. 266). He believes that it is the first of these pairs of facts and theoretical dispositions that is compelling.

Simmons does not advance any reasons in favour of the theoretical disposition he prefers, and I, too, accept that the theoretical dispute 'is too substantial and complex to be usefully addressed here' (Simmons,

1996, p. 266). However, it may be worth calling into question whether he is right to formulate the issue in relation to universality in quite the way that he does. Although the claim that universality, at least in any interesting, non-trivial sense, is an *essential* feature of morality is not one that the approach adopted here need embrace, it is possible to defend something like the normative independence thesis in a way that poses no significant challenge to at least a weak form of universalism. For the claim that political obligations are owed to a polity by virtue of people's membership of it can be quite properly presented as itself universal in form (or at least very general). This is just what Kent Greenawalt does in characterizing a natural duty as:

> 'one that arises because one is a person or a member of a society or because one occupies some narrower status, such as being a parent. Because such duties do not depend upon voluntary actions that bring one within their reach, their application is potentially broader than duties based on promises or fair play. In contrast with utilitarianism, theories of natural duty may explain why obedience to law is a genuine duty, not just a question of morally preferable action and why obedience may be called for though no untoward consequences will flow from disobedience.' (Greenawalt, 1987, p. 159)

Although I prefer not to defend associative obligations in quite these terms, the contention that we have obligations to parents or to legitimate political authorities could be presented in a way consistent with at least a moderate interpretation of the principle of universality. So, there is no compelling reason to think that proponents of the normative independence thesis *must* be of a strongly anti-universalist theoretical disposition, although there may be reasons for them to incline that way. But at least this may help those who are firmly committed to a weak form of universalism to accept the idea of associative obligations; although there are stronger forms of universalism with which it may well be incompatible (Vernon, 2007; Horton, 2007b).

One of Simmons's principal arguments for denying the normative independence thesis – the 'obvious fact' – is that on any plausible view there must be general moral constraints on what local practices can justify: 'this suggests that local associative obligations, conceived as independently generated by local practice, are at best a reasonably weak sort of moral obligations' (Simmons, 1996, p. 269). However, Simmons's conclusion would appear to follow only if it is true that 'the more weighty general moral concerns' are also so extensive as to greatly restrict the scope of local practices to generate obligations. If, however, we hold, with theorists like Michael Walzer (1994) or John Gray (2000), that these general moral concerns are themselves fairly weak, in that they leave scope for a wide diversity of local practices, then obligations independently generated by local practices could comprise a large and significant part of people's ethical life. Nor, importantly, does it follow that, because local practices must not violate some general moral constraints, it is the general moral constraints that really underpin associative obligations and make them morally binding. All that the general moral constraints do is to set limits to what (those who endorse them) can recognize as a genuinely moral obligation, and hence to the kinds of association that can give rise to them. With respect to political obligation, therefore, obligations can be owed to very different kinds of polity, so long as they do not systematically violate what may be some pretty minimal moral conditions, perhaps expressed through a very basic and restricted list of human rights. Nothing in the associative account denies this possibility. But, similarly, nothing in what Simmons says shows that what local practices are able to justify cannot be both extensive and significant.

The whole question of what might be called 'the moral standing' of groups that generate associative obligations is, as has been seen, often thought to be the crippling defect of theories of associative political obligations. As Richard Dagger expresses the point:

> 'Tracing political obligations to obligations of membership, especially of membership in nonvoluntary or noncontractual associations, presents [a] problem because membership is not confined to groups or associations that are decent, fair or morally praiseworthy . . . All families have members, but some families are so abusive or dysfunctional that some of their members presumably have no obligation to abide by family rules. The same is certainly true of political societies. If the character of a polity is such that some or even many of its "members" are routinely exploited and oppressed, it is difficult to see how they are under an obligation to obey its laws.' (Dagger, 2000, p. 110)

Dagger concedes that an answer along the lines just given – that only those groups or associations that are valuable give rise to obligations – is perfectly possible. However, he claims that this move undermines the defence of associative obligations because, as he puts it, 'membership is not itself sufficient to generate an obligation. Something extra must be added – an appeal to justice or to the nature of a true community – to supply what a straightforward appeal to membership lacks' (Dagger, 2000, p. 110). This, though, seems to me to misstate the matter in a way that does a serious disservice to the robustness of the idea of associative obligations.

As has already been mentioned, one feature of this criticism of associative obligation that usually appears to go unnoticed, or at least unremarked, by those who advance it is that it applies equally to obligations arising from voluntary commitments. Such a commitment – whether the result of a promise to perform a particular act or of voluntarily joining an association – can just as easily involve an undertaking to do wrong. Presumably, in these cases people will not be regarded as having acquired an obligation, or whatever obligation that they have acquired will be overridden by their duty not to do wrong. (For the purposes of this argument, although not for all purposes, it does not much matter which of these formulations we adopt.) However, although voluntarily assumed obligations can be rendered void or overridden in a wide variety of circumstances, there appears to be no comparable inclination to want to deny that voluntary commitments can ever generate moral obligations, or to claim that they must be 'a reasonably weak sort of moral obligation'. It is unclear, therefore, why the fact that some associations may not be 'decent, fair or morally praiseworthy' should undermine or trivialize the significance of associative obligations *in general*, any more than it does voluntarily assumed obligations. Moreover, this line of argument acquires additional force once the case for associative obligations is better understood.

What the defender of associative obligations should appeal to is the nature of the group or the relationship that generates these obligations (Mason, 2000). So, for instance, familial obligations are to be explained in terms of the value of familial relationships. This need not involve any general appeal to justice or even to the nature of a *true* family – valuable familial relationships can and do take many different and diverse forms. It does require one to say *something* about familial relationships that show them to be valuable; but this is surely not an unduly demanding requirement. Most of us, at least, do believe that in a minimally decent family there is something valuable about those relationships, and we would not be too hard put to say what it is. In characterizing what is valuable about such relationships one need not be driven to arguing that their value is, therefore, purely instrumental. It is not that families are only a means of achieving independently valuable ends (although of course they may also be that) but that the relationships that comprise a family are themselves part of the value that it realizes. Similarly, although many of the benefits arising from membership of a polity are instrumental in character, there are some goods that can plausibly be argued to be internally related to what it is to be a member of at least some polities; for instance, some of the political goods of citizenship, which cannot be had without being a member of a polity. There is one kind of good – peace and security – that, it will be argued in the next chapter, the polity has a special responsibility to provide, which although obviously instrumentally valuable can also be understood as the *raison d'être* for a polity.

Nor, it should be added, are the bonds between members of a family or those in other obligation-generating relationships properly understood as merely 'psychological' (Wellman, 1997, p. 107). They are indeed likely to have a more or less strong emotional dimension, but they are also typically subject to a rich ethical vocabulary that allows us to distinguish 'right' and 'wrong' ways of behaving and to praise or blame members accordingly. Characterizing what it is that is valuable in particular relationships or groups will no doubt draw on values that are not unique to those relationships or groups – in the case of the family, intimacy, emotional support, a secure environment for the raising of children, and so on. However, this in no way compromises the idea of associative obligations by surreptitiously implying that they must in some damaging respect depend upon an 'external justification' (Simmons, 2001, ch 5). The 'justification' is to be found in part in the relationships that constitute the group and the corresponding goods associated with membership.

The major problem with Simmons's treatment of the normative independence thesis as being the claim that local practices are *entirely* independent of all broader moral considerations is that it has the effect of rendering it more implausible than it need be. The claim of normative independence is not the claim that local practices should bear *no* relationship to, or be completely unconstrained by, any general moral values. Some basic constraints on how people should treat each other, and values such as truthfulness, loyalty, integrity and so on, are naturally part of the bigger picture. Rather, the thesis should be understood as, at least in part, proposing that local practices give these values a particular substance or content, a particular shape, ordering and meaning within a specific social or institutional setting or way of life.

It must be emphasized that nothing that has been said so far precludes the possibility of disagreement about whether or not any *particular* kind of group or association does have value. This is as it should be. In some cases there will be a large measure of agreement, supported by a broad range of reflection and argument, though in other cases much less so. It is also likely that most groups or associations will have both valuable and negative aspects, so that disagreements will often partly revolve around how those valuable and negative aspects are to be 'weighed' in relation to each other. It is perhaps this fact that explains how even members of what are judged to be seriously morally deficient groups may still legitimately regard themselves as having obligations towards the group. Moreover, some relationships – friendship for instance – have an openness or elasticity such that when one person behaves badly towards another, the other may not immediately conclude that therefore the moral bonds that are part of that relationship are dissolved. So, too, within quite severely 'dysfunctional' families mature children may reasonably regard themselves as having obligations to parents who are morally and emotionally deficient in significant respects. It is these features of associative relationships that show why they cannot *simply* be reduced to relations of reciprocity or gratitude, and are also very different from contractual relations. Thus, although even the best polities will never be entirely just (whatever one's understanding of justice), and most will no doubt have a number of serious ethical failings, this is not of itself enough to show that people in such polities are without any political obligations, so long as the polity also has some value. But perhaps there is more to be said specifically against the idea of associative *political* obligations.

Certainly Simmons believes that 'the case against associative *political* obligations is stronger than the case against the normative independence thesis' (Simmons, 1996, p. 271, my emphasis). So, even if it is possible, in general terms, to vindicate the normative independence thesis, this will not count decisively in favour of associative political obligations. There are two reasons why Simmons thinks this. First, he says that communal, associative obligations are typically 'vague and indeterminate at best . . . By contrast, most people have quite a clear sense of the content of their political obligations' (Simmons, 1996, p. 271). This latter assertion, however, is highly contestable, to say the least; and he offers no reasons or evidence in its support. Contra Simmons, surely people can be, and often are, uncertain of exactly what the bonds to their polity require of them, about what can be legitimately demanded of them, and about how strong those bonds are in relation to other moral concerns. Nor is it clear why, if we do think that political obligations are to some degree open-ended or indeterminate, 'we simply threaten the basis of the entire argument' (Simmons, 1996, p. 271). Simmons, though, is not alone in his view about the need for a determinate content to political obligations: George Klosko takes a similar view (Klosko, 1998). He, like Simmons, characterizes their content in traditional terms as 'obligations to obey the state or to submit to political authority', arguing that 'strong moral requirements to obey the law would counter widespread current scepticism about the possibility of a workable theory of political obligation founded on liberal premises' (Klosko, 1998, p. 53). Maybe so, and I am not unsympathetic to Klosko's motives; but perhaps this is rather too limited a view of political obligation. Although any account will need to say something specifically about the questions he identifies, it can be argued that there are good reasons to move away from an understanding of political obligation as exhausted by a narrow duty to obey the law. Once political obligations are understood to be those ethical responsibilities that we have by virtue of being members of a polity then their content becomes potentially richer, but also more open-ended (Parekh, 1993).

Simmons's second objection raises a different kind of point, and one that merits a fuller reply than can be given here. This is his contention that, at least in modern states, there is nothing sufficiently substantial to constitute a common life or a shared identity that can plausibly be thought to entail political obligations. It is, though, worth noting that if this is a historical claim about the loss of the conditions under which political obligations are meaningful then it involves a significant concession to the general idea of associative political obligations. For this claim does not deny the *possibility* of associative political obligations under different circumstances from those that we have come to inhabit. But, of course, this would not turn out to be much of a defence if it amounted to no more than empty possibility.

It is a problem that arises from the claim that under the conditions of modernity – conditions of pervasive ethical diversity and pluralism within polities – there is no political community because the essential precondition of moral consensus is absent. Hence, there can be no political obligation, because government is only a bureaucratic imposition that has no moral claims on its subjects. From a very different philosophical perspective than that of Simmons, Alasdair MacIntyre expresses a somewhat similar concern:

> 'In any society where government does not express or represent the moral community of the citizens, but is instead a set of institutional arrangements for imposing a bureaucratic unity on a society which lacks genuine moral consensus, the nature of political obligation becomes systematically unclear. Patriotism is or was a virtue founded on attachment primarily to a political and moral community and only secondarily to the government of that community; but it is character-

istically exercised in discharging responsibility to and in such government. When however the relationship of government to the moral community is put in question both by the changed nature of government and the lack of moral consensus in the society, it becomes difficult any longer to have any clear, simple and teachable conception of patriotism. Loyalty to my country, to my community – which remains unalterably a central virtue – becomes detached from obedience to the government which happens to rule me.' (MacIntyre, 1981, pp. 236–7)

This is a serious issue, but it can be argued that MacIntyre paints too bleak a picture of the modern state and far too rosy a one of earlier forms of political organization. However, a fuller response to how this challenge might be met will have to await the elaboration of the associative theory in Chapter 7, where it will be suggested that it is not so much moral consensus or homogeneity that is needed to underpin associative obligations as a reasonably cogent sense of belonging to a single political community that provides a distinctive and important good. But, it is only fair to remark, even there I do not claim to have a fully satisfactory response, and the concern to which MacIntyre's point gives rise is, if overstated in the form that he presents it, a legitimate one with potentially worrying implications for modern political life.

Conclusion

In this chapter I have sought to sketch in broad and general terms the contours of an associative account of political obligation and to lay the ground for the elaborated version of that account that follows in Chapter 7. I have found the conceptual argument to have some merit, but ultimately to be no less flawed than the views that it seeks to displace. We have begun to assess the merits of another approach: that of an associative account of political obligation. Although Margaret Gilbert's version of an associative account is undeniably impressive, there are aspects of it that give rise to doubts about its success, particularly her denial that political obligation needs an ethical dimension. However, the general criticisms of this approach by A. J. Simmons and others have been found less than compelling. Thus, the upshot of what has been argued so far is that an associative understanding of political obligation, which seeks to articulate an account of a polity as a form of nonvoluntary association that has sufficient and distinctive value to generate moral bonds and corresponding obligations, remains a viable approach. In the next chapter, therefore, an attempt is made to flesh out one particular associative account, seeking to show how the general approach can be developed so as to offer a broadly satisfying explanation of what it means to have political obligations and why they matter.

7 Elaborating the Associative Theory

In the preceding chapter I began to sketch in broad and general terms the key components of an associative understanding of political obligation. Such an understanding centres on what it is to be a member of a polity and how being a member of a polity, like being a member of a family, involves corresponding obligations of membership. I also sought to show that although the very idea of associative obligations, and in particular the idea of associative political obligations, has been subject to extensive criticism, these criticisms are less damaging than their advocates maintain. So far, however, beyond these generalities about membership, little has been said to give real substance to the account of associative political obligations. That is the task of this chapter.

I will attempt to show how the widespread sense common among people in a variety of different polities, that as members they do have political obligations of some sort, can be vindicated through an associative account. Before embarking on that task, though, there are a few preliminary points that need to be made to avoid raising expectations that will not be met. First, I shall not in fact say very much about the specific content of political obligations. This is because, to some extent at least, such obligations will vary between polities: that is one of the implications of an associative account. While they will share a broad content or orientation that is grounded in what it is to be a member of any polity and the generic good of a polity for its members, it is the character of the particular polity to which one belongs that precisely determines what one's obligations will be. Furthermore, there may well be some legitimate disagreement about exactly what they are. This does not, however, undermine, let alone invalidate, the associative account. The associative account seeks to explain the sense that we have obligations to the polity of which we are members, but it does not claim to determine in detail what these must be or leave no room for reasonable disagreement, and still less does it try to tell people how they should act on any particular occasion. Thus, while the associative account does not leave the content of political obligation entirely empty and indeterminate, it quite properly leaves space for differences between polities and for argument and debate between members within a polity about what their obligations precisely are: a theoretical account of political obligation should not seek to displace political contestation about such matters.

Second, the account that follows does not purport to explain the political obligations of everyone, or even of everyone who believes that they have political obligations. This is an important qualification. The nature of political life is a source of endless frustration to tidy-minded philosophers, who seek above all logical precision and clear-cut arguments, and to avoid vagueness and messiness. However, some untidiness and a substantial measure of contingency is the political condition; so, unsurprisingly, there is no single account of political obligation that covers every case. Thus, what the associative account aims to do is explain political obligation in the standard, but also most difficult, case: the obligations of people simply born into polity. The account may additionally contribute something to the understanding of other cases, but in some it will no doubt need to be modified or supplemented in various ways. Again, this should not be thought to be a damaging concession. The idea that one principle, theory or narrative must explain all possible political obligations for everyone for all time is to set the bar far too high. This is the truth that underlies pluralist theories. For, if we can explain the standard case, we can then explore how and why this needs to be revised or qualified to cope with more unusual circumstances, although this is not a task that is undertaken in what follows. Moreover, we should also accept that it may not be applicable to times and places with very different political landscapes from our own.

Although, as would be expected, I believe that the particular version of the associative account of political obligation set out below has at least something to commend it, that does not mean that it does not stand in need of further development and, no doubt, qualification and correction in various respects. In particular, it is important to distinguish the attractiveness of an associative account of political obligation in general from the merits or otherwise of any particular version of it, including the version that is articulated here. The associative account should not, therefore, be understood to stand or fall on the merits or otherwise of the precise specification of this particular version of it; although, of course, if it is not to fall, there has to be some version of it that is at least more satisfactory than any of the other approaches, including philosophical anarchism. In part, therefore, it is hoped that this version will generate further work aimed at strengthening and enriching the associative account: it does not pretend to be definitive and is certainly not intended to be the last word in elaborating such an account. It remains very much work in progress.

The sense of political obligation

I begin with some commonplaces, some 'reminders', about the sense that a very large number of us have about our relationship to our polity, which should be fairly uncontroversial. We relate to the polity of which we are members in a multiplicity of diverse and complex ways that are qualitatively different from how we relate to other polities. We think and speak of *our* government or country, and we think of ourselves as *belonging* to our polity. We distinguish members from non-members, and our actions reveal the significance of that distinction in a wide range of circumstances. We see our government, at least in many contexts, as acting in our name and our relation to it as involving an ethically significant connection: our government's actions can *commit* us, both prospectively and retrospectively. We may hold ourselves to some extent responsible and think that we are answerable in various ways for the actions of our government, whether or not we approve of what it does. There is an important, if limited, sense in which we understand ourselves as the authors of such actions, even when we oppose them: they are the actions of our polity, the polity of which we are members. This is the kind of relationship expressed, for instance, in the comments of the late Polish film director Krzysztof Kieslowski in reflecting on capital punishment prior to his making 'A Short Film About Killing'. He said that the practice was 'being done in my name' and 'I am a member of this society' as indications of his own sense of responsibility for what he saw as a barbaric and unjustified practice. Whether or not one agrees with Kieslowski about capital punishment, it is this sense of identification with the political community, of which his remarks are indicative, which is central to understanding political obligation.

We recognize that our government is entitled to make claims on us and we may have legitimate expectations of it, which cannot be explained without reference to the thought that it is *our* government and we are *citizens* of the state it governs. We pay taxes, which we well understand are morally and conceptually distinct from, for example, charitable donations to good causes and from theft (despite the attempt of some libertarians to pretend otherwise), and in doing so, however reluctantly, we recognize that the threat of punishment if we do not is fundamentally different in kind from a threat of harm by, say, an 'overenthusiastic' collector for a charity or a criminal. (And this remains true even if we would prefer the money to go to a charity and think that they would probably make better use of it.) We acknowledge that over many areas of our life our government has *authority*, which means that we recognize that it has the right, within very broad limits, to make decisions that we are under an obligation to accept as legitimate just because it is the government (once again, whether or not we happen to agree with those decisions). It elicits a great many feelings from us, some of which imply an emotional bond, including the possibility of feelings of pride and shame in relation to the actions of our polity and its members. These latter feelings are especially significant, because they characteristically indicate some sense of being part of our polity and complicit in its actions. They are predicated on our, at least to some degree, identifying with it: we can and do quite naturally talk of an 'us' and a 'we' in relation to our polity. Not all of this is equally true for everyone; but much of it is true for a great many of us. Our membership of our polity not only shapes our lives in a causal sense, it also enters conceptually and morally into the ways in which we think about ourselves, our relationships with others, and in what we feel and how we think about what we should do.

What, though, it may be asked, are these reminders of? They are reminders of a few of the many and varied ways in which our membership of a polity figures in our lives. They also remind us that membership of a particular polity is not a 'bare' fact about us, but what might be called an 'internal relation'. As Rush Rhees in his discussion of the relationship between the citizen and the state writes:

> 'The "relation" seems to be an internal one, not like my relation to the park when I am in it. When I am not in the park, this will make no difference to the park or to me. But we cannot think of the state without thinking of individual citizens or vice versa. But neither is "the relation of the individual to the state" at all like "the relation of the individual wolf to the pack" or "the relation of the individual to the crowd". These could be understood as quasi-physical relations and the relation of the individual to the state is not that. It has rather to be studied, apparently, in terms of obligation.' (Rhees, 1969, pp. 81–2)

Rhees's point here is an important one. Being a member of a polity is not merely a matter of happening to live in a particular geographical area, even though the facts of one's place of birth and residence usually play an important role in one's acquiring political obligations. Nor is it a fact like how tall one is or one's date of birth, facts that under normal circumstances have no particular ethical import for us. Being a member of a polity is a fact that already has an ethical colouring and significance.

In understanding ourselves *as* members of a particular polity we employ what Bernard Williams has called 'thick' ethical concepts to characterize that understanding, and the fact of our membership of our polity figures routinely in our processes of ethical deliberation and practical reasoning (Williams, 1985, ch. 8). These reminders do not 'prove' that we have political obligations (whatever that might mean), and nor are they intended to do so, but they are an important part of any remotely accurate phenomenology of our ethico-political experience: they show how people commonly think, feel and act, at least *as if* being members of a polity were something meaningful. In doing so, we acknowledge that being members of a polity has ethical significance for us; a significance that is partly cashed out in terms of relations involving responsibilities and obligations. But, more than this, they show how deeply implicated and enmeshed we are in such ways of thinking, feeling and acting. For these are not marginal or trivial features of our lives, but typically play a significant role in the way in which we locate and orient ourselves in relation to other individuals, groups and institutions both within and without our polity. In short, although their importance will vary between people, across polities and over time, they form part of the conceptual and ethical fabric through which we make sense of our lives.

It is this kind of understanding of what it is to be a member of a polity, for example, which explains the very real difference between the relationship to the Iraq war of those French and American citizens who opposed it. This might be expressed briefly, glossing over a great many complexities, by saying that because the United States was responsible for waging that war while France was not, this meant that only American citizens could have some sorts of response. Thus, while many Americans who oppose the war, perhaps paradoxically if one thinks only of personal responsibility, may feel a deep sense of *shame* and even *guilt* about what has been done in Iraq, as well as *anger* or even *outrage*, French citizens who oppose it can feel only the latter. French citizens can perhaps feel *shame* or *guilt* in so far as they think that their government has been insufficiently robust in its opposition to American policy or that they are beneficiaries in some way from it, but they cannot (at least unless there is some unusual story to be told about their relation to American involvement) feel it about what the US has done in Iraq. Nothing depends on this particular example, and it would not be difficult to find others if the interpretation of this one is regarded as perhaps unduly tendentious. The general point is that we can feel shame or guilt only for things we are or have done; but, it is because we identify with our polity, we can intelligibly experience these feelings.

This also constitutes part of a reply to the criticism that associative obligations are merely 'institutional' or 'positional' obligations, and as such have no morally binding quality (Stocker, 1970; Simmons, 1979; Green, 1988). Institutional affiliations, such as being a member of a polity, it is claimed, 'may have an identificatory function in showing which duties their incumbent has, but they have no justificatory function in grounding those duties' (Green, 1988, p. 211). Or, as A. J. Simmons bluntly expresses the point:

> 'The existence of a positional duty (i.e., someone's filling a position tied to certain duties) is a morally *neutral* fact. If a positional duty is binding on us, it is because there are grounds for a moral requirement to perform that positional duty which are independent of the position and the scheme that defines it. The existence of a positional duty, then, never establishes (by itself) a moral requirement.' (Simmons, 1979, p. 21)

More will be said about the possibility of immoral associations later in the chapter, but the point here is that our membership of groups such as a family or a polity are not just morally neutral facts about us. They are already typically understood in normative terms and experienced by their members as having a moral dimension.

How, then, is it possible for us to have these feelings and think in such way, and is it reasonable to do so? How is it that we are able to think of ourselves as being connected to our polity in a way that having political obligations makes sense? Basically, there are three broad lines of argument that can be sketched in response. The first concerns the general significance of membership of groups that we do not voluntarily choose to join. The other two lines of argument engage more directly with the polity, as a distinctive form of association. One explores what it is that is generically valuable about a polity. The other, which in turn has two distinct but related strands, concerns our relationship to the particular polity of which we are members. In pursuing these arguments, the aim is to bring out more fully what it means to be a member of a polity, and thus how and why being a member supports the idea that we have corresponding obligations.

Groups, membership and the good of a polity

To begin with it is necessary to say something about what is meant by a group or an association, although this discussion is both brief and general. In particular, a group or association (and I shall use the terms interchangeably) must be distinguished from a mere *category*. Andrew Mason has usefully defined a group as 'a collection of individuals who either act together, or who cooperate with one another in pursuit of their own goals, or who at least possess common interests' (Mason, 2000, p. 21). In addition, some sort of structure and persistence over more than very brief periods of time mark the kind of groups that are of concern here. Groups are to be understood as real; not in the sense of constituting peculiar metaphysical entities such as a group mind, but in that *inter alia* they can act and be the subject of actions people define themselves and are defined by others as members or not; and they routinely figure in practical reasoning and deliberation, including moral reasoning and deliberation (Graham, 2002). What groups there are and on what criteria they are based or organized varies within and between societies and cultures, and also temporally. Groups come into and go out of existence – although not always at a precise moment in time – exist for some purposes and not others, and their membership can, to some extent at least, be indeterminate and contested. While all this is rather vague and very general, the kind of groups that are of concern here are usually easily recognized, if not necessarily so easy to define.

There is nothing especially problematic in the idea that membership of groups or associations can, at least under some circumstances, give rise to obligations. Indeed, it is hard to see how any worthwhile human society, certainly any remotely complex and economically advanced society such as a modern state, could exist without this being the case. However, people's membership of many groups is clearly and obviously the result of a voluntary choice to join; and in such cases it is generally the voluntariness of the decision to join that is thought to play a crucial part in explaining any corresponding obligations. Typically, it is said, these are obligations that we have created or chosen to take on for ourselves, and because we have taken them on voluntarily they do not, for example, offend against individualist ideas of personal autonomy or give rise to other objections that render them morally problematic. And this is, in fact, the best explanation of the obligations that we have to those groups, such as various kinds of clubs, to which we would have no obligations unless we had voluntarily joined them. These truly are 'voluntary associations'.

The difficulty with political obligations is that, as was argued in Chapter 2, notwithstanding some heroic attempts to show otherwise, it does not appear that they can be explained in this manner at all convincingly: polities are not voluntary associations. Most of us do not, in any sense, voluntarily decide to join the polity of which we are members. We do not, for instance, standardly choose our polity from a range of options, either from a variety of different polities or between a polity and some other kind of group or association. Rather, as we might say, we *find* ourselves to be members of a particular polity; and there is a straightforward sense in which most of us are 'born into' our polity, something that we experience as a 'normal' feature of our lives. It is the idea that we could acquire obligations to a particular group or association that we did not voluntarily choose to join, which has met with considerable resistance. As was discussed in the preceding chapter, this resistance may be directed towards all such obligations or focused specifically on political obligations. On the latter view, while it is conceded that some non-voluntary groups, usually the family, may give rise to obligations, it is claimed that this is true only for small, closely-knit, face-to-face groups, of which a modern polity is clearly not one. It needs to be shown, therefore, that not only can we have obligations arising from membership of some groups we have not chosen to join, but also that a polity is one of those groups.

Let us then return to the general thought about the indispensability of at least some groups, membership of which gives rise to obligations. Could we envisage any worthwhile society in which only those groups that we voluntarily choose to join would give rise to obligations? I do not think so: we are necessarily born into a web of social practices and relationships that already structure and give weight and depth to our lives. For instance, although something that we would recognize as 'the family' may not be universal, there will always need to be some institutional arrangements for raising and educating children. It is quite hard to see how any such institution could entirely eschew all ethical bonds between its members that were not the result of a voluntary choice. But, even if I am wrong about this, it is still harder to see why anyone should want to insist that we *must* reject the thought that membership of such groups can give rise to obligations. For it certainly seems that not only are non-voluntary groups integral to social life, they can be (and often are) important sources of value for us. And this, in turn, is at least sufficient to support the claim that we can intelligibly and defensibly understand ourselves to be ethically bound to at least *some* non-voluntary groups. There is no good reason to believe, therefore, that it is *only* the voluntary membership of groups that can give rise to obligations to them.

However, while this shows that it is implausible to think that voluntarism is the only option, it does not show that it is specifically *membership* of non-voluntary groups that explains any corresponding obligations. In the case of the family, for instance, it could be argued to be a principle of gratitude, and with respect to political obligations it could be something like reciprocity or fair-play (Klosko, 1992; Dagger, 2000). Without wanting to deny that these principles can also play a part in our deliberations about how we should act towards our parents or our polity, they are surely not the whole story, and indeed seem secondary to what is fundamental. Thus, with respect to our parents, they cannot account for one crucial thought that also figures in such deliberations: that this particular person is *my* parent, and it is just this that has moral significance for me. In thinking about our obligations to parents, characteristically, it is not a matter, for example, of simply assessing to whom among those numerous individuals who happen to have helped us in various ways we have most reason to be grateful. However any putative calculation of gratitude might turn out, it can be enough simply to respond, 'but he is my father' or 'she is my mother' for their moral claims on me (and of course *only* on those who stand in that relationship) to be acknowledged. The obligation is partly constitutive of the social relationship of parent and child: it is a dimension of the shared concern and commonality that *is* that particular relationship. This is not to suggest that such relationships cannot take a variety of different forms – the family need not take the form of the 'traditional' nuclear family. Nor is it to suggest that such relationships are immune from moral criticism; that would be manifestly absurd. However, it is this acknowledgement of the ethical significance of the relationship that provides an essential element of the context for any such criticism. Nor is it to suggest that general moral principles or other moral considerations are irrelevant in advancing such criticisms. It is, though, to insist that the relationship has its own distinctive moral standing: its own place, often deeply embedded, in our patterns of thought and feeling. And with regard specifically to the polity, we have already seen that the other theories are in various ways insufficient as an explanation of political obligations. So, if there are political obligations, these other theories do not explain them.

These general points about the value and significance of groups that we do not voluntarily choose to join are certainly not enough to clinch the argument for associative political obligations. For one thing, it may be that the polity is not one of the groups to which these arguments apply. At best, the argument to this point only shows that there can be *some* groups, with respect to which the idea of associative obligations offers a highly plausible explanation for the ethical bonds that characterize them. And, it will be rightly said, a family is in many respects a very different sort of group to a polity, and there are correspondingly many differences between our moral and emotional relationships to them. Moreover, it would show too much if the argument established that any and every group that one is 'born into' entailed an ethical bond. This would make the associative account hostage to the possibility of there being obligations to essentially immoral or pointless groups. The argument so far, therefore, needs to be supplemented to show that a polity is indeed the kind of group from which associative obligations can arise. There are two aspects to this. One is to show how a polity is a form of association that can have value for its members. However, while an argument along these lines is necessary, it is not sufficient. Such an argument is well adapted to showing why we can plausibly think of ourselves as having obligations to *a* polity, but is less so to showing that we stand in a special relationship to *our* polity; that is, to the particular polity of which we are members. It can, perhaps, say something about why it will often be contingently true that the polity of which we are members is of greater consequence to us, but it is the wrong sort of explanation to account for the distinctive nature of that relationship. Thus, this argument needs to be supplemented by an explanation that focuses not just on the generic good of a polity, but the character of the relationship between a polity and its members: this is the second aspect of the account. The latter I take to be the specifically 'associative' strand of the argument, and it forms the subject of the next section. For the remainder of this section, though, it is first necessary briefly to sketch the argument about the value of a polity. For convenience and in honour of its inspiration, I label this 'the Hobbesian argument'.

What is it about a polity that could lead us to acknowledge obligations towards it? Or, to put it slightly differently, what explains the notion that the polity is the kind of non-voluntary group to which it is reasonable to think that we could have obligations? One crucial feature (or set of features), I want to suggest, and one that explains the most distinctive element of the polity as a form of human association, is the need for an effective coercive authority to provide order, security and some measure of social stability. Some anarchists apart, it is almost universally accepted that if human beings are to live together for any length of time and have any prospect of worthwhile lives, at least in groups that extend beyond those that could be held together entirely by strong bonds of natural affection, there needs to be some reasonably effective regulatory body. The basis of the need for order and security, backed by coercion, is to be found in the many differences between people, differences of belief, temperament, morals and interests, which lead to conflict, suspicion, hostility, insecurity and sometimes, ultimately, violence. This is not to assume that human beings are naturally selfish or evil; but only that, on any plausible assumptions about human relations, there will always be contention, partiality, competition, dispute and, even among people generally well disposed to each other, problems of coordination.

Without a body that establishes a set of common rules, which adjudicates their interpretation when there is disagreement and which, when necessary, enforces them by protecting people against their violation, there is no realistic, long-term prospect of a minimally secure, let alone prosperous, life together. If human beings are to flourish, on any remotely plausible account of what it is for them to flourish, certain minimal conditions must be established and maintained. Principally, there needs to be a recognizable and viable social order – some measure of predictability and security, some level of reliable expectations and some degree of trust, which enables people to have confidence in and to cooperate with each other to develop complex and stable social institutions and predictable patterns of behaviour. This, I claim, is the generic good of a polity. It also constitutes a response to those who suggest that the idea of 'a general project by all people in a large geographical area for which implicit standards of performance could realistically be posited is patently absurd' (Utz, 2004, p. 304; see also Green, 1988, p. 233). There is nothing absurd in the idea that everyone in a territory has an interest in social order and security or that we have at least a rough idea of how to judge whether or not, or rather how far, they obtain. Of course, many people will want much more from their polity, and many polities will furnish more, but whatever else they want they will need the generic good of order and security. And it is the particular nature of this generic good of a polity that in turn explains the indispensable role of coercion within a polity, typically differentiating it from other groups: the possibility of legitimate coercion is *essential* to a polity's *raison d'être*.

In saying that something like this minimum core is essential for a polity to have value. It should not be interpreted as asserting, a priori, that every polity necessarily possesses this minimum core, and that therefore every polity must in fact have value. There are ample reasons for doubting that some polities in human history have met even this minimal standard, at least for a significant number of their members, and that some today continue to do so. Assessments as to whether this minimal standard has been met in any particular case are in large part an empirical matter, a question of practical judgement, and not of philosophical assertion. But, and this is an important qualification, to have this value a polity does not need to be very admirable, and certainly does not need to be liberal democratic or just, or even nearly just. A polity may have this minimal value while being, for instance, thoroughly illiberal and undemocratic. In this respect, the argument here differs fundamentally from that advanced by Ronald Dworkin. For Dworkin, associative obligations of membership are tied to highly idealized conceptions of fraternity and the integrity of a political community that turn out to be extremely demanding moral requirements that few, if any, polities actually meet. For example, he writes that 'members must suppose that the group's practices show not only concern but an *equal* concern for all members' (Dworkin, 1986, p. 200). However, in terms of the argument here, this 'must' has no warrant: a polity may provide the generic good for all its members without showing an equal concern for each of them. We may hold that such equal concern is morally desirable; but it is not essential for the realization of the generic good of a polity.

It is a mistake, in my view, to tie political obligations generally to any particular favoured political *ideal*, rather than to meeting a minimal threshold of value that is almost entirely uncontroversial and in most circumstances, if there is the will, could be easily achieved. Two points in particular are worth making in this regard. First, we should remember that most polities in human history have been inegalitarian, and have been neither liberal nor democratic; and, indeed, on any moderately strenuous account of what these involve, probably none have truly possessed these qualities. However, many illiberal and inegalitarian polities have successfully secured the minimal conditions of order and security, and therefore have had value for their members, even if they have not been, by some standard, anything like as good as they could and should have been. Second, to agree that a particular polity realizes this generic value is not at all to say that people must accept without demur the polity as it is – that they should not seek to change its political structure or ethos. There is no such quietist agenda implicit in this view. Arguments about the best form of a polity or about how any existing polity should be reformed are not matters of concern here, but proposals for radical political change are certainly not precluded or rendered in any way illicit. All that is being argued is that once a polity is accepted as having value it provides an ethical basis for the claim that it is the kind of association to which members can have obligations: it gives specific substance to the thought that a polity is a non-voluntary group that can have value for its members. Moreover, the nature of that value plays a crucial role in explaining, in general terms, the form and minimal essential content of the associated obligations.

In accepting that a polity does need to have at least minimal value for its members, if they are to have obligations to it, I may seem to be disagreeing with another defender of the idea of associative obligations, Yael Tamir. She claims that if 'only morally valuable communities could generate associative obligations, the latter would become a meaningless concept' (Tamir, 1993, p. 102). The context of this remark is one of expressing her dissent from Ronald Dworkin's position, whose view I also rejected a little earlier. In so far as his argument is the target, then the appearance of a disagreement with Tamir may be misleading. That there may be no real disagreement between us is further supported by the example she gives of the mafia. This presents no challenge to my argument, because there is no reason to think that membership of the mafia must be without any value. Although the mafia is very different from a polity, and it would be misguided to assimilate them, one of the reasons why the mafia was able to flourish in parts of the US, for example, was because it really did offer a measure of protection (and not only against itself!) for otherwise vulnerable Italian Americans. It is not entirely clear how exclusive Tamir intends her focus on *moral* value to be: does this allow that a group could have some other sort of value? Presumably, too, she would not want to suggest that having moral value actually *disqualifies* a group as a candidate for associative obligations, which would be decidedly odd. However, although I suspect this is not really her view, it may still be that she wants to claim that a non-voluntary group can have no value at all and yet still generate associative obligations among its members. *If* this is her view then there is indeed a disagreement between us. For, if a non-voluntary group is entirely without value, then it is very hard to see what there is about it that gives rise to moral obligations among its members, at least if they have not voluntarily chosen to join (Utz, 2004, p. 303).

What appears to motivate Tamir's claim is the worry that, if one concedes that a group must have moral value if it is to generate obligations, there is no useful work left for the concept of associative obligations to do, and thus that 'it would become a meaningless idea'. After all, it may be said, what then explains the obligation is not really membership of the group, but its value – in the case of a polity, the value of order and security. However, this conclusion does not follow; the fact that a group has value may be necessary, but it is not sufficient to explain the obligations. And so it is; for while this argument seeks to explain what it is about a polity that makes it valuable, as it stands it does not explain why we have a special relationship to the *particular* polity of which we are members. It would mean that, for example, when on holiday in Australia, a US citizen would have political obligations to the Australian government if it were providing the order and security for him or her to enjoy the holiday. It is generally true that the locus of the order and security that is likely to be of most value to us is that of the polity in which we normally reside and conduct most of our lives. This, though, does not take us far enough in understanding the particular bond that we have with *our* polity. It is precisely this 'particularity requirement' – our having political obligations specifically to our polity – that is central to political obligation (Simmons, 1979, pp. 31–5). The account so far, therefore, needs to be supplemented by an argument that is addressed specifically to the relationship between a polity and its members.

Identity, polity and political obligation

It is in meeting the particularity requirement that the distinctively 'associative argument' comes in. This argument weaves together notions of a (valued) group, membership and identity in a particular way. The general philosophical underpinning of this kind of argument is, perhaps, familiar enough from what has become known as the 'communitarian' literature (MacIntyre, 1981; Taylor, 1989; Miller, 1995; Scheffler, 2001). At root, it is the idea that our self-understanding, and the way that others understand us, is shaped and constrained in fundamental respects by the various social contexts and practices, including our membership of particular social groups, which constitute the fabric of our lives. It is the meanings afforded by our language, culture and history that determine the social possibilities that are available to us. Only some ways of living and understanding ourselves make sense in the societies in which we live. In Jim Jarmusch's film, *Ghost Dog*, the eponymous hero, who lives in contemporary urban America, seeks to live in accordance with the code of 'The Way of the Samurai'. While a few features of this code, in a more or less mangled form, can be adapted to the circumstances in which Ghost Dog finds himself, he cannot *be* a samurai. This is not just because he does not try hard enough, or because of other personal failings on his part, or even because the life of a samurai is a very demanding one to live (although some or all of these may be true). It is simply that the social context for such a life is entirely absent. He cannot adopt the identity of a samurai because such a way of life is not a genuinely meaningful option in late-twentieth-century, urban America. At best, he can adopt a few ersatz approximations of some features of such a life.

Just as some social identities are effectively precluded, however, so others, I want to suggest, 'come with the territory', so to speak. This is rather more controversial than the contention that some ways of life are not real options. It amounts to the claim that some identities are, at least initially, ascribed rather than chosen. Moreover, there is at least one important difference, which is that it may be possible to find a way of rejecting or escaping such an ascribed identity without the world being magically transformed in some way, whereas Ghost Dog can never be a samurai without such a magical transformation. But, the very fact that this is the most 'natural' description of what is going on when such identities are shed – we can also, to some extent, be stripped of them against our will – presupposes that the identity already has some real purchase, even if it is subsequently cast off. To renounce an identity is always to engage with it in some way or other, even if only negatively. It is important to grasp that the possibility of rejecting an identity does not presuppose that it must have been voluntarily chosen in the first place. This can be seen clearly enough in the case of the family: the possibility of rejecting my relationship to my family of origin does not imply that I must initially have voluntarily chosen it, because as I did not choose it that would make such a rejection impossible. Nor is it sufficient merely to *say* that one rejects a particular identity: we can of course say all kinds of things, but that does not make what we say true or authentic. If one is serious about such a rejection, one also has to act (for the most part) consistently with it.

So, for example, in relation to familial bonds, one cannot consistently renounce any meaningful bond with one's parents and continue to appeal to them for aid when in difficulties on the very grounds that they are one's parents, with parental obligations to help. To sever the familial bond, if it is to be more than merely a rhetorical gesture or adolescent play-acting, *is* to cease relating to other members of the family in a certain sort of way, as father or mother, as son or daughter, or as brother or sister; a point I shall return to specifically in the context of political obligation later. This is not 'a bizarre behaviouristic twist' to an argument that otherwise focuses on beliefs and feelings (Higgins, 2004, p. 154). It is, rather, little more than a commonplace that we judge how seriously people mean what they say, at least in part, by how they act. If someone claims that they think or feel one thing, but always act in a way that suggests they think or feel something else, then that casts serious doubt on whether they really do think or feel what they claim to. While people's beliefs, feelings and actions need not be a seamless continuum, they clearly need to bear some kind of coherent relationship to each other, if we are to make much sense of what they think and do.

Notwithstanding suspicions to the contrary, the idea that we acquire identities that we have not chosen is neither metaphysically suspect nor morally objectionable. It is simply the way things are, a consequence of being born into the world at a particular time and place, with specific forms of social life in which we find ourselves already situated: we all start from somewhere, and that somewhere is to a large extent not of our choosing. Alasdair MacIntyre eloquently expresses the point when he writes:

> 'We all approach our own circumstances as bearers of a particular social identity. I am someone's son or daughter, someone else's cousin or uncle; I am a citizen of this or that city, a member of this guild or that profession; I belong to this clan, that tribe, this nation. Hence what is good for me has to be good for one who inhabits these roles. As such, I inherit from the past of my family, my city, my tribe, my nation, a variety of debts, inheritances, rightful expectations and obligations. These constitute the given of my life, my moral starting point. This is in part what gives my life its own moral particularity.' (MacIntyre, 1981, pp. 204–5)

This is surely a much more plausible description of our social condition generally than one in which we are reducible to autonomous, rational bearers only of natural rights, entirely unencumbered by any social identities. We are never just that, and never could be.

Thus are we born into a particular polity; and, as members of that polity, we assume an identity and acknowledge a relationship to its institutions, practices and members that shows itself in the myriad ways described earlier. So, for instance, if I cease to be a British citizen (perhaps by becoming a member of another state), I come to lose that particular political identity. My relationship to those who were my fellow citizens and what was once my government change. That government is no longer *my* government. I may still approve or disapprove of its actions, but I am no longer connected to it in the same way: it ceases to act in my name. There are claims that I can no longer justifiably make against it, and demands that it can no longer legitimately make of me. Similarly, people who were formerly my *fellow citizens* are such no more; and various kinds of concern or lack of it towards their well being, and that of my polity, take on a different ethical colouring. In short, one dimension of my life does not remain unchanged if the connections that constitute membership of a polity are severed: my self-understanding and my understanding of my relations to other people and institutions, and how they regard and relate to me, are in various respects transformed.

There are two aspects, or sides, to this associative argument, which can be labelled loosely as 'objective' and 'subjective'. The objective side draws attention to the fact that membership of a polity is normally something that is simply assumed in accordance with established conventions: nothing particular needs to be *done* in the vast majority of cases to acquire such membership, which is, in a perfectly straightforward sense, non-voluntary. (The mistake of tacit consent theory, it might be said, lies not so much in the account it gives of the conditions of political obligation as in the attempt to present these as the expression or manifestation of a clear, if implicit, voluntary choice.) For example, membership may be conferred on one by place of birth or through descent. In this sense the political identity that derives from membership of a polity can be understood as a kind of ascribed status; in the contemporary world, typically that of a citizen. Thus, one has, say, the status of a British citizen, which carries with it certain rights and duties, expectations and such like. As noted earlier, the precise content of such rights and duties inevitably change over time and vary between polities, reflecting differences of circumstance, history, culture, political system and such like, but at its core is a legal status. This legal status includes expectations about behaviour, held by both the government and other members of the polity, including the expectation that the authority of the law be recognized, backed by the threat of coercion. I call this the 'objective' side because, from this perspective, our political identity does not depend upon our personal sentiments, emotions, attitudes or point of view: it is concretely manifested in a range of social practices and institutions. Political identity is in this respect real; and it has moral and political implications for us and for others.

If this understanding of membership is not to be one-sided, but shared by the member, as well as being objectively manifested in the practices of the polity, this ascribed identity needs to be complemented and supported by an acknowledgement of membership by the member. This will involve at least a minimal sense of belonging to, or identification with, the polity on the part of the member. It is 'subjective' in the sense that it relates to a more or less explicit self-understanding, incorporating many of the moral sentiments, beliefs, emotions and attitudes listed earlier as 'reminders'. 'To *identify* with a group and its practices is to commit oneself to it in a way that normally involves endorsing its practices and seeking to promote its interests, whilst regarding one's wellbeing as intimately linked to its flourishing' (Mason, 2000, p. 23). While I broadly agree with Mason, the qualification *normally* is significant with regard to identification with a polity. It is a mistake, or at least very misleading, to draw the connection between identification and *endorsement* at all tightly in this context. First, because a polity is typically a large and diverse group, endorsement of the many practices that comprise it is always likely to be qualified and partial. It would be a singularly compliant and unreflective person who endorsed *all* the practices of his or her polity. But, secondly, in any case, this does not seem necessary, even in groups much more limited than a polity. We are all familiar with the figure of the internal critic, the insider, often fiercely loyal to the group but forever critical of it, frustrated that it is not as good as it should be. Indeed, in some cases it may *only* be an insider who has the standing to make certain kinds of criticism of the group. Identification with one's polity can be expressed in a variety of ways, some more minimal and less positive than others, but does not require endorsement of all its current practices or values, or even all the important ones. While an ongoing and comprehensive refusal to embrace *any* of its practices or values would, to say the least, raise serious questions about whether, or in what sense, someone could truly be said to identify with his or her polity, there is a good deal of ground between the two extremes.

Generally, the idea that we must endorse or approve of its practices and values does not quite capture what is central to identification with a polity and hence to political obligation. More important to such identification is the acknowledgement of a common political authority: this is the core content of political obligation. This, in turn, will be embedded in something like a narrative of political identity, undoubtedly open to differing interpretations and emphases, and held with varying degrees of sophistication, but in which the history, actions and future of the polity, in general its fate, are seen as connected in a meaningful way with the member's own. Such narratives 'situate' us in relation to our polity and include most obviously stories of our history – authentic and mythical – but can also take many other forms. They are instances of what, following Rogers Smith, can be called 'ethically constitutive stories'. This idea refers to:

'a wide variety of accounts that present membership in a particular people as somehow intrinsic to who its members really are, because of traits that are imbued with ethical significance. Such stories proclaim that members' culture, religion, language, race, ethnicity, ancestry or history, or other such factors are constitutive of their very identities as persons, in ways that both affirm their worth and delineate their obligations. These stories are almost always intergenerational, implying that the ethically constituted identity espoused not only defines whom a person is, but who her ancestors have been and who her children can be.' (Smith, 2003, pp. 64–5)

As well as being narrowly 'political' in content, these stories can be cast in biological, religious, historical or cultural forms, but in so far as they relate to membership of a polity they help articulate, through defining and redefining, sustaining, modifying and transforming, a sense of political identity. This is typically what happens, for instance, to give some trite examples, when Americans call on the Founding Fathers of the Republic, the French appeal to the ideals of the Revolution or the British summon the Dunkirk spirit.

These stories may also be about symbols, such as the flag, and about values. The latter are frequently embedded in characterizations of ways of life, and not only through narratives of actions or events. They are stories that are often invoked most dramatically and urgently when a polity is seen as confronting questions of great moment or in times of crisis, but it is also important to recognize that they are frequently deployed more mundanely in familiar and routine situations. Almost every day we reiterate, revise or create small narratives of decline, improvement or continuity in our country, stories of its achievements or failures, of how the actions of our government relate to our past or future, and so on, which overlap and interlock with one another. And, it should be acknowledged, in modern liberal democracies at least, these are not infrequently narratives of complaint!

These interrelated, or 'nested', narratives in which the story of our own life is embedded, permit a host variations, and will neither all be shared nor be wholly uncontested (although what the limits are to such variety and contestation might be is an interesting question, although one to which, perhaps, no general answer can be given). Recent immigrants, for example, although not just them, are likely to have distinctively different narratives that need to be connected in some way to (possibly revised) pre-existing narratives within the polity. And, one of the narratives people can have, however idealized they may be, is that theirs is a polity that is open and receptive to outsiders, such as for example the narrative of the United States as a nation of immigrants or the narrative about a core British value being one of toleration. There is, though, no guarantee that the narratives will not sometimes be in tension with one another, sometimes uncomfortably so and with possibly damaging or destructive effects. Narratives of political identity are also almost by definition, in some respect exclusionary: they distinguish 'us' from 'them'; those who are in an important respect not us. This can be entirely harmless, but sometimes these narratives can create or exacerbate frictions and conflicts within a polity.

Political narratives can easily conflict with narratives that sustain other identities, such as religious or cultural identities. And there is no guarantee that there must always be ways for such narratives to be harmoniously reconciled. Correspondingly, political obligations can not only conflict with other obligations, but may do so 'tragically'. One such example is the story of Antigone, as presented in Sophocles' eponymous drama. Forbidden by Creon, her acknowledged and rightful ruler, from burying her rebellious dead brother, Polynices, as familial duty and piety required, Antigone is confronted with a dilemma that is ultimately deeply destructive for all those involved. Thus, our political identity need not be simple and is always but one of many of our identities, with their associated obligations. Furthermore, our political identity may well not be the most important to us, and so we may regard our political obligation as overridden by a higher duty, for instance to God. Nothing in the account of political identity defended here seeks to deny any of these, as I see them, undeniable facts, and it does not assume a general harmony of interests, identities or obligations.

Thus, through our political identity we acknowledge or recognize our corresponding political obligations. However, talk of recognizing or acknowledging the obligations of membership may give rise to a potential misunderstanding. For this aspect of the subjective strand of the associative account does not, as might be alleged, reintroduce consent or some other voluntarist principle through the back door. Acknowledging or recognizing our obligations does not imply that the act of acknowledgment or recognition is what *creates* the obligations. To return for a moment to the family, the obligation of a man to his brother, for example, does not arise from a voluntary act, and in this respect is quite different from, say, his obligation to pay someone five pounds because he promised to do so. The man has to acknowledge his obligations in both cases, but only in the latter case is the obligation created by a voluntary act: in this case through the act of promising. But there is nothing analogous to a promise with respect to his fraternal obligations. Similarly, for the polity; acknowledging our political obligations does not create them. Normally, we identify ourselves as members of the polity and in so doing acknowledge the obligations that being a member of the polity entail: we do not decide whether or not to create such obligations. In short, although self-understanding plays an important role in the associative account of political obligations, this is quite unlike the role that choice or decision plays within voluntarist theories.

When a polity possesses its generic value, and both objective and subjective aspects of political identity are in place, we have a situation in which all the conditions of political obligation are fully met. This is the paradigm case of political obligation. However, one obvious question that may be asked about the two aspects of the associative argument is what happens when they come apart, especially if they radically diverge, as there is no strictly necessary connection between them. They can come apart in at least three different ways. First, people may identify with an actual or potential polity that is distinct from that of which they are 'objectively' taken to be members. Where such an alternative identification is extensive, persistent and deep then, for example, secession or affiliation to another polity is likely to be a live issue. Political obligations for such people are problematic because there is real contestation over membership. This is the story, for instance, of many movements of national independence. Note, however, that to renounce or deny political obligations to one polity in favour of another is not to deny any idea of political obligation or to deny the validity of the associative account of it: indeed, it can without strain be interpreted as supporting both.

Second, it may be that people obey the law, have no political allegiance elsewhere, but identify very weakly if at all with 'their' polity, perhaps having only the most narrowly instrumental attitude towards it. Here, the dangers are apathy, cynicism and political alienation. No doubt polities can and do survive a fair measure of these potentially dysfunctional attitudes, at least under relatively favourable circumstances. However, if extensive, persistent and deep-rooted, the bonds of a polity are in time likely to be corroded, even though this would have to reach pretty extreme levels for its ability to secure the generic good of a polity to be undermined. But, because in many polities more than this generic good is both promised and expected, the consequences of such attitudes for the vitality of a polity can still be serious, including giving rise to questions about the extent of, although not the existence of, members' obligations.

Third, there is the case of people who identify with a polity that effectively rejects or excludes them. This can be a source of great anguish and material deprivation to such people, but may or may not have serious implications for the polity, depending upon the basis and scale of the exclusions. And, much though we might like there to be, there may not always be a straightforward answer in such cases as to where this leaves their political obligations; although, if the polity no longer offers them *any* security, it would seem that subjective identification may not be sufficient to support the attribution of political obligations.

It should be stressed, though, that if we want an account of political obligation that is adequate to the complexities of our experience, what is 'difficult' about such situations should be accommodated and explained by it, rather than simply denied. So, I do not think that we should necessarily see such cases as an embarrassment, for it can be regarded as a virtue of an account of political obligation that it has at least *some* difficulty with them – they are after all difficult cases – especially if it is able to help us understand why they are difficult. Thus, for instance, in circumstances where the integrity of the polity is itself subject to widespread and fundamental contestation, political identity and political obligation are likely to be uncertain and confused. While a theory of political obligation may reduce such uncertainty and confusion, there is no reason to think that it should eliminate it. In this regard, pursuing the logic of the account defended here, I would argue, helps us to locate the source of what is problematic about political obligation in these cases.

Political obligation, authority and obedience

So far, various comments have been made in passing about the limits to what can be said generally about the content of political obligation. In particular, it has been argued that in explaining what it is to be a member of a polity, without reference to the specificities of particular polities, it is possible only to pick out very general features of the relationship. As political obligations express one's membership of a particular polity, much will depend upon the characteristics of the polity through which that relationship is defined and sustained. However, because polities do, as we saw earlier, have a certain kind of generic value, at least where they have value at all, in terms of providing some measure of order and security, our political obligations can be expected to focus particularly on the conditions of this good and the specific practices and institutions through which it is realized. Because they are fundamental to any polity, the defence of the realm, upholding the law and the authority of properly constituted governmental bodies are bound to figure prominently in articulating the content of political obligations. Moreover, the nature of the generic good of a polity also does much to explain the specifically coercive aspect inherent in political authority. For coercive authority is fundamental to a polity's realizing its generic good, as the experience of both chronically weak and brutally tyrannical polities, in their different ways, clearly demonstrate. In this respect, the traditional formulation of the problem of political obligation as being concerned with obedience to law or government is not altogether mistaken but, as was remarked in Chapter 1, it is misleading and too limited. It is misleading because acknowledging political authority is not as such merely a matter of obeying the law, even if that is how it will frequently manifest itself in practice. Moreover, an exclusive focus on obedience to the law will often be too narrow to capture all that is at stake in complex discourses of political obligation (Parekh, 1993).

It is, though, worth drawing out a couple of the implications of this account for how the content of political obligation can be understood, and in particular why acknowledging the authority of law and political institutions is not simply a matter of obedience to them. To be a member of a specific polity is standardly to recognize the authority of its laws and governmental institutions. This, as has been explained, is the core of the content of political obligation. However, acknowledging political authority does not imply that people must always act in accordance with the law or with the commands of government. For example, it need not preclude conscientious disobedience to laws, or even, in some admittedly unusual instances, the denial that a de facto government is authoritative. Both of these claims, though, may be thought problematic and perhaps to undermine the whole idea of political obligation. Thus, in briefly explaining them I shall try to make a little clearer the relationship of political obligation to both law and government.

To deal with the more straightforward point first, acknowledging the authority of the law does not mean that all laws must always be obeyed. There are at least two important but different kinds of circumstances in which disobedience to the law may be consistent with acknowledging one's political obligation. First, particular laws may not have been made in accordance with the established legal procedures or other legitimate processes of the political community. Such laws may be unconstitutional, ultra vires, contrary to accepted principles of natural justice without good cause, and so on. In this way, perhaps, they might be deemed not to be laws at all; but the important point is not terminological: it is that such 'laws' or commands are not authoritative; and though a government may seek, and indeed have the power, to enforce them, people are under no obligation to take account of them in their deliberations (although it may of course be prudent to do so!). Second, and more interestingly, the law may be recognized as authoritative, even when disobeying a specific procedurally valid law. The most familiar instance of this is the classic conception of civil disobedience (Cohen, 1971). The civil disobedient acknowledges the authority of the law and the government's right to enforce it by willingly accepting a punishment for violating it. Additionally, and more tentatively, it may even be possible for a person to invoke his or her political obligation as a reason for disobeying this or that law. Obviously, *political* obligation cannot normally consist in pervasive and consistent disobedience to the laws of one's polity, but where, for example, a particular law is believed to be seriously and demonstrably at variance with the prevailing structure of law, one might appeal to the integrity of the political community as itself a reason for disobedience (Dworkin, 1986, ch. 6). Disobedience to a law may express the sense that this is what is owed to one's polity in this particular instance. Certainly, these last cases are not without difficulties, and even more certainly they cannot be the norm; but it is far from clear that disobedience to a particular law cannot, on occasion, be consistent with, or perhaps manifesting, one's political obligation.

What, though, of the still more counter-intuitive claim that political obligation could even be consistent with denying the authority of the de facto government of one's polity? Again, this can hardly be the norm, but such a possibility results from the gap that can arise between acknowledging the authority of the law and recognizing the authority of a government. For example, there are circumstances where an effective government has recently attained power by unlawful means. This case is like that of an invalid law, but more radical in its implications. An interesting historical example might be that of the Vichy government in wartime France. Many French citizens did not recognize the Vichy government as having legitimate political authority, yet they can sensibly be said to have retained their sense of belonging to the French state. They could plausibly claim that their political obligation not only implied no recognition of the authority of the Vichy regime, but that it actually required opposition to it. (Historically, there were other reasons for resistance but these are not to the point in this context.) In fact, many French citizens recognized the authority of the de Gaulle government in exile, although it had no effective political power within France at the time. Yet, the French people loyal to de Gaulle would have acknowledged the authority of much of the law that was left unchanged by the government of usurpation. In such a situation political obligation would seem to be consistent with the denial of the authority of the *de facto* government; but how long an intelligible sense of *political* obligation could really be said to survive this sundering from the effective government is a moot point and would no doubt depend on an array of contingent and circumstantial factors. In any case, the account of political obligation set out here provides a fruitful context for exploring the issues to which such cases give rise, rather than trying simply to settle them by philosophical fiat.

It should be emphasized that the kinds of cases considered in the two preceding paragraphs are in a sense 'special cases' and cannot be the norm. But they do help to show that political obligation is not reducible simply to obeying the government or law. Moreover, there is more to political life than law, regulation and government, fundamental though those are. Thus, one can manifest one's political obligations by supporting one's polity in other ways, such as voting (even when this is not a legal obligation), participating in political affairs and generally being a good citizen, whatever that amounts to in any particular polity. Political obligation need not be limited only to whatever is essential to realize the generic good of a polity, although in the standard case that will necessarily be an important part of it. This does not render political obligation vacuous or meaningless, but incorporated the sense that it is both complex and contextual.

Conclusion

In this chapter I have sought to show how a theoretically sound and morally unobjectionable conception of associative political obligations can be fleshed out. The fundamental claim I have advanced is that there is a robust and cogent understanding of associative political obligations that provides a highly plausible explanation of how it is intelligible, reasonable and morally defensible for people to think that they have such obligations. The principal arguments for these conclusions have been that political obligations are a concomitant of membership of a particular polity; a polity being a form of association that has as its generic value the goods of order and security. Membership of a polity can be, and usually is, a status that one assumes without any voluntary decision to join, and which is internalized through various forms of identification. The precise content of political obligations will vary according to the character of any particular polity but, because of the nature of the generic good of a polity, political authority backed by tlegitimate coercion will inevitably be at its heart. This completes the main argument of the book. In Chapter 8 I briefly to return to the questions of why political obligation matters and what kind of theoretical account of it we should be seeking.

8 Conclusion

The principal tasks of this book have now been completed. Several general theories of political obligation have been considered, and what I claim to be a more promising alternative approach has been sketched. The fundamental contention that I have sought to defend is that there is robust and cogent understanding of associative political obligations that provides a highly plausible explanation of how it is intelligible, reasonable and morally defensible for people to think that they have such obligations. I have also claimed that there are good, though not logically compelling, reasons as to why pretty much all of us should take the idea that we have political obligations seriously. The main arguments for these conclusions have been that political obligations are a concomitant of membership of a particular polity; a polity being a form of association that has as its generic value the good of order and security. Membership of a polity can be, and usually is, a status that one assumes without any voluntary decision to join and which is internalized through various forms of identification. The precise content of political obligations will vary according to the character of a particular polity but, because of the nature of the generic good of a polity, political authority in the form of governmental institutions backed by legitimate coercion will inevitably be at its heart. It has also been argued that it is hard to see how we could flourish, at least under conditions of modernity, outside of a polity. All of these arguments stand in need of greater refinement and further elaboration, but it is perhaps worth remarking that, while I can easily envisage many aspects of the particular account set out in Chapter 7 being qualified, revised and improved upon, and some rejected as mistaken, it is to the broad contours of an associative account of political obligation that my commitment is firmest.

There are, however, at least two matters to which it is, perhaps, useful briefly to return in this conclusion, by way of a coda to the arguments about political obligation set out in the main body of the book. One involves exploring a little further the philosophical approach that has been adopted in the course of the argument. In particular, it requires some brief reflection on a few of the assumptions underlying this approach and what can and cannot (or, perhaps, should not) be expected from a general theory of political obligation. The other involves reminding ourselves why political obligation matters. This will also provide one last opportunity for engaging with those theorists who are generally sceptical about there being any political obligations, and in particular with the philosophical anarchist. It is with this second point that I begin.

Why political obligation matters

Political obligation matters: it is important that we understand ourselves as members of a polity with corresponding obligations. And it matters even more that those who do so understand themselves are not misled into thinking that they are confused or mistaken for so thinking. To see why it matters it may be helpful to return to the anarchist, construed simply as someone who rejects the whole idea of being under any political obligations. In terms of the argument advanced earlier, the political anarchist is very likely to deny the claim that the polity has value, will not identify with it, and will reject the ascribed status of member. As was seen earlier, there is an honourable tradition of political thinking, probably at its apogee in the second half of the nineteenth century but continuing into the present, which rejects the state in particular as always illegitimate. Correspondingly, political anarchists reject the thought that people could have obligations to it, although they have great difficulty in envisaging a plausible conception of society in which political authority in some shape or form, and therefore something suspiciously like political obligations, do not reappear. If my earlier arguments are basically sound then this should come as no surprise. There is reason, too, to think that political anarchists will have to give up a lot else as well. So much of life in even moderately complex societies is inextricably bound up with there being a state that we should have to change so fundamentally the way in which we live that it is difficult to envisage, in the foreseeable future, a genuinely viable alternative. Of course, many anarchists (and perhaps some globalization theorists) believe otherwise. However, it is not merely coincidental that classical anarchism often took the form of a reaction against the conditions of modernity, and that it characteristically (although not always) went along with a more small scale, localized and rural vision of social life. And, whatever the merits of the latter, once lost, it is hard to see how it can be re-created, at least through intentional action rather than as, for instance, the result of an ecological catastrophe. In so far, however, as political anarchists struggle to live their lives in a way that manifests this rejection of the state, there can be integrity to their rejection of political obligation, even if that struggle is sometimes mired in confusion, and others, like me, believe such a rejection to be fundamentally misguided.

The position of the philosophical anarchist in a modern state, however, is rather different. There is, I believe, an inherent tension in such a position. On the one hand, philosophical anarchists seem content to accept the benefits that membership of a particular state confers on them; and because they do not claim to want to abolish the state, unlike political anarchists, or even to overthrow the political system, they are excused from engaging in the onerous and discomforting business of actively opposing it, and of trying to live a kind of life that eschews any dependence on the state. But they do deny any corresponding political obligations, owed by virtue of membership of the polity (or on any other basis), although they may often support particular laws for independent moral reasons or on prudential grounds. The viability of such a position, however, is, I suggest, dependent upon most people not adopting it. Both of and not of the polity, inside and outside, philosophical anarchists can certainly *say* that they deny that any of us have any general political obligations, but is it a principled position that can be coherently lived? Could we plausibly envisage a viable polity comprised entirely of philosophical anarchists? If not, then philosophical anarchists are caught in something like a performative contradiction. Although ostensibly denying that (almost) anyone has any political obligations, the possibility of a viable polity capable of delivering the generic goods from which they are happy to benefit seems to be dependent on most people not being philosophical anarchists. If this is so, then in this respect the philosophical anarchists' denial of political obligation has lost contact with the role that it plays in our lives, and in so far as philosophical anarchists have lost contact with the unacknowledged role that it plays in making their *own* lives possible, philosophical anarchism may be thought to manifest, if not bad faith exactly, at least an embarrassing lack of awareness of its own parasitic status.

There appears to be something artificial and unreal, even perhaps self-indulgent, in the philosophical anarchist's denial that the vast majority of people have or can have, except under the most improbable of circumstances, any political obligations (Gans, 1992). It is a symptom of a way of thinking that is deeply corrosive of any sense that, in some respects at least, we share a collective fate and of our sense of the indispensability and worth of non-voluntary collective entities, and of our ability and will to sustain them. For good historical, moral and political reasons, we have rightly learnt to be suspicious of sanctifying the state; but that does not mean, at least under any conditions remotely approximating those in which we currently live, that we can do without it. And, it is hard to see how any viable, worthwhile, collective, political life is possible without acknowledging some political obligations. For most of us, political relations are not the most important in our day-to-day lives. But when political relations go badly awry, we are likely to come very quickly to understand how our day-to-day lives none the less depend on them. If for no other reason, that is why political obligation should matter (to almost all of us).

Philosophy and political obligation

One reason for many philosophical anarchists adopting the view they do is that they have an extremely demanding conception of what would count as a satisfactory justification of political obligation. This leads naturally on to the other matter to be discussed. In the opening chapter I suggested that there is something of a mismatch between the kind of account of political obligation defended here and some of the theories considered in earlier chapters. The nature of this mismatch should by now be rather clearer. The account of political obligation that I have articulated draws heavily on our ordinary thinking and tries to make sense of, what I take to be, the widely shared view that people have some sort of ethical bond or moral commitments to the political community of which they are members: that is, as the term is used here, they have political obligations. It is less concerned with trying to justify political obligation in terms of fundamental moral principles or some more or less comprehensive moral theory. As an exercise in *political* theory or philosophy it tries to take seriously the realities of social and political life, and so does not start with the isolated but fully socialized individual and then ask why he or she has any obligations to his or her polity. It also accepts that there will be numerous exceptions, special circumstances, hard cases, and so on. It is not necessarily a weakness of the kind of account of political obligation offered here that it does not answer every question or cover all cases, and such phenomena should not be taken as refutations. What it tries to do is provide the best account of the standard case, leaving room for further work on what we might want to say about other cases that do not easily fit within that account.

The kind of account of political obligation set forth here is to a considerable extent interpretative or hermeneutic. It aims to explain the idea of political obligation in a way that both comports well with ordinary thinking in the area and shows that thinking to be reasonable and morally unobjectionable. It can also be thought of as an exercise in the phenomenology of political morality. In this regard it takes its inspiration from an approach perfectly articulated by Bernard Williams in discussing moral philosophy more generally. It is worth quoting him at some length:

'There could be a way of doing moral philosophy that started from the ways in which we experience our ethical life. Such a philosophy would reflect on what we believe, feel, take for granted; the ways in which we confront obligations and recognize responsibility; the sentiments of guilt and shame. It would involve a phenomenology of ethical life. This could be good philosophy, but it would be unlikely to yield an ethical theory. Ethical theories, with their concern for tests, tend to start from just one aspect of ethical experience, beliefs. The natural understanding of an ethical theory takes it as a structure of propositions, which, like a scientific theory, in part provides a framework for our beliefs, in part criticizes or revises them. So it starts from our beliefs, though it may replace them.' (Williams, 1985, p. 93)

In the sense in which Williams characterizes ethical theory, the argument here is not aimed at offering an equivalent political theory. Rather, it has sought to exemplify the kind of alternative to such a theory that Williams briefly but illuminatingly sets out. It is aimed, in large part, at trying to understand the idea of political obligation and its place in our thinking about how we are related to our polity.

However, it would be misleading to imply that there is no normative dimension to the argument: clearly, there is. For, in explaining why it is reasonable and morally unobjectionable (in many circumstances) to think of ourselves as having political obligations, there is a more or less explicit challenge to those who claim not to have them. In this respect, it could be argued that there is something of a tension between the descriptive and normative aspirations of the argument. If there is – and I am not inclined to deny it – then it is, I suggest, a creative one, but also one that it is perhaps impossible for political philosophy altogether to avoid. A political philosophy entirely without a normative dimension is hard to envisage, but anyway not something that would necessarily be of much value, even if it could be attained. But, there is an important distinction between political philosophy with a normative dimension, and a political philosophy that has as its sole aim normative instruction.

Because it has this normative dimension, however, the hermeneutic or phenomenological approach as practised here cannot be dismissed as merely descriptive and entirely uncritical. The approach allows that our ordinary beliefs, feelings and assumptions may be incoherent, contradict each other or be disordered in other respects. There is never a guarantee to be had in advance that we will find our ordinary patterns of thought and feeling coherent, and indeed it seems highly unlikely that they would turn out to be fully coherent and entirely defensible. Such an approach, therefore, can retain significant critical purchase on our ordinary ways of thinking and feeling. It may help us in revising our beliefs or in trying to restructure some of our moral emotions; by showing which beliefs or feelings are most incongruous or aberrant; by drawing out implications or revealing assumptions of those beliefs or feelings that would lead us to doubt their cogency or viability; or by a series of other interpretative or hermeneutic techniques. But it certainly begins by taking those thoughts and feelings seriously and treating them with respect, and not simply as something to be dismissed as irrational or an ideological illusion in the name of a preconceived political theory.

However, it would also be wrong to exaggerate the difference between the two approaches that Williams identifies. For example, it would be an error to think that what Williams calls 'ethical theories' can have nothing to contribute to a phenomenology of ethical life. This would be a mistake, because ethical theories themselves frequently include a more or less substantial phenomenological component. As Williams says, most ethical theories at least start from some genuine, if limited, aspect of our ethical experience, even if many of them move on very rapidly, often losing sight of where they began. Moreover, such theories can also sometimes help to shape ordinary thinking. Thus, in arguing against other theories of political obligation, we have been able to see that few, if any, of them having nothing to be said in their favour. Some common good and natural duty theories, in particular, have been seen to have useful contributions to make to our understanding of political obligation, especially when placed within the context of an associative account. The kind of philosophical approach adopted here, therefore, is able to draw on, and learn from, the work of other philosophical approaches and theories. As with most things, it is a matter of degree and emphasis, although differences of degree and emphasis can still be highly significant.

It is most unlikely that the arguments set out in this book will persuade everyone who reads them, and probably at least sometimes for very good reasons. I have tried to provide an understanding of political obligation that the reader will find interesting and illuminating and therefore will think it worth trying to improve upon, or even if ultimately found unconvincing at least worth taking seriously. It is in the nature of the kind of inquiry in which we have here been engaged that there never is a last word, a definitive solution, a final answer, a QED. But every book must necessarily have a last word, and I have now reached mine.

Guide to Further Reading

Probably the best general introduction to political obligation remains that of A. J. Simmons (1979). He offers incisive critical discussions of the major theories of political obligation and, though this book takes issue with the philosophical anarchism he endorses, I have learned a great deal from his work. His later thoughts, essentially offering further arguments in favour of philosophical anarchism, but also including his criticisms of associative accounts of political obligation, can be found in Simmons (2001). Higgins (2004) offers a thorough and careful critical discussion of most of the arguments about political obligation; and she, too, takes a fairly sceptical view of general theories of political obligation. Knowles (2010) was published just as this manuscript was submitted and I have not had the opportunity to engage with his arguments. But, based on the quickest of readings, it is clearly an interesting work, with a distinctive interpretation of the philosophical justification, written in a lively and engaging style. Klosko (2005) defends a multiple principle approach, basically a natural duty theory supplemented by additional principles. Although it contains some important criticisms of other views, Gilbert (2006) is not really a general overview, but, in my view, unquestionably the most fully developed and original theory of political obligation of the last several decades: unfortunately, the very complexity of her view means that I have not been able to do it justice here, and it has to be admitted that it is tough going in places.

Other good systematic and more or less general discussions can be found in Flathman (1972), Green (1988), Greenawalt (1987), Plamenatz (1968) and Zwiebach (1975). Briefer general discussions are provided by Dagger (1977), Dunn (1980) and (1991), and Raz (1986). Edmundson (1998) presents an original defence of the idea of a legitimate state without political obligation. Two useful collections of articles on various aspects of political obligation are those edited by Harris (1990) and Pennock and Chapman (1970).

Socrates's discussion, which can be regarded as the first sustained consideration of political obligation, can be found in Plato (1969) and is critically assessed by Woozley (1979). An interesting recent discussion of Aristotle of particular relevance is Rosler (2005). The classic works of the social contract tradition are Hobbes (1968), Locke (1967) and Rousseau (1973). Seventeenth-century contract and consent theory is especially interestingly explored in Herzog (1989), while more extended historical discussions can be found in Gough (1967), Hampton (1986), Lessnoff (1986) and Steinberg (1978). The classic critique of contract theory is Hume (1953). The best and most ingenious modern defence of consent theory is that by Beran (1977) and more fully (1987). Other recent defenders of some form of consent theory include Plamenatz (1968) and Tussman (1960). DeLue (1989) focuses specifically on liberal theorizing, including consent theory; and Walzer (1970) offers some unusually stimulating reflections within the consent tradition, which are subject to critical assessment by Euben (1972). The philosophical literature on various aspects of consent and social contract theory is very extensive, and most books on political obligation include substantial discussions of it. Pateman (1985) presents perhaps the most detailed and sustained critique of consent theory; and in her (1988) and (1989) books she has explored ideas of contract and consent specifically in the context of feminist theory. Hirschmann (1989), too, imaginatively relates political obligation to wider feminist themes.

Political obligation is not much discussed by utilitarians, other than to criticize contract and consent theory. Hume (1978) set out a proto-utilitarian account, but Bentham (1988) has little to say about political obligation. In addition to the brief account in Hare (1976), criticized by Dagger (1982), Flathman (1972) provides a sustained predominantly utilitarian defence of political obligation, rare among recent political philosophers. There exist a large number of general discussions of utilitarianism, and Lyons (1965) is especially useful on the distinction between act- and rule-utilitarianism. Green (1986) offers the classic statement of a common good theory of political obligation. It is criticized by Plamenatz (1968) and Pritchard (1968), but partially defended in Harris (1986), Milne (1962) and (1986), and Nicholson (1990). O'Sullivan (1987) discusses Green in the context of the idealist approach to political obligation more generally. Several of the essays in Harris (1990) discuss the possibilities and problems of a common good theory in a modern context.

Modern hypothetical contract theory has its origins in Kant (1991) and is defended by Pitkin (1972) and Stark (2000). The moral force of hypothetical consent generally is discussed in Zimmerman (1983) and Lewis (1989). The fairness theory is articulated by Hart (1967), elaborated by Rawls (1964) and further developed by Klosko (1992). It is extensively criticized by Simmons (1979, 2001) and in his contribution to Wellman and Simmons (2005). The best modern attempt to justify political obligation in terms of a principle of gratitude is that by Walker (1988) and (1989), but see also Card (1988), Klosko (1989) and Knowles (2002). The samaritan defence is presented most fully by Wellman in his contribution to Wellman and Simmons (2005). The natural duty to support and promote just institutions is set out in Rawls (1999) and discussed in Greenawalt (1987) and Simmons (1979). A modern natural law account of political obligation is presented by Finnis (1980). In addition to Klosko (2005), a pluralist theory is defended by Wolff (2000).

An especially helpful historical and analytical introduction to anarchism is provided by Miller (1984); while Carter (1971), Ritter (1980) and Woodcock (1963) provide further supplementation and development. Woodcock (1977) offers some useful introductory readings. Among the important works of individualist anarchism are Spooner (1966) and Tucker (1893): the modern proponents include D. Friedman (1973) and Rothbard (1978). Some classic statements of communal anarchism can be found in Bakunin (1972) and Kropotkin (1970). An early precursor of philosophical anarchism is Godwin (1976), but the canonical modern statement is that of Wolff (1976). Wolff's many critics include Bates (1972), Frankfurt (1973), Pritchard (1973) and Smith (1973b). He replies to two of them in Wolff (1973). The weaker form of philosophical anarchism is defended by Simmons (1979) and Green (1988) among others. Simmons is criticized by Klosko (1987) and Senor (1987) to whom he replies in Simmons (1987).

Those particularly interested in civil disobedience will be spoiled for choice, but might usefully consult Childress (1971), Cohen (1971), Singer (1973) or Bedau (1991). The problem of the obligation to obey the law is discussed in Carnes (1960), Mackie (1981), Raz (1979), Smith (1973a), Smith (1976), and is a central topic of legal philosophy. Political authority is discussed in De George (1985), Flathman (1980), Friedman (1973), Tuck (1972), Watt (1982) and Winch (1972). Coordination problems as a foundation for political obligation are discussed in Taylor (1976). Versions of the conceptual argument are defended by MacDonald (1951), Rees (1954), McPherson (1967) and Pitkin (1972), while Pateman (1973) presents the most extensive critique of it.

Dworkin (1986) appears to have coined the term 'associative obligations', and Hardimon (1994), Gilbert (1996 and 2006) and Scheffler

(2001) have also contributed to the development of the associative view. It is criticized by Wellman (1997) and Simmons (1996), and the account in this book is questioned by Vernon (2007). Also relevant is the work of Jeske (1996, 1998, 2001). Charvet (1990) offers an account of political obligation with some affinities to that presented here, while Oakeshott (1975) presents a characteristically individual but deeply pondered account of what he calls 'civil obligation'. The moral significance of the nation state is discussed by Miller (1989) and (1989), and the relationship between the self and society is explored in Taylor (1989). Finally, Tyler (1990) offers some empirical reflections about political obligation.

Bibliography

Bakunin, M. (1972) *Bakunin on Anarchy* (1842–76) ed. S. Dolgoff (New York: Vintage Books).

Bates, S. (1972) 'Authority and Autonomy', *The Journal of Philosophy*, vol. 69.

Bedau, H. (ed.) (1991) *Civil Disobedience in Focus* (London: Routledge).

Bentham. J. (1988) *A Fragment on Government* (1776) ed. R. Harrison (Cambridge: Cambridge University Press).

Beran, H. (1976) 'Political Obligation and Democracy', *Australasian Journal of Philosophy*, vol. 50.

Beran, H. (1977) 'In Defense of the Consent Theory of Political Obligation and Authority', *Ethics,* vol. 87.

Beran, H. (1987) *The Consent Theory of Political Obligation* (London: Croom Helm).

Berry, C.J. (1986) *Human Nature* (London: Macmillan).

Brandt, R. B. (1965) 'The Concepts of Obligation and Duty', *Mind,* vol. 73.

Cameron, J. R. (1971) 'The Nature of Institutional Obligation', *Philosophical Quarterly,* vol. 22.

Card, C. (1988) 'Gratitude and Obligation', *American Philosophical Quarterly*, vol. 25.

Carnes, J. (1960) 'Why Should I Obey the Law?', *Ethics,* vol. 71.

Carr, C. (2002) 'Fairness and Political Obligation', *Social Theory and Practice*, vol. 28.

Carter, A. (1971) *The Political Theory of Anarchism* (London: Routledge & Kegan Paul).

Carter, M. (2003) *T. H. Green and the Development of Ethical Socialism* (Exeter: Imprint Academic).

Charvet, J. (1990) 'Political Obligation: Individualism and Communitarianism', in P. Harris (ed.) *On Political Obligation* (London: Routledge).

Childress, J. (1971) *Civil Disobedience and Political Obligation* (New Haven: Yale University Press).

Cohen, C. (1971) *Civil Disobedience: Conscience, Tactics and the Law* (New York: Columbia University Press).

Dagger, R. (1977) 'What is Political Obligation?', *American Political Science Review, vol.* 71.

Dagger, R. (1982) 'Harm, Utility and the Obligation to Obey the Law', *Archiv fur Recht und Social Philosophie,* vol. 68.

Dagger, R. (2000) 'Membership, Fair Play, and Political Obligation', *Political Studies*, vol. 48.

Daniels, N. (ed.) (1975) *Reading Rawls* (Oxford: Basil Blackwell).

De George, R. T. (1985) *The Nature and Limits of Authority* (Kansas: University of Kansas Press).

DeLue, S. (1989) *Political Obligation in a Liberal State* (New York: State University of New York Press).

Dunn, J. (1967) 'Consent in the Political Theory of John Locke', *Historical Journal,* vol. 10.

Dunn, J. (1980) 'Political Obligation and Political Possibilities', in his *Political Obligation in its Historical Context: Essays in Political Theory* (Cambridge: Cambridge University Press).

Dunn, J. (1991) 'Political Obligation', in D. Held (ed.) *Political Theory Today* (Oxford: Polity Press).

Dworkin, R. (1975) 'The Original Position', in N. Daniels (ed.) *Reading Rawls* (Oxford: Basil Blackwell).

Dworkin, R. (1986) *Law's Empire* (London: Fontana).

Edmundson, W. (1998) *Three Anarchical Fallacies* (Cambridge: Cambridge University Press).

Euben, J. P. (1972) 'Walzer's *Obligations*', *Philosophy and Public Affairs,* vol. 1.

Filmer, R. (1991 [1680, 1685]) *Patriarcha and Other Writings* ed. J. Sommerville (Cambridge: Cambridge University Press).

Finnis, J. (1980) *Natural Law and Natural Rights* (Oxford: Clarendon Press).

Flathman, R. (1972) *Political Obligation* (New York: Atheneum).

Flathman, R. (1980) *The Practice of Political Authority: Authority and the Authoritative* (Chicago: University of Chicago Press).

Frankfurt, H. (1973) 'The Anarchism of Robert Paul Wolff', *Political Theory,* vol. 1.

Friedman, D. (1973) *The Machinery of Freedom* (New York: Harper).

Friedman, R. B. (1973) 'On the Concept of Authority in Political Philosophy', in R. Flathman (ed.) *Concepts in Social and Political Philosophy* (New York: Macmillan).

Gans, C. (1992) *Philosophical Anarchism and Political Disobedience* (Cambridge: Cambridge University Press).

Gaus, G. (1990) 'The Commitment to the Common Good', in P. Harris (ed.) *On Political Obligation* (London: Routledge).

Gilbert, M. (1989) *On Social Facts* (London: Routledge).

Gilbert, M. (1993) 'Group Membership and Political Obligation', *The Monist,* vol. 76.

Gilbert, M. (1996) *Living Together: Rationality, Sociality and Obligation* (Lanham, MD: Rowman & Littlefield).

Gilbert, M. (2006) *A Theory of Political Obligation* (Oxford: Oxford University Press).

Godwin, W. (1976) *Enquiry Concerning Political Justice* (1793) ed. I. Kramnick (Harmondsworth: Penguin).

Goodin, R. (1995) *Utilitarianism as a Public Philosophy* (Cambridge: Cambridge University Press).

Gough, J. W. (1967) *The Social Contract,* 2nd edn (Oxford: Oxford University Press).

Graham, K. (2002) *Practical Reasoning in a Social World* (Cambridge: Cambridge University Press).

Gray, J. (2000) *Two Faces of Liberalism* (Cambridge: Polity Press).

Green, L. (1988) *The Authority of the State* (Oxford: Clarendon Press).

Green, T. H. (1986) *Lectures on the Principles of Political Obligation and Other Writings* (1881–8), P. Harris and J. Morrow (eds) (Cambridge: Cambridge University Press).

Greenawalt, K. (1987) *Conflicts of Law and Morality* (Oxford: Clarendon Press).

Griffin, J. (1986) *Well-Being: Its Meaning, Measurement and Moral Importance* (Oxford: Clarendon Press).

Hampton, J. (1986) *Hobbes and the Social Contract Tradition* (Cambridge: Cambridge University Press).

Hardimon, M. (1994) 'Role Obligations', *The Journal of Philosophy*, vol. 91.

Hare, R. M. (1963) *Freedom and Reason* (London: Oxford University Press).

Hare, R. M. (1976) 'Political Obligation', in T. Honderich (ed.) *Social Ends and Political Means* (London: Routledge & Kegan Paul).

Hare, R. M. (1981) *Moral Thinking* (Oxford: Clarendon Press).

Harris, P. (1986) 'Green's Theory of Political Obligation and Disobedience', in A. Vincent (ed.) *The Philosophy of T. H. Green* (Aldershot: Gower).

Harris, P. (ed.) (1989) *Civil Disobedience* (Lanham: University Press of America).

Harris, P. (ed.) (1990) *On Political Obligation* (London: Routledge).

Hart, H. L. A. (1967) 'Are There any Natural Rights?' (1955), in A. Quinton (ed.) *Political Philosophy* (Oxford: Oxford University Press).

Hegel, G. W. F. (1952) *The Philosophy of Right* (1821) trans. with notes by T. M. Knox (Oxford: Clarendon Press).

Herzog, D. (1989) *Happy Slaves: A Critique of Consent Theory* (Chicago: University of Chicago Press).

Higgins, R. (2004) *The Moral Limits of Law: Obedience, Respect and Legitimacy* (Oxford: Oxford University Press).

Hirschmann, N. J. (1989) 'Freedom, Recognition and Obligation: A Feminist Approach to Political Theory', *American Political Science Review*, vol. 83.

Hirschmann, N. J. (1992) *Rethinking Obligation: A Feminist Method for Political Theory* (Ithaca, NY: Cornell University Press).

Hobbes, T. (1968 [1651]) *Leviathan* ed. C. B. Macpherson (Harmondsworth: Penguin).

Honoré, A. M. (1981) 'Must We Obey? Necessity as a Ground of Obligation', *Virginia Law Review,* vol. 67.

Horton, J. (2005) 'Peter Winch and Political Authority', *Philosophical Investigations*, vol. 28.

Horton, J. (2006) 'In Defence of Associative Political Obligations: Part One', *Political Studies*, vol. 54.

Horton, J. (2007a) 'In Defence of Associative Political Obligations: Part Two', *Political Studies*, vol. 55.

Horton, J. (2007b) 'Defending Associative Obligations: A Response to Richard Vernon', *Political Studies*, vol. 55.

Hume, D. (1953) 'Of the Original Contract' (1742), in C. W. Hendel (ed.) *David Hume's Political Essays* (Indianapolis: Bobbs-Merrill).

Hume, D. (1978) A. *Treatise of Human Nature* (1739–40) ed. L. A. Selby-Bigge, 2nd edn rev. by P. H. Nidditch (Oxford: Clarendon Press).

Hunter, J. F. M. (1966) 'The Logic of Social Contracts', *Dialogue,* vol. 5.

Jenkins, J. (1970) 'Political Consent', *Philosophical Quarterly,* vol. 20.

Jeske, D. (1996) 'Associative Obligations, Voluntarism and Equality', *Pacific Philosophical Quarterly*, vol. 77.

Jeske, D. (1998) 'Families, Friends and Special Obligations', *Canadian Journal of Philosophy*, vol. 28.

Jeske, D. (2001) 'Special Relationships and the Problem of Political Obligation', *Social Theory and Practice*, vol. 27.

Johnson, K. (1976) 'Political Obligation and the Voluntary Association Model of the State', *Ethics,* vol. 86.

Joll, J. (1971) 'Anarchism a Living Tradition', in D. Apter and J. Joll (eds.) *Anarchism Today* (London: Macmillan).

Kant, I. (1991) *Political Writings* (1784–98) ed. H. Reiss, trans. H. B. Nisbet (Cambridge: Cambridge University Press).

Kelly, P. J. (1990) *Utilitarianism and Distributive Justice: Jeremy Bentham and the Civil Law* (Oxford: Clarendon Press).

Klosko, G. (1987) 'Presumptive Benefit, Fairness and Political Obligation', *Philosophy and Public Affairs,* vol. 16.

Klosko, G. (1989) 'Political Obligation and Gratitude', *Philosophy and Public Affairs*, vol. 18.

Klosko, G. (1990) 'Parfit's Moral Arithmetic and the Obligation to Obey the Law', *Canadian Journal of Philosophy,* vol. 20.

Klosko, G. (1992) *The Principle of Fairness and Political Obligation* (Lanham: MD: Rowman & Littlefield).

Klosko, G. (1998) 'Fixed Content of Political Obligation', *Political Studies*, vol. 46.

Klosko, G. (2005) *Political Obligations* (Oxford: Oxford University Press).

Klosko, G. (2009) 'Cosmopolitanism, Political Obligation, and the Welfare State', *Political Theory*, vol. 37.

Knowles, D. (2002) 'Gratitude and Good Government', *Res Publica*, vol. 8.

Knowles, D. (2010) *Political Obligation: A Critical Introduction* (London: Routledge).

Kropotkin, P. (1970) *Kropotkin's Revolutionary Pamphlets* (1877–1920) ed. R. N. Baldwin (New York: Dover).

Le Baron, B. (1973) 'Three Components of Political Obligation', *Canadian Journal of Political Science,* vol. 16.

Lefkowitz, D. (2004) 'The Nature of Fairness and Political Obligation: A Response to Carr', *Social Theory and Practice*, vol. 30.

Lessnoff, M. (1986) *Social Contract* (London: Macmillan).

Lewis, T. J. (1989) 'On Using the Concept of Hypothetical Consent', *Canadian Journal of Political Science*, vol. 22.

Locke, J. (1967 [1690]) *Two Treatises of Government*, 2nd edn, ed. P. Laslett (Cambridge: Cambridge University Press).

Lyons, D. (1965) *Forms and Limits of Utilitarianism* (Oxford: Oxford University Press).

Lyons, D. (1981) 'Need, Necessity and Political Obligation', *Virginia Law Review,* vol. 67.

MacCormick, N. (1982) *Legal Right and Social Democracy* (Oxford: Clarendon Press).

MacDonald, M. (1951) 'The Language of Political Theory', in A. G. N. Flew (ed.) *Logic and Language*, 1st series (Oxford: Basil Blackwell).

MacIntyre, A. (1981) *After Virtue* (London: Duckworth).

Mackie, J. L. (1981) 'Obligations to Obey the Law', *Virginia Law Review,* vol. 67.

MacPherson, C. B. (1962) *The Political Theory of Possessive Individualism* (London: Oxford University Press).

Mapel, D. (1990) 'Democratic Voluntarism and the Problem of Justifying Political Bonds', *Polity,* vol. 23.

Martin, R. 'Political Obligation', in R. Bellamy and A. Mason (eds) *Political Concepts* (Manchester: Manchester University Press)

Mason, A. (1997) 'Special Obligations to Compatriots', *Ethics,* vol. 107.

Mason, A. (2000) *Community, Solidarity and Belonging* (Cambridge: Cambridge University Press).

McDermott, D. (2004) 'Fair-Play Obligations', *Political Studies,* vol. 52.

McMahon, C. (1987) 'Autonomy and Authority', *Philosophy and Public Affairs,* vol. 16.

McPherson, T. (1967) *Political Obligation* (London: Routledge & Kegan Paul).

Miller, D. (1981) *Philosophy and Ideology in Hume's Political Thought* (Oxford: Clarendon Press).

Miller, D. (1983) 'Linguistic Philosophy and Political Theory', in D. Miller and L. Siedentop (eds) *The Nature of Political Theory* (Oxford: Clarendon Press).

Miller, D. (1984) *Anarchism* (London: Dent).

Miller, D. (ed.) (1987) *The Blackwell Encyclopaedia of Political Thought* (Oxford: Basil Blackwell).

Miller, D. (1989) *Market, State and Community: Theoretical Foundations of Market Socialism* (Oxford: Oxford University Press).

Miller, D. (1995) *On Nationality* (Oxford: Oxford University Press).

Milne, A. J. (1962) *The Social Philosophy of English Idealism* (London: Allen & Unwin).

Milne, A. J. (1986) 'The Common Good and Rights in T. H. Green's Ethical and Political Theory', in A. Vincent (ed.) *The Philosophy of T. H. Green* (Aldershot: Gower).

Milne, A. J. (1990) 'Political Obligation and the Public Interest', in P. Harris (ed.) *On Political Obligation* (London: Routledge).

Newey, G. (2008) *Hobbes and Leviathan* (London: Routledge).

Nicholson, P.P. (1990) *The Political Philosophy of the British Idealists* (Cambridge: Cambridge University Press).

Nickel, J. W. (1989) 'Does Basing Rights on Autonomy Imply Obligations of Political Allegiance?', *Dialogue,* vol. 28.

Norman, R. (1983) *The Moral Philosophers* (Oxford: Clarendon Press).

Nozick, R. (1974) *Anarchy, State and Utopia* (Oxford: Basil Blackwell).

Oakeshott, M. (1975) *On Human Conduct* (Oxford: Clarendon Press).

O'Sullivan, N. (1987) *The Problem of Political Obligation* (New York: Garland).

Parekh, B. (1993) 'A Misconceived Discourse on Political Obligation', *Political Studies,* vol. 55.

Parekh, B. (1996) 'Citizenship and Political Obligation', in P. King (ed.) *Socialism and the Common Good* (London: Frank Cass).

Parfit, D. (1984) *Reasons and Persons* (Oxford: Oxford University Press).

Pateman, C. (1973) 'Political Obligation and Conceptual Analysis', *Political Studies,* vol. 21.

Pateman, C. (1985) *The Problem of Political Obligation: A Critique of Liberal Theory,* 2nd edn (Oxford: Polity Press).

Pateman, C. (1988) *The Sexual Contract* (Oxford: Polity Press).

Pateman, C. (1989) *The Disorder of Women* (Oxford: Polity Press).

Pennock, J. R. and Chapman, J. W. (eds.) (1970) *Nomos XII: Political and Legal Obligation* (New York: Atherton Press).

Perkins, L. (1972) 'On Reconciling Autonomy and Authority', *Ethics,* vol. 82.

Pitkin, H. (1972) 'Obligation and Consent', in P. Laslett, W. G. Runciman and Q. Skinner (eds) *Philosophy, Politics and Society,* 4th series (Oxford: Basil Blackwell).

Plamenatz, J. P. (1968) *Consent, Freedom and Political Obligation,* 2nd edn (Oxford: Oxford University Press).

Plato (1969) *Crito* (395–389 BC) trans. and intro. H. Tredennick, *The Last Days of Socrates* (Harmondsworth: Penguin).

Pritchard, H. A. (1968) *Moral Obligation and Duty and Interest* (London: Oxford University Press).

Pritchard, M. (1973) 'Wolff's Anarchism', *Journal of Value Inquiry,* vol. 7.

Proudhon, P.-J. (1979) *The Principle of Federation* (1863) trans. and intro. R. Vernon (Toronto: University of Toronto Press).

Raphael, D. D. (1976) *Problems of Political Philosophy,* rev. edn (London: Macmillan).

Rawls, J. (1964) 'Legal Obligation and the Duty of Fair Play', in S. Hook (ed.) *Law and Philosophy* (New York: New York University Press).

Rawls, J. (1985) 'Justice as Fairness: Political not Metaphysical', *Philosophy and Public Affairs,* vol. 14.

Rawls, J. (1999) *A Theory of Justice,* rev. edn (Oxford: Oxford University Press).

Raz, J. (1979) *The Authority of Law* (Oxford: Clarendon Press).

Raz, J. (1986) *The Morality of Freedom* (Oxford: Clarendon Press).

Rees, J. C. (1954) 'The Limitations of Political Theory', *Political Studies,* vol. 2.

Reiman, J. (1972) *In Defense of Political Philosophy* (New York: Harper & Row).

Rhees, R. (1969) *Without Answers* (London: Routledge & Kegan Paul).

Riley, P. (1973) 'How Coherent is the Social Contract Tradition?', *Journal of the History of Ideas,* vol. 34.

Ritter, A. (1980) *Anarchism: A Theoretical Analysis* (Cambridge: Cambridge University Press).

Rogowski, R. (1981) 'The Obligations of Liberalism: Pateman on Participation and Promising', *Ethics,* vol. 91.

Rorty, R. (1989) *Contingency, Irony and Solidarity* (Cambridge: Cambridge University Press).

Rosler, A. (2005) *Political Authority and Obligation in Aristotle* (Oxford: Oxford University Press).

Ross, W. D. (1930) *The Right and the Good* (London: Oxford University Press).

Rothbard, M. (1978) *For a New Liberty: The Libertarian Manifesto* (New York: Collier Macmillan).

Rousseau, J.-J. (1973) *The Social Contract* (1762) trans. and intro. M. Cranston (Harmondsworth: Penguin).

Ruben, D.-H. (1972) 'Tacit Promising', *Ethics,* vol. 83.

Sandel, M. J. (1982) *Liberalism and the Limits of Justice* (Cambridge: Cambridge University Press).

Sartorius, R. (1981) 'Political Authority and Political Obligation', *Virginia Law Review,* vol. 67.

Scheffler, S. (2001) *Boundaries and Allegiances: Problems of Justice and Responsibility in Liberal Thought* (Oxford: Oxford University Press).

Schochet, G. J. (1975) *Patriarchalism and Political Thought* (Oxford: Basil Blackwell).

Senor, T. D. (1987) 'What If There Are No Political Obligations? A Reply to A. J. Simmons', *Philosophy and Public Affairs,* vol. 16.

Sibley, M. (1970) 'Conscience, Law and the Obligation to Obey', *The Monist,* vol. 54.

Sidgwick, H. (1874) *The Methods of Ethics* (London: Macmillan).

Siegler, F. (1968) 'Plamenatz on Consent and Obligation', *Philosophical Quarterly,* vol. 18.

Simmons, A. J. (1979) *Moral Principles and Political Obligations* (Princeton: Princeton University Press).

Simmons, A. J. (1987) 'The Anarchist Position: A Reply to Klosko and Senor', *Philosophy and Public Affairs,* vol. 16.

Simmons, A. J. (1996) 'Associative Political Obligations', *Ethics*, vol. 106.

Simmons, A. J. (2001) *Justification and Legitimacy: Essays on Rights and Obligations* (Cambridge: Cambridge University Press).

Singer, P. (1973) *Democracy and Disobedience* (Oxford: Clarendon Press).

Smith, J. C. (1976) *Legal Obligation* (London: Athlone Press).

Smith, M. B. E. (1973a) 'Is There a Prima Facie Obligation to Obey the Law?', *Yale Law Journal,* vol. 82.

Smith, M. B. E. (1973b) 'Wolff s Argument for Anarchism', *Journal of Value Inquiry,* vol. 7.

Smith, R. M. (2003) *Stories of Peoplehood: The Politics and Morals of Political Membership* (Cambridge: Cambridge University Press).

Soper, P. (2002) *The Ethics of Deference* (Cambridge: Cambridge University Press).

Spooner, L. (1966) *No Treason: The Constitution of No Authority* (1870) (Larkspur, CO: Pine Tree Press).

Stark, C. (2000) 'Hypothetical Consent and Justification', *Journal of Philosophy*, vol. 97.

Steinberg, J. (1978) *Locke, Rousseau and the Idea of Consent* (Westport, CT: Greenwood Press).

Stirner, M. (1921) *The Ego and His Own* (1844), trans. S. Byington (London: Jonathan Cape).

Stocker, M. (1970) 'Moral Duties, Institutions and Natural Facts', *The Monist,* vol. 54.

Tamir, Y. (1993) *Liberal Nationalism* (Princeton, NJ: Princeton University Press).

Taylor, C. (1975) *Hegel* (Cambridge: Cambridge University Press).

Taylor, C. (1985) *Philosophy and the Human Sciences: Philosophical Papers,* vol. 2 (Cambridge: Cambridge University Press).

Taylor, C. (1989) *Sources of the Self* (Cambridge: Cambridge University Press).

Taylor, M. (1976) *Anarchy and Co-operation* (London: Wiley).

Tuck, R. (1972) 'Why is Authority Such a Problem', in P. Laslett, W. G. Runciman and Q. Skinner (eds) *Philosophy, Politics and Society,* 4th series (Oxford: Basil Blackwell).

Tucker, B. (1893) *Instead of a Book* (New York: B. R. Tucker).

Tussman, J. (1960) *Obligation and the Body Politic* (New York: Oxford University Press).

Tyler, T. (1990) *Why People Obey the Law* (New York: Yale University Press).

Utz, S. (2004) 'Associative Obligation and Law's Authority', *Ratio Juris*, vol. 17.

Vernon, R. (2007) 'Obligation by Association? A Reply to John Horton', *Political Studies*, vol. 55

Waldron, J. (1993) 'Special Ties and Natural Duties', *Philosophy and Public Affairs*, vol. 22.

Walker, A. D. (1988) 'Political Obligation and the Argument from Gratitude', *Philosophy and Public Affairs,* vol. 17.

Walker, A. D. (1989) 'Political Obligation and Gratitude', *Philosophy and Public Affairs,* vol. 18.

Walter, E. (1981) 'Personal Consent and Moral Obligation', *Journal of Value Inquiry,* vol. 15.

Walzer, M. (1970) *Obligations: Essays on Disobedience, War and Citizenship* (Cambridge, MA: Harvard University Press).

Walzer, M. (1994) *Thick and Thin: Moral Argument at Home and Abroad* (Notre Dame, IN: University of Notre Dame Press).

Ward, C. (1973) *Anarchy in Action* (London: Allen & Unwin).

Wasserstrom, R. (1968) 'The Obligations to Obey the Law', in R. S. Summers (ed.) *Essays in Legal Philosophy* (Oxford: Basil Blackwell).

Watt, E. D. (1982) *Authority* (London: Croom Helm).

Wellman, C. (1997) 'Associative Allegiances and Political Obligations', *Social Theory and Practice*, vol. 23.

Wellman, C. (2000) 'Relational Facts in Liberal Political Theory: Is There Magic in the Pronoun "My"?', *Ethics*, vol. 110.

Wellman, C. (2001a) 'Friends, Compatriots, and Special Political Obligations', *Political Theory,* vol. 29.

Wellman, C. (2001b) 'Toward a Liberal Theory of Political Obligation', *Ethics*, vol. 111.

Wellman, C. and Simmons, A. J. (2005) *Is There a Duty to Obey the Law?* (Cambridge: Cambridge University Press).

Williams, B. (1973) *Problems of the Self* (London: Cambridge University Press).

Williams, B. (1985) *Ethics and the Limits of Philosophy* (London: Fontana).

Winch, P. (1972) 'Authority and Rationality', *The Human World,* vol. 7.

Wolff, J. (1991–2) 'What is the Problem of Political Obligation?', *Proceedings of the Aristotelian Society*, vol. 91.

Wolff, J. (2000) 'Pluralistic Models of Political Obligation', in M. Berghramian and A. Ingram (eds) *Pluralism* (London: Routledge).

Wolff, R. P. (1973) 'Reply to Professors Pritchard and Smith', *Journal of Value Inquiry,* vol. 7.

Wolff, R. P. (1976) *In Defense of Anarchism,* 2nd edn (New York: Harper & Row).

Woodcock, G. (1963) *Anarchism* (Harmondsworth: Penguin).

Woodcock, G. (ed.) (1977) *The Anarchist Reader* (London: Fontana).

Woozley, A. D. (1979) *Law and Obedience: The Argument of Plato's Crito* (London: Duckworth).

Zimmerman, D. (1983) 'The Force of Hypothetical Commitment', *Ethics,* vol. 93.
Zwiebach, B. (1975) *Civility and Disobedience* (Cambridge: Cambridge University Press).

Index